ODYSSEY OF A
DERELICT GUNSLINGER

A Saga of Exposing TV Preachers, Corrupt Politicians,

Right-Wing Lunatics...and Me

John B. Camp

Cover Photograph by David Trufant

ISBN: 1-4392-3006-4
ISBN-13: 9781439230060

Visit www.booksurge.com to order additional copies.

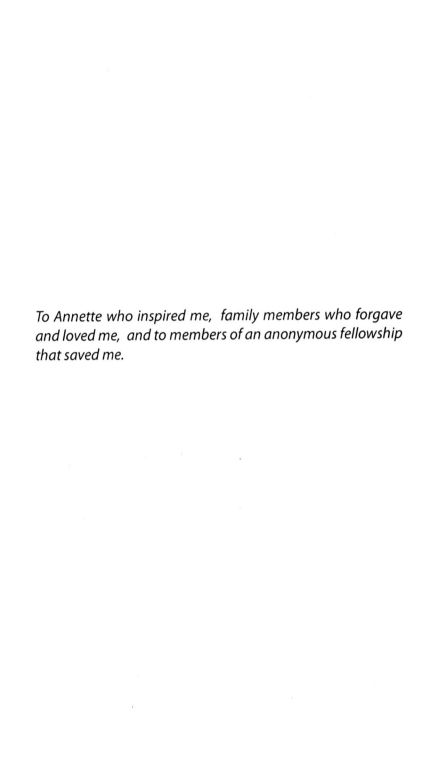

To Annette who inspired me, family members who forgave and loved me, and to members of an anonymous fellowship that saved me.

CONTENTS

Introduction 1

1 Witnesses to the Persecution 11

2 With Malice 47

3 Genesis of a Myth 77

4 Dancing on Barry's Grave 107

5 A Rogue Governor and a Horny Preacher 131

6 "One of the Finest Investigative
Reporters in the World" 155

7 Fateful Encounters 187

8 Muckraking Nirvana 213

9 Kicking Sand in the Faces of Bad Guys 249

10 A Loss of Faith 275

11 A Redneck in Blueblood Land 299

12 Real Reporters Don't Do Happy Talk 331

13 Past, Present and Future 353

14 It Seemed Like a Good Idea at the Time 381

15 At Least I Got a New Face 417

16 The Nerve of CNN 439

Epilogue 475

INTRODUCTION

By any measure, I seemed destined to spend my life in redneck honky-tonks, drunkenly bitching about the liberal news media, corrupt politicians and delivering Rush Limbaugh inspired commentary about the state of the nation. That's a best case scenario. Dead is the worst. Miraculously, sobriety intervened. I vacated my barstool, joined the liberal news media, won a bunch of journalism prizes, and eventually became Senior Investigative Correspondent for CNN. My implausible journey is a remarkable blend of serendipity and necessity.

A scoundrel Louisiana Governor once called me a "derelict gunslinger." Regrettably, the label is accurate. But as English novelist Virginia Wolfe noted, "If you do not tell the truth about yourself, you cannot tell it about other people."

The truth is that I've spent nights in jails, undergone treatment for booze-related ailments at halfway houses and hospitals, and lost and regained jobs based on my blood alcohol level. This shameful résumé is replete with messy divorces, and estrangements from my children, parents and friends. In short, I am an unlikely character to have cast stones at anyone. But truth is a major topic of this tome, so I can't sugarcoat my seedy background as a teenage alcoholic, child groom and daddy, Air Force slacker, door-to-door Bible and book huckster, wannabe rock and roll disc jockey. And gutter drunk.

Until I was twenty-seven-years old, I never once considered being a journalist, broadcast or otherwise. I wanted to be a rock and roll disc jockey. My disc jockey ambitions were unfulfilled. Indeed, I never got to spin one rock and roll record. A few weeks into my first radio job at a 250-watt station in the Sierra Nevada Mountains of Northern California, United Press International repossessed the newswire. To keep the lights lighting and the transmitter transmitting, somebody needed to fill two sponsored newscasts. I knew nothing about reporting. Nonetheless, I was sent forth in the small town of Sonora to gather all the news fit to broadcast.

The station's signal didn't reach much farther than two tin cans tethered by string. However, KVML called itself *The Voice of the Mother Lode*. And as the only fulltime "Voice of the Mother Lode," I was given the task of collecting ten minutes of local news each day. I reported petty crimes, traffic accidents and funeral notices. My only "journalism" skills consisted of typing and bullshit. The latter talent ultimately formed the foundation of my muckraking career—a business that is the antithesis of playing records and entertaining listeners with witty patter.

Investigative reporting is the only craft I know in which practitioners celebrate being called assholes. This aberrant appreciation of verbal assaults used to be quite evident at annual conventions sponsored by Investigative Reporters and Editors, known as IRE. During four days of narcissistic displays of braggadocio, muckrakers shared secrets of winning big awards, pissing off people and acquiring rectal identities. Between workshops and seminars, reporters prowled hotel corridors, bars, and reception areas to beguile one another with accounts of their journalism heroics—gloating about reputations they tarnished, folks they sent to jail, lawsuits filed against them, and the number of people who honored them with nasty epithets.

A perverse pride in quantifying success in terms of loathsome nicknames was a sign of an arrogant sense of infallibility that characterized many investigative reporters. To reinforce egos, mud-slingers presented awards to one another each year. Prize-winners fondled the trophies when beset with doubts about the virtue of their vocation.

As an early award-fondling IRE member, as well as a former member of the organization's Board of Directors, my critique of the muckraker psyche is a confession of personal flaws, rather than a blanket condemnation of the imperfections of investigative reporters. Still, I observed my own shortcomings in a lot of journalists, who deemed themselves qualified to act as judges, juries and character assassins.

The IRE acronym supposedly reflects a mindset of members. But it has become a misnomer. Most muckrakers only get mildly irritated nowadays. In the wake of media consolidation, old-fashioned scandal-mongering that sent people to jail has diminished to a point of invisibility — especially on television. As a "Peabody award-winning" head-hunter for three decades, my exposés did, in fact, put people in jail and exposed systemic evils that brought about significant changes.

Emblematic of contemporary television's surrender to drivel was the reaction of an LSU journalism class I spoke to in the spring of 2007. Dumbfounded students may have thought I was lying when I bragged of exposing the misdeeds of Presidential candidates, Governors, Congressmen, TV preachers, and a colorful assortment of crooks. I told of traveling the revival circuit with televangelist Jimmy Swaggart, secretly filming Mafia dons and flying alongside the country's most notorious dope smuggler.

My investigative stories also defended the worst kinds of criminals by revealing the unscrupulous tactics of ambitious prosecutors, overzealous cops and corrupt FBI agents. Exposing the "good guys" often made me a target of scorn, including attacks by lunatics that Hillary Clinton described as part of a "vast right-wing conspiracy."

Detractors had plenty of ammunition to attack me since I literally staggered into investigative reporting—a lurch that began around midnight on February 4, 1971.

Holding onto an empty wine bottle, I sat on a curbside in the New Orleans French Quarter, forlornly contemplating my failures. I couldn't even succeed as a skid row drunk. The onset of delirium tremens was cutting short my plan to become a full-time wino. A couple of street people—my dearest friends during a chaotic three-day bender—had notified a girlfriend that her missing darling was in terrible condition. Rushing to my side, she hauled my sorry ass to a Baton Rouge halfway house. It was the genesis of an amazing transformation—personally, spiritually and professionally.

In the years that followed, my sober face appeared in newspapers, on the cover of a national journalism magazine, and the cover of a book profiling the country's leading muckrakers. My reporting was hyped as "legendary." Lucky was a more appropriate portrayal. Investigative reporters are only as good as the commitment of people they work for. During my career, I landed in television's best muckraking venues.

Riding the crest of a tsunami spawned by the Watergate scandal, my rise from gutter drunk to acclaimed reporter was inextricably intertwined with lessons I learned at meetings of an anonymous organization that taught me how to stay sober. Denial is the foremost trait of drunks, making self-honesty a crucial component of sobriety. The same attribute is also a prerequisite for investigative reporting. By filtering my judgments through a prism of painful personal experiences, I benefited from pragmatic insights of denial mechanisms that are triggered when people get caught in embarrassing and/or felonious situations. My alleged acuity in discerning truth—or my version thereof—evolved from accepting stark truths about me.

But before I get carried away with high-mindedness, it's important to disclose my occasional reliance on questionable tactics that I now condemn. Television reporting requires compromises. And so does ambition. Slicing through layers of self-deception is a gradual process that is never mastered. My ethics of convenience would probably result in failing grades in journalism classes. I say "probably" because I never spent time in journalism classes—other than posturing before students about my purity.

The only alphabet graffiti behind my name represents the previously mentioned substance found in cow pastures. Except for a single semester of seldom attended classes prior to my expulsion from the University of Alabama and a brief stop at a Los Angeles disc jockey school, my scholastic pursuits ended at Tuscaloosa, Alabama Senior High School—an institution identified more with kudzu than ivy. I learned journalism basics in small radio stations. My advanced degree was acquired in Louisiana, a superb classroom for on-the-job training. I don't advise budding muckrakers to follow my path.

A year after my failed skid row audition, the Baton Rouge radio station that fired me for being a drunk heard rumors I had stopped drinking and offered me a return engagement. My old job as News Director and host of a popular daily talk show was filled. So having nothing better to do, I made myself useful by rummaging around for original stories. Six months later, I uncovered a bribery scheme that put local bankers and a government official in prison. Eureka! I was an investigative reporter.

The career-altering exposé entailed all the adventures people associate with investigative reporting, but rarely happen in reporting a single story. There were back alley meetings with a "deep throat," days of digging through documents, a search for a missing witness in Latin America, and the drama of a stunning confession by a bank executive who believed I knew he paid bribes to the Louisiana official. My story won the Radio Television News Directors International Award for investigative reporting, along with several other major journalism prizes.

The accolades prompted me to proclaim myself an "award-winning reporter" and flood major radio and television stations with résumés. My timing was remarkable. The bribery story aired June 21, 1972—just four days after burglars were caught inside the Watergate offices of the Democratic National Committee. The ensuing scandal caused journalists across America to adopt the title of investigative reporter. I figured I was one.

Until my self-anointment, the only investigative reporter of note I had met was syndicated columnist Jack Anderson. Following his 1972 Pulitzer Prize for disclosing clandestine deals between the United States and Pakistan, he went on a speaker's tour. At LSU, he warned students of a conspiracy by the American government officials to hide important policy decisions from U.S. citizens. Anderson's fervor suggested to me that he was nuts—an indication of my naiveté.

Anyway, my bloated résumé got results. In early 1973, Miami, Florida's NBC television affiliate hired me as its chief muckraker. WCKT—now WSVN—pioneered a genre of investigative reporting that featured undercover video and "gotcha" ambush interviews. During my three years of uncovering south Florida scandals, I was able to modify my title to "Peabody award winning reporter." Twice over, although my medallions were shared with colleagues whose stories were also submitted for awards. Years later, I received two Peabody prizes that were mine all mine.

But whether shared or awarded solely for my exposés, the first line of all job applications began, "Dear Sir or Madam, I am a Peabody award winning reporter, etc." The impressive title got me hired as head of one of television's first multi-member investigative reporting units at Boston's ABC affiliate, then described by the *New York Times* as the "best local station in the country." However, "Blue blood" Beacon Hill wasn't ready for my brand of "redneck" muckraking. The unit closed after four years.

Subsequent visits to unemployment lines were interrupted by part-time reporting for a New England syndicated news service and a freelance gig at ABC *Close Up* in New York. The *Close Up* experience convinced me that documentaries were the only venue for serious investigative reporting. All I needed to prove the theory was a job. It came about in the city where I began mucking.

As an alternative to food stamps and a promise that I could produce investigative documentaries, I reluctantly returned to Louisiana. As Baton Rouge's mini-Mike Wallace for seven years, I collected my third and fourth Peabody medallions, along with enough journalism awards to build a self-aggrandizing shrine. I had no intention of leaving investigative reporting Nirvana until CNN called. Money talks and muckrakers walk.

So, how does an under-educated ex-drunk escape his honky-tonk, trailer trash destiny to become a semi-prominent journalist for a network that once billed itself as "the world's largest newsgathering organization?" I've often pondered the question.

Watching myself on the TV screen, seeing my face on the cover of magazines, a book and in newspapers, and reading flattering stories of my achievements as an investigative reporter, I have wondered if this is the same guy who set out to be a rock and roll disc jockey at "the *Voice of the Mother Lode*."

This book tells the story of an improbable odyssey in which I was a witness to the transformation of television news to "infotainment."

CHAPTER ONE

WITNESSES TO THE PERSECUTION

In August, 2004, I sat in a nearly empty movie theater in Atlanta, Georgia watching myself play the role of pompous journalism critic in a feature length documentary titled, *The Hunting of the President*. It could just as easily been called the *Revenge of Harry Thomason*. He was the film's Executive Producer. A longtime Bill Clinton friend and apologist, Thomason is credited with helping compose the infamous Monica Lewinsky denial, "I never had sexual relations with that woman."

My screen time was brief. But given my seedy and academically-deficient background, it seemed absurd to be sandwiched between prominent pundits like *Newsweek*'s Jonathan Alter and the *Washington Post*'s Howard Kurtz. Daddy would have been proud of the audaciousness of his only child. For a few seconds, the film suggested I was a journalistic "somebody." And being "somebody" was a household mantra when I was growing up—a process that took many more years than for most children.

The Hunting of the President exposed the "Clinton Rules," a form of reporting in which political terrorists are given more credibility by mainstream journalists than irrefutable evidence contradicting their propaganda.

I was the lone television investigative reporter in the film, possibly because Thomason couldn't find another TV guy willing to say that the so-called Whitewater "scandal" was a scam perpetrated on the news media. Whitewater was the genesis of an era of complicity between journalists, right-wing zealots and partisan prosecutors. Skepticism, the best quality of good reporters, degenerated into toxic cynicism. Myths transcended logic. The travesty was a low point in responsible investigative journalism.

"Coming up with the story was more important than coming up with the truth," I stated in the documentary film.

The "Clinton Rules" exempted journalists from asking questions and providing context that would have exposed Whitewater as a hoax in its early stages. Instead, the bogus scandal increased the influence of the extreme right-wing, added momentum to Newt Gingrich's ongoing Republican revolution in Congress, contributed to the growth of Fox "News," and ultimately led to the election of George W. Bush.

Although the "Clinton Rules" have not been repealed, the 2008 election of Barack Obama suggests modest changes. Enamored by the candidate, reporters did not give credibility to claims of a Muslim background and his alleged association with domestic "terrorists." Except for Fox News, the *Drudge Report* and Internet blogs, the rumors failed to gain momentum. However, if journalists follow past patterns, they will overreact and end the love affair with Obama by reporting trivia and misspeak as scandal.

Journalistic responsibility—if it ever returns—comes too late to repair the damage to the nation caused by baseless right-wing attacks on Bill Clinton, Al Gore and John Kerry—the latter a target of the 2004 lunatic-generated "Swift Boat" political ads that questioned his heroism during the Vietnam War. The fate of Clinton, Gore and Kerry was affected by a deterioration of investigative reporting before and after Whitewater.

My claim of expertise—such as it is—began three years before Bill Clinton gave his Jimmy Swaggart impersonation. As CNN's Senior Investigative Correspondent, I was sent to Little Rock to bring honor to the network by gathering evidence that would vault me to Watergate-like journalism fame. To that end, I read hundreds of blurred, oil-slick microfiche documents that were supposed to tell a tale of misdeeds by the leader of the free world. But rather than revealing high crimes of Bill and Hillary, the documents disclosed the crimes of reporters in accepting as truth all that was printed in the *New York Times*—the original source of allegations leading to the Whitewater investigation.

When I arrived in early 1994, reporters were already chasing stories in Little Rock like drunken revelers searching for beads at Mardi Gras parades. Instead of joining the pack, I decided to first read material that was the basis of the "scandal." The documents eventually became a centerpiece of a story that I believed would blow Whitewater out of the water. Nobody paid attention. The original purpose of the Whitewater inquiry had been forgotten. Sex had obscured less titillating issues surrounding a minor league Clinton real-estate investment that triggered the probe. Paula Jones' portrayal of Bill's private parts, and Monica Lewinsky's knee calluses ultimately became a national mania.

While journalists sat around bars speculating about the President's sex life, an out-of-control investigation expanded into one of the worst cases of partisan prosecutorial abuses in the annals of the American justice system. The investigation eventually cost taxpayers an estimated $70 million—$12.5 million of which taught citizens lessons about Bill Clinton's sexual proclivities and a semen-stained blue dress.

It requires considerable hubris to question the venerable *New York Times*. It is our nation's "newspaper of record." As a rule, TV correspondents don't dispute the *Times*— especially reporters with my kind of checkered background. In the end, though, my CNN reporting paralleled many of the conclusions in an Independent Counsel's final report, as well as interim findings released in the course of the costly inquiry.

The official report took eight years to compile. I reached the same conclusions in two months. I'm not bragging. Well, maybe a little. But I believe that most reasonably competent reporters could have done the same story— maybe in less time. Regrettably, the national media was predisposed to finding the Clintons guilty. CNN was no exception. I fought an internal battle to even get my story on the air. It was considered un-reporter-like to disclose exculpatory material favoring the President. Most journalists assigned to the story were terrified of being labeled "Clinton apologists."

As an equal opportunity muckraker, my only agenda was finding the truth. Throughout my career, Republicans and Democrats alike had gone to jail or otherwise been disgraced by my exposés. Moreover, I arrived in Little Rock under the assumption that there was a factual basis for the Whitewater investigation. After Robert Fiske was named Independent Counsel—the first of three prosecutors to head the probe—reporters were speculating about possible indictments. Who and for what was unclear.

A former United States Attorney for the Southern District of New York, Fiske had a reputation for thoroughness and fairness. And from the outset of the inquiry, his office moved quickly to resolve questions related to Bill Clinton's dealings before, during and after three terms as Arkansas Governor. Fiske may have moved too fast. He was replaced six months later by Kenneth Starr, the moralistic son of a fundamentalist preacher.

The appointment was orchestrated by a powerful cabal of Republican Senators. "Judge" Starr, as the former federal appeals court judge preferred to be addressed, was given an opportunity to inflict damage on the President. A life-long supporter of right-wing causes, he served his sponsors well by creating the illusion of doing something.

The Independent Counsel's office under his direction took credit for indicting twenty people and obtaining eighteen convictions. Six cases were guilty pleas to misdemeanors. None were directly linked to the Clintons or the original purpose of the investigation. It was an expensive brand of justice—$3.5 million per defendant.

The most notable cases were those of Arkansas Governor Jim Guy Tucker and former Associate U.S. Attorney General Webb Hubbell. Both went far afield from the initial intent of the Independent Counsel's appointment. Hubbell, a close friend and golfing buddy of Bill Clinton, pleaded guilty to cheating the IRS and his partners in Little Rock's prestigious Rose Law Firm. The devious dealings were first discovered by Hubbell's colleagues. However, Starr's office took credit for the investigation.

Governor Tucker, a longtime Clinton adversary, was convicted of bankruptcy fraud. The indictment involved convoluted non-Whitewater financial dealings so insignificant that the presiding judge sentenced him to house arrest. His co-defendant was James McDougal—a former partner of Bill and Hillary in the Whitewater real-estate development. He was convicted and sentenced to prison. Again, the case had no direct connection to the Clintons, or the initial purpose of the Whitewater investigation.

Have I forgotten anything? Oh yeah, the President was impeached. It was reported in all the newspapers and on TV, too—especially the lurid passages in Kenneth Starr's report to Congress accusing the President of lying about adulterous behavior. To Starr's chagrin, the U.S. Senate acquitted Clinton, and the First Lady forgave her horny husband. Or so she says. Regardless, would I or most married men tell a fib under similar circumstances? For damn certain. Sometimes, two wrongs do make a right.

The biggest share of the blame for Whitewater's voyeuristic chapter in American politics and injustice is the fault of Starr's hardcore religiosity and the narrow views of his born-again assistant, Hickman Ewing. When recruited by Starr, the former U.S. Attorney for the Western District of Tennessee was practicing law in Memphis on weekdays and preaching at a fundamentalist church on weekends. The men were two of a kind. In my opinion, neither was able to distinguish between sin and crime. Aiding and abetting the moral crusade was an assortment of Clinton-haters that included devious TV preachers, unscrupulous Congressmen, radio propagandists and a mob of negligent reporters.

But the person most responsible for the Whitewater investigation was a dead Friend of Bill, an "FOB" as the President's Arkansas pals were known. If Deputy White House Counsel Vincent Foster had conducted a news conference in July 1993 to announce his reasons for committing suicide, I doubt there would have been a Whitewater investigation, or stories of Presidential sex games, or reports of a semen-stained blue dress, or an impeachment, or the election of George W. Bush, or an endless war in Iraq. Nor would there have been sideshows like "Travelgate," Hillary's commodities profits, and other controversies that meant little and accomplished nothing more than costing tax-payers money. Kenneth Starr and his minions could have enjoyed pornography in private and spared the nation a debate over whether blow-job is one word, two words, or hyphenated.

My supposition is not a far stretch. Foster's taste-test of the barrel of an ancient 38-caliber Colt revolver post-humously produced all sorts of sinister scenarios that were propagated by many characters I suspected of being escapees from mental hospitals. Near the top of the loony list were a few columnists of the otherwise respectable *Wall Street Journal*. The newspaper's op-ed page was a repository of Whitewater disinformation, including con-jecture that Foster was possibly murdered, or committed suicide because of his knowledge of dark Clinton secrets.

The Arkansas lawyer's medically diagnosed clinical de-pression was disregarded as a factor in his death, although the condition has long been a cause of early exits from the living. Ludicrously, tabloid writers and conspiracy theorists suggested murder. Maybe at the behest of his former Rose law firm partner, Hillary. Maybe they were lovers. Maybe she broke off the relationship. Maybe, maybe, maybe. The rumors were nonstop.

My assignment to join the ever-expanding horde of journalists traipsing around Little Rock in pursuit of Pulit-zer Prizes and Peabody awards seemed a waste of time.

Investigative reporters from the *New York Times*, *Washington Post* and other major news organizations had been digging away ever since Vince Foster left without saying goodbye. I would be gathering left-over crumbs. After all, *Times* and *Post* investigative journalists are supposed to be the best in the business.

Therefore, I was astonished to learn that a trove of official documents disputed Whitewater allegations reported in the nation's leading newspapers. Equally remarkable, many reporters—network television correspondents in particular—were nothing more than recyclers of articles in the *Times* and *Post*. They were desperate for the tiniest bit of new information to supplement their plagiarism.

It seemed to me that both television and print journalists displayed an appalling ignorance of the basics of real estate partnerships, law firm distributions of profits and functions of state government. Reporters often characterized Whitewater as too complicated for "Joe six pack"—"Joe the plumber" in 2008 parlance. Amazingly, most correspondents assigned to the story didn't take time to understand the transactions. That required leaving Little Rock's Capital Hotel bar—a gathering place where muckraker wannabes corroborated each other by repeating the latest rumors.

Sure, I'm being judgmental. But facts support the judgment. When I got to Little Rock I only knew what I read in newspapers. I was starting from scratch. Washington-based *Special Assignment* producer Matthew Saal had arrived two weeks before me and gathered documents from various state agencies. He said most of the stuff didn't make sense to him. My job was to interpret the material.

As it turned out, Matt and I were an odd but complementary duo. Manhattan-born and raised, he was a young Harvard graduate. In contrast, I was a semi-redneck graduate of Tuscaloosa, Alabama High School where my academic record was barely mediocre prior to rapidly going downhill. I lasted only one semester at the University of Alabama. Except for a "D" in ROTC, I compiled a perfect record by failing every class. My contribution to our reporting was twenty-two years of experience in digging through bureaucratic records. His smarts and my pragmatism combined to make us a good team.

From the beginning, we both assumed there must be substance to the Whitewater clamor. The *New York Times* had accused Bill and Hillary of doing something. Just what was imprecise. Eight months before Bill Clinton's election—March 8, 1992—a dense *Times* "exposé" gave details of a land deal involving the Clintons and a controversial business partner. As far as I could discern, the article made four primary allegations:

...Without financial risk, the Clintons became partners in a real estate development known as Whitewater Estates

...A Whitewater partner—James McDougal—owned a state regulated savings and loan company that later needed help from friends in high places.

...As Governor, Clinton appointed a state regulator of financial institutions who delayed taking action when McDougal's S&L was declared insolvent.

...At the behest of Rose Law Firm partner, Hillary Clinton, the regulator approved a "novel" financial arrangement to salvage the sinking company.

If I'm going to accuse the *New York Times* of screwing up the country as a result of sloppy and inaccurate reporting, it's necessary to explain Whitewater to readers who don't remember, don't understand, or don't give a shit about anything more complicated than Monica Lewinsky blow-jobs, Paula Jones' alleged shock over seeing Bill Clinton's crooked penis, and Jennifer Flowers' self-described affair with Bill. Actually, the Whitewater transactions were not nearly as complicated as people believe. Just boring.

In 1978, Hillary and then Arkansas Attorney General Bill Clinton formed a partnership with Jim (not-nuts-yet) McDougal and his wife, Susan. They bought and subdivided land on the White River near the tiny north Arkansas town of Fillipin. Bill and Jim McDougal became good friends ten years before while working in the re-election campaign of U.S. Senator William Fulbright. Jim was a likable ex-drunk who got sober in 1967 in Alcoholics Anonymous. However, he never got over dipsomaniacal traits of grandiosity and self-importance—shortcomings common to most alcoholics, me included. Sober, most of us get better.

Based on McDougal's record as a successful real-estate developer, Whitewater Estates seemed like a good investment opportunity. Bill Clinton previously made a couple of thousand dollars investing in another McDougal-promoted project. So relying on bank loans, the partnership paid $202,000 for two-hundred-twenty acres of riverside land. The property was subdivided into forty-two parcels with sales prices ranging from $5000 to $14,000. If every lot had sold at the asking price, the partnership would have split about $80,000 in profits after expenses and real estate sales commissions.

Like many similar recreation-oriented developments in the late seventies and early eighties, Whitewater was designed to attract World War Two and Depression era retirees who were looking for the good life in small towns. But Fillipin was too small, too far from urban areas, and interest rates were soaring. Sales never reached expectations.

Attorney General Clinton's investment was reported in several Arkansas newspapers. When he was elected Governor in 1979, McDougal was appointed as an economic development liaison. The Little Rock *Democrat-Gazette*'s account of the appointment raised the issue of conflict of interest. But Jim's tenure was brief, and there was never a hint of hanky-panky. Until the *New York Times* "exposé," Whitewater failed to cause a ripple. Even then, the *Times* story was so ambiguous and poorly written, it was ignored. And besides, Bill Clinton was not yet the Presidential nominee, let alone elected.

But six months after the inauguration, Vince Foster killed himself. His death gave life to right-wing conspiracy nuts. Anti-Clintonites speculated that his suicide was somehow connected to the real estate deal. Most were perpetual malcontents easily influenced by radio rabble-rousing. They blamed "liberals" like Bill Clinton for their angry and empty lives. Exploiting the bile were conservative groups like Citizens United—source of the disgraceful 1988 "Willie Horton" ads accusing Michael Dukakis of opening prison gates so rapists and other violent criminals could prey upon society.

The Clintons apparently failed to learn damage control from the Dukakis campaign. Because of an innate distrust of the news media, they failed to adequately respond to speculation of Whitewater wrongdoing. Their silence gave rise to even more rumors. Minor discrepancies in their finances evolved into full-fledged accusations.

In the fourteen years since forming a real estate partnership with the Clintons, Jim McDougal had fallen on hard times. By 1992, a bi-polar condition made him eligible for a straightjacket. His wife had left him, and he was the target of an investigation into self-dealing as the owner of an insolvent savings and loan company called Madison Guaranty. The Clintons either didn't know or chose to ignore his mental state.

Following the election, Vincent Foster was given the task of wrapping up the Clintons' Arkansas business affairs. Hence, documents relating to Whitewater were kept in his

White House office. The Clintons' personal records were removed a few hours after his death—a standard procedure to protect lawyer-client confidentiality. Moving the documents set the rumor mill in motion. The *Times*, *Washington Post*, *Wall Street Journal* and other publications entered a competition to see which news organization could be more wrong. I planned to set the nation's major newspapers straight.

During my initial trip to Little Rock, I read all the material that producer Matt Saal collected. Indeed, he became concerned that I had abandoned him after I remained in my Capital Hotel room for three days. It took that much time to put the documents in chronological order and read through the state government gobbledygook. The reward was a revelation. I discovered that the *Times* article was dead wrong.

When I informed Matt of my discovery, he worried that after two decades of sobriety; I had gone on a drunken binge in Little Rock and was now hallucinating. The Clintons must be crooks. Why else would the nation's "newspaper of record" accuse them of wrongdoing? But after taking Matt on a guided tour through the documents, he agreed that the material provided a clear-cut contemporaneous record contradicting the *Times*.

...The partnership deal was not a free ride for the Clintons. They co-signed $250,000 in bank loans with the McDougals to finance Whitewater Estates.

...Bill Clinton was not Governor when he entered into the business arrangement, nor was McDougal then the owner of a state regulated S&L. He acquired the financial institution after the Whitewater partnership agreement.

...As Governor, Clinton appointed a regulator who delayed closing McDougal's insolvent federally insured Madison Guaranty. The delay, however, was at the request of the Federal Home Loan Bank Board.

...A so-called "novel" financing proposal for Madison cited in the story wasn't novel at all. Nor was it approved. The state regulator simply stated in response to Ms. Clinton's inquiry as an attorney that regulations allowed an S&L to sell stock if it met certain stringent conditions.

But the most shocking blunder in the *Times* seminal Whitewater story was an omission rather than a commission. Ace investigative reporter Jeff Gerth failed to acknowledge information given him eleven days before publication of the article.

Beverly Bassett Schaffer, the former Arkansas regulator accused of doing favors for McDougal's Madison Guaranty, faxed Gerth an eighteen page memorandum that gave a detailed account of her actions. Another five page memo was sent a week later. The documents definitively answered several questions raised in the "exposé." Yet, Gerth implied that Bassett Schaffer couldn't recall her role in the disputed transactions.

For example, she was accused of a conflict of interest for doing legal work for McDougal prior to becoming a state regulator. Bassett Schaffer was then a young associate assigned to do research at a firm representing McDougal.

"I've never met him," she told me in an interview. "I've never had a phone conversation with him, or received a letter from him, or memoranda. Nobody has called me and suggested that he knew me or that we had ever met. I don't know that we've ever been in the same room together."

Until my interview, the former state official repeatedly refused to talk to national reporters. Jeff Gerth's article and the news media's blind parroting of its inaccuracies made her wary. Particularly disturbing was a confrontation with an NBC producer and camera crew outside her Fayetteville, Arkansas law office. Schaffer took photographs of the news team as it stalked her between business appointments. Television ambushes are not unusual. I've done more than I care to admit. What made the NBC incident noteworthy was the producer's traveling companion, a man named David Bossie. He was the political director of Citizens United—Willie Horton's public relations firm.

The right-wing dirty trickster regularly bragged about his relationship with reporters. He even did their research, collecting documents at courthouses and other government agencies. Thick dossiers that were distributed to newsmen by Bossie looked impressive but revealed nothing illegal.

Doing our own homework, Matt Saal and I inspected archival records disclosing that Bassett Schaffer was the first to establish Madison Guaranty's insolvency and to initiate action. Our research helped persuade her that I wasn't just another TV jerk looking for a one-night stand-up. Knowing the documents clearly outlined the steps she took relating to McDougal's firm, she agreed to her first in-depth interview since the Independent Counsel's appointment.

"Mind boggling" is the way she described the *Times* story. "You can spend a lot of time making a record for yourself and building a good name. But you had better not hope it counts for anything when it matters."

The former securities regulator said she gave Governor Clinton a heads-up courtesy call to let him know that his business partner's S&L was going under. At the same time, she took action to close the firm. Clinton made no effort to intervene. Before she could act, though, the Federal Home Loan Bank Board in Dallas requested a delay. The delay eventually increased Madison's losses from $15 million to $68 million.

Former FHLBB Senior Vice President Walter Faulk confirmed Bassett Schaffer's account of what happened. "I don't see how anyone could say that knew the history of this case, or who would look into the history of the case, could say that she acted irresponsible or delayed or drug her feet in any manner whatsoever."

Faulk said he had no choice but to temporarily keep Madison open, sans Jim McDougal. The Federal Savings and Loan Insurance Corporation had run out of funds to cover depositor losses. The delay was crucial in preventing a run on other Arkansas S&L institutions. And besides, Madison Guaranty was a low priority in a nationwide S&L crisis—number one hundred eighty-nine on a list of failures.

Despite the federal official's key role in closing Madison Guaranty, Gerth never contacted Faulk. In fact, the only journalist other than me to interview him prior to the investigation's spiraling out of control was a Washington bureau correspondent for the *Minneapolis Star-Tribune*. The lapse in responsible reporting seemed inexplicable.

Faulk not only defended Bassett Schaffer, he also contradicted the half-truths of another perpetrator of the Whitewater myth—then GOP Congressman Jim Leach. The mild-mannered Iowa Representative has never received proper discredit for his role in the travesty. "In a nutshell, Whitewater is about the arrogance of power," he stated in a speech before Congress, suggesting that high crimes were committed.

Leach was known for his diffidence in criticizing opponents. Hence, reporters and pundits assumed he was above the partisan fray. Like a tail-wagging Cocker Spaniel, Leach was not expected to be an attack dog. But his leash was yanked by threats from the Republican leadership to deny him Chairmanship of the House Banking Committee if he didn't toughen up and take bites out of Bill Clinton's ass.

In our contentious 1994 interview, Leach feigned ignorance of the reasons for the delay in dealing with Madison

Guaranty's insolvency. He pretended to be unaware that the Federal Savings and Loan Insurance Corporation went broke because Congress failed to provide sufficient funds to cover S&L losses. "Oh, if you say who's at fault, I think you have a combination of people at fault. You have the state, you have the federal government, all of whom were slow," he conceded before hastily ending the interview. Leach was upset because unlike other reporters, I disputed his claim that Bassett Schaffer should have closed Madison, even if no money was available to protect depositors.

Apparently, much of Jeff Gerth's bad information came from Leach. While waiting in his office to do our interview, Matt Saal pointed to notes on the Representative's desk showing that he and Gerth were passing information to each other. Trade-offs are how reporters obtain a lot of proprietary records. In House speeches, the Congressman was lavish in praising the *Times* reporter as an originator of information that came from his office. So I guess I'm jealous. My sources were never so duplicitous in handing out accolades on my behalf.

All things considered, Representative Leach was more reliable than another key source for the first Whitewater story. Jim McDougal initially misled Gerth by giving him erroneous information that essentially formed the basis of the March, 1992 article. Egged on by a Little Rock Republican operative, McDougal told untrue and inflated yarns about the Whitewater partnership and his dealings with the Clintons and Beverly Bassett Schaffer. But in the manic stage of a bi-polar illness, he was apt to say anything.

By relying on a mentally deranged source, the *Times* set a precedent later adopted by hare-brained reporters questioning Vince Foster's suicide. Gerth played psychiatrist. He observed that "Mr. McDougal appeared stable, careful and calm." The story failed to mention that only months before, his source tried to enter an insanity plea in a bank fraud case. Financial setbacks and a belief that he had been cast aside by Bill Clinton left Jim in a near paranoid state.

McDougal was ultimately found innocent in the case—a verdict that he considered a miracle since he was guilty as hell. In the wake of his good fortune, he was ready to move forward and expected help from his friend, Bill. Although the Governor promised him a job, he failed to deliver. Despite the promises, McDougal's mental health and the publicized criminal trial made it politically impractical to appoint him to any government position. Regardless, Jim felt betrayed.

In most of my conversations with McDougal, he "appeared stable, careful and calm." That didn't change a psychiatric diagnosis. By the time of our on-camera interview, Matt and I had finished inspecting boxes of Whitewater documents. I had also interviewed Bassett Schaffer, Walter Faulk, Congressman Leach and several Arkansas bureaucrats. Confronted with the results of the research, Jim backed away from early allegations. He claimed Gerth misquoted and/or misinterpreted what he said.

Following the McDougal interview, I was ready to expose the "real truth" about Whitewater. However, I was in for a big surprise. Ed (no relation to Ted) Turner—then CNN's top newsgathering executive—reacted in a way that ran counter to the network's reputation as the *Clinton News Network*.

"I don't give a goddamn if the *New York Times* is wrong," he said angrily. "Either you come up with something on Clinton's crooked deals or we'll get somebody else to investigate the story."

Insulted, I promptly resigned. But not in Ed's presence. He had a terrible temper and would have helped me pack. So rather than have a quit fit in front of Ed, I announced my resignation to *Special Assignment* Executive Producer, Pamela Hill. I knew she would dissuade me of such a notion. And she did. After hearing me out, Pam defused the conflict by sending Ed a diplomatically worded memo supporting my research. He finally approved the story so long as I omitted references to the *Times*.

His reluctance to question the newspaper's accuracy epitomizes an attitude indigenous to television executives. Lacking faith in the skills of their correspondents, they cringe at the prospect of contradicting the printed word. Stories in the *Times*, *Washington Post* and other major publications are considered sacrosanct. As a result, CNN and its cable news imitators repeat newspaper and magazine stories twenty-four hours a day without independent research. More disturbing, networks fail to make corrections if published articles are proven wrong. Inaccuracies are simply disregarded.

Prior to our run-in over the Whitewater story, Ed and I were quite friendly. He was the executive who recruited me to the network. A solid newsman, he had been with CNN since its inception. For whatever reasons, he intensely disliked Clinton. Nor did he trust any of the Arkansas political crowd—the so-called Friends of Bill.

I got an early preview of Ed's animosity toward the President prior to our Whitewater run-in. The *American Spectator* published a lengthy exposé about Bill's supposed babes in January 1994. The article's author, David Brock, has since disavowed the story. Anyway, the conservative magazine gave CNN an exclusive copy of the story, which Ed was eager to use. I was included in a group who read the article and discussed how it should be handled.

Disgruntled Arkansas state cops formerly assigned to Clinton's security detail at the Governor's Mansion were named as sources of the story, and I suggested we make an effort to determine their credibility. I also expressed concerns about collaborating with the partisan publication in the absence of substantial independent research. My opinion didn't carry much weight. So I shut up. I was leaving on vacation the next day and didn't really care what was decided as long as I wasn't assigned to do the dirty work.

Whether the troopers told the truth is questionable. The President never received high marks for marital fidelity. But as it turned out, the troopers had a history of integrity problems that were documented in public records. A few hours of research would have revealed their tendencies to bend the truth. CNN didn't check. The network was among the first mainstream news organizations to proselytize "Babegate."

Two months later, my half-hour report offered a different spin on the nascent Clinton "scandals." Titled *Whitewater: A Changing Tide*, the documentary predicted a quick end to the inquiry. My simplified account of the Clinton/McDougal partnership gave details of transactions for a real-estate project that fell short of expectations. Due to lagging sales, a desperate and mentally disturbed partner cut corners to salvage the deal.

Documents and interviews with Bassett Schaffer, Walter Faulk, McDougal and other officials provided indisputable evidence that no favors were done by Bill Clinton on behalf of his partner. Nor did anyone intervene to save Madison. CNN buried my report and labeled me an ass-kissing Clinton apologist.

I wasn't completely alone in my contrarian take on Whitewater. A few journalists—notably Little Rock political pundit Gene Lyons and *New York Observer* columnist Joe Conason — were influenced by facts rather than cynical speculation. They were co-authors of *The Hunting of the*

President: The Ten-Year Campaign to Destroy Bill and Hillary Clinton, the book from which the film was adapted.

Not long after my documentary, Lyons wrote a one-hundred-fifty-three-page treatise titled, *Fools For Scandal: How the Media Invented Whitewater.* Published by *Harpers,* its theme was the same as my exposé. Unlike CNN, *Harpers* allowed Gene to name Gerth and the *Times* as the root cause of the tumult surrounding the bogus scandal.

In October, 1994, the magazine sponsored a National Press Club forum that was aired on C-Span. Gene and I were participants, along with reporters from *The Wall Street Journal, Business Week, U.S. News & World Report,* the Minneapolis *Star Tribune* and the *Columbia Journalism Review.* The *Times* declined an invitation.

Gene and I were the most outspoken critics of Whitewater reporting, although others on the panel expressed similar concerns. By coincidence, I had witnessed one of the most flagrant examples of journalistic irresponsibility the week before. The right-wing *Washington Times* ran a front page story under a headline, "Trooper Recalls Clinton Seeking Loan Help." The cop, L.D. Brown, had been a source for the *American Spectator's* "Bill's babes" exposé. The *Washington Times* tale quoted him as overhearing a conversation in which Bill Clinton supposedly help arrange a controversial Small Business Administration loan for Jim McDougal.

A day later, the Little Rock *Democrat-Gazette* picked up the story under the headline, "Arkansas Trooper said He Saw Clinton Pressure Judge for Money." Amazingly, an adjacent article stated "Trooper Denies Story on SBA Loan." On the same day, the *Washington Post* apparently plagiarized its cross-town rival under the byline of eager-beaver investigative reporter, Susan Schmidt, another perpetrator of the Whitewater hoax. The *Post* headline read "Arkansas Trooper Offers Partial Support to Allegation." But Brown was lying. The *Post* ran a correction two days later conceding the story was wrong—a rarity in its abysmal reporting of Whitewater-related issues.

"You start to wonder what's happening when you see this kind of reporting," I said during the C-Span discussion. "The *Washington Times* has not been known as a beacon of high-quality journalism, and yet you have the *Washington Post* in its fear of being scooped coming up with its own story, then having to correct it."

And downward Whitewater journalism descended. Nothing ever emerged to give credence to the *New York Times* original allegations or to many other "investigative" stories that followed. Despite the apathy that greeted my CNN documentary, it received an Emmy nomination, and I got to sit with TV news bigwigs at an ostentatious awards ceremony in a fancy New York City hotel ballroom, eating steak and feeling like "somebody." After collecting four Peabody medallions and numerous other journalism prizes, one more award was not a big deal. Good thing, too. I didn't win.

The biggest award was the Independent Counsel's 2002 final report validating my belief that the inglorious

Whitewater sham should have ended years before. That likely would have happened if Robert Fiske had continued in the job. This is evident by the release of a progress statement six months into investigation.

A June 30, 1994, interim report stated unequivocally that Vince Foster's death was a suicide. The document also cleared the White House and U.S. Treasury Department of interfering in a federal investigation of Jim McDougal's defunct S&L company—an allegation that surfaced a few days after Foster's demise. Crazed Clinton critics like Indiana Republican Representative Dan Burton were outraged by Fiske's expeditious findings. In one of the strangest events surrounding Whitewater, Burton shot a watermelon. Evidence such as the melon murder led to the appointment of Ken Starr.

Before leaving Little Rock, Robert Fiske recommended that the Independent Counsel's office be allowed to expand its investigation to include collateral crimes. Unwittingly, he gave Starr carte blanche to go on a political witch-hunt. I doubt that he imagined the kind of abuses that would occur over the next eight years. The provision was all that Starr needed to launch a partisan mockery of the justice system. Fairness, truth and integrity were forgotten in conducting the investigation.

Journalists joined the crusade, losing sight of context and proportion. Dozens of reporters on temporary duty in Little Rock were expected to quickly develop stories. All relied on the inaccurate *New York Times* article as a starting point. Very few tried to substantiate Gerth's reporting. The result—especially the reporting of television correspondents—was trivial tidbits interwoven into recaps of the *Times* stories.

Jim McDougal was a prime supplier of Whitewater disinformation. His bi-polar condition pushed him way over the edge of mental stability. Basking in notoriety at a *Western Sizzler* steakhouse in Arkadelphia where he conducted business, he took great pleasure in his fifteen-minutes-plus of recognition. Even as we set up CNN cameras for an interview at his residence, Jim kept busy on the phone doing radio interviews. His small manufactured home was on property owned by Claudia Riley, widow of former Arkansas Lieutenant Governor, Bob Riley. The couple had remained McDougal's loyal friends in good and bad times.

Notwithstanding his unpredictable behavior and frequent absences from reality, I was quite fond of Jim. Ex-drunks see reflections of ourselves in each other. His booze background helped us establish rapport. Though he probably said the same thing to all journalists, he claimed I was the only newsman who truly understood him and his deals. He told CNN reporter Bob Franken in a live interview in Washington that if indicted, he planned to call me as a defense witness. Jim made the statement after showing up as an observer at a Congressional hearing on Whitewater. He was decked out in one of his trademark pastel suits and a fedora. A *Western Sizzler* waitress was at his side.

As Jim feared, he was indicted, convicted and sentenced to prison in a bankruptcy fraud case involving Governor Jim Guy Tucker. By then, neither I nor anyone else could save him. Ignoring the advice of attorneys, he testified in his own defense. A bad choice. Though outwardly cavalier, witty and outrageous, he was a terrible witness.

The former high-roller deeply regretted his part in the scandal. He was heartbroken when a jail sentence was imposed on his ex-wife, Susan. Granted immunity, she still refused to testify before the Whitewater Grand Jury and spent eighteen months in the slammer. Susan said she feared being indicted for perjury if she told the truth because her testimony would be favorable to the Clintons. The fear was not unusual. Other witnesses claimed to have been intimidated by threats of perjury when their stories failed to mesh with the preconceived notions of prosecutors. Susan emerged as a martyr among the Clinton supporters. Before leaving office, Clinton issued her a Presidential Pardon.

I stayed in contact with Jim McDougal until late 1997. Our final conversation occurred when he called from a federal prison in Fort Worth, Texas offering a tip about an obscure aspect of the investigation. Busy on other stories, I brushed him off and later felt guilty about my abruptness. He died in March, 1998 in a prison cell—almost exactly six years to the day of the first *New York Times* Whitewater story. He was 57.

As a matter of personal disclosure, Bill Clinton's White-water attorney, David Kendall, was a co-counsel in success-fully defending me in a libel case in 1981. He was puzzled that I had not called him. But after thirteen years, I had forgotten his involvement in the case until he reminded me of our connection following my CNN documentary. I hoped he would become a key source. However, his Quaker conscience prevented him from engaging in the sieve-like tactics of the Independent Counsel's office. The only help I got was an accurate prediction that my reporting would prove prophetic.

Throughout 1994 and into early 1995, I reported con-trarian Whitewater stories and continued to fight battles to get them on the air. After a while, I began to worry about my reporting. When Pulitzer Prize winner James Stewart's book — *Blood Sport* — took up the banner of Ken Starr's crusade, I was ready to return to Tuscaloosa High School for a refresher course in perception, or perhaps schedule an appointment with an optometrist to examine my lying eyes. Thankfully, Gene Lyons and Joe Conason assuaged my fears by exposing countless errors in Stewart's book.

Remarkably, the Independent Counsel's final White-water report released in 2002 failed to set off a wave of soul-searching among journalists responsible for the eight year debacle. Nor were there mea culpas by Stewart, Jeff Gerth, the *Times*, *Post*, and others who were demonstrably inaccurate in their reporting. Gerth eventually left the *Times* to co-author a book titled, *Her Way: The Hopes and*

Ambitions of Hillary Rodham Clinton. He described "her way" as disingenuous, manipulative and ambitious — all qualities of a successful politician, but short of making her the 2008 Democratic Presidential nominee.

Regarding Whitewater, Gerth wrote, "Her likely indiscretions were altogether modest." Then he offered an incredible excuse for stirring up a $70-million hoax. Buried in footnotes, he stated that his initial article "had been rewritten by editors to include a number of mistakes," which were immediately corrected. However, there is no evidence of corrections in the newspaper's archives. Gerth's Hillary book made no mention of Beverly Bassett Schaffer and others he falsely accused of improprieties.

Whitewater is an egregious example of the dangers of distorting the truth under the guise of investigative journalism. Inaccurate reporting in the nation's "newspaper of record" was responsible for the appointment of a right-wing prosecutor whose obsessive search for dirt on the President had a devastating effect on the country. Impeachment proceedings, endless investigations by Congressional committees and years of partisan bickering brought government to a near standstill. Whitewater also had tributaries.

—

Although Ken Starr's office was the worst of the bunch, he had plenty of bad company in the Independent Counsel business. Between 1994 and 1998, U.S. Attorney General Janet Reno created a quasi-welfare agency for publicity hungry lawyers. She facilitated the appointment of eight separate Independent Counsels.

While spending $100-million, they obtained convictions for obscure crimes in cases that have long since been forgotten. The investigation of Housing and Urban Development Secretary Henry Cisneros is a glaring instance of much-to-do about sins best kept secret. In an FBI interview prior to his Senate confirmation, the former San Antonio Mayor lied to agents about payments to a mistress. Big deal—literally. It cost $9-million before he copped to a misdemeanor plea and paid a $10,000 fine. Independent Counsel David Barrett wasn't finished. Another $10-million was spent in an unsuccessful search for evidence that the Clinton White House impeded the Cisneros investigation.

Equally outrageous, if not more so, was the $21-million investigation of Secretary of Agriculture Michael Espy, a former Congressman who could not break his ingrained Congressional habit of accepting gratuities. When the *Wall Street Journal* reported that he was wined, dined, and entertained by Tyson Foods and other companies regulated by the Department of Agriculture, Espy's reaction was, "no big deal." But like the Cisneros probe, it was a big deal in terms of taxpayer money.

Independent Counsel Donald Smaltz conducted a four year investigation to prove to the freeloading regulator that Congressional rules were different than those in the Executive branch of government. Espy was finally indicted for accepting freebies, along with companies and individuals who gave him gifts. However, following a four month trial, a jury didn't take long to find him innocent. The panel may have concluded that his years in Congress rendered him incapable of saying "no." Moreover, Smaltz failed to produce evidence that Espy reciprocated by doing favors for anyone.

Because of a longstanding friendship with Espy, Arkansas-based Tyson Foods was the major target of the investigation. As a Congressman, he represented chicken-plucking Mississippi where poultry is a billion-dollar industry. After Espy became Secretary of Agriculture, his travel and lodging were paid by the company to two Tyson-sponsored events. His girlfriend also got assistance from a Tyson college scholarship fund. The beneficence amounted to only a few thousand dollars. But to quickly settle the case, the company pleaded guilty to giving Espy gratuities and paid a $6-million fine.

In an extraordinary overreach by the prosecutor, Tyson's chief spokesman, Archie Schaffer, was convicted under a vague statute usually applied to butchers. If Archie's surname sounds familiar, it's because he is married to former securities regulator, Beverly Bassett Schaffer. In the confines of Arkansas politics and commerce, everybody who is anybody is linked by no more than two degrees of separation. Archie is also the nephew of former U.S. Senator Dale Bumpers.

The conviction of bribing Espy with perks and getting nothing in return, was twice overturned by federal Judge

James Robertson. However, his exoneration of Archie was reversed on appeal. In September, 2000, Judge Robertson reluctantly sentenced Schaffer to a year in prison. Before serving a day, though, President Clinton signed a Pardon. He had plenty of justification. Nearly every Arkansas politician of prominence —Democrat and Republican— petitioned him on behalf of the popular Tyson employee.

Other firms and individuals were also convicted of relatively minor charges in the course of the investigation, but they were really inconsequential players in the probe. Donald Smaltz had set his sights on getting into history books. Under the delusion that Tyson Foods had a corrupt relationship with President Clinton, his office took off on several tangents unrelated to Agriculture Commissioner Espy.

In reality, Tyson's ties to the President were tenuous. While Governor, he pushed through highway weight limitations on trucks, and environmental laws that were detrimental to the corporate bottom line—actions that sometimes prompted the company to back Clinton opponents, like Bob Dole in the 1996 Presidential election.

But Friends of Bill worked for the company. The closest FOB was Tyson chief legal counsel Jim Blair, the husband of one of Hillary's closest friends. Before becoming Tyson's in-house lawyer, Blair helped Mrs. Clinton parlay $1000 into $100,000 in commodities market profits. *New York Times* reporter Jeff Gerth turned her good fortune into an exposé that linked her good luck in 1978 to a

$9-million Arkansas government "loan" to Tyson seven years later. The "loan" turned out to be a tax credit available to all companies as an incentive to expand operations in Arkansas. The Gerth story was front page news. The *Times* buried a loosely worded one paragraph correction.

Donald Smaltz was unable to conjure a way to investigate the Blair/Hillary commodities connection since it was far removed from the purpose of his inquiry. However, any doubt that the President was the Independent Counsel's intended target was erased when Smaltz confirmed to *Time* magazine that his office was probing a bizarre tale by a disgruntled former Tyson pilot, who claimed to have delivered envelopes stuffed with cash to Governor Clinton years before. The accuser had been fired by Tyson because of erratic behavior. And according to co-workers, he would have been the last person entrusted with such a mission. His mental health issues didn't deter prosecutors.

FBI agents were sent to interview his former Tyson boss, a Northwest Airlines Captain. When he labeled the allegation preposterous, agents threatened to charge him with perjury, warning that his Northwest job was in jeopardy. The pilot's lawyer filed a complaint with the Justice Department about the heavy-handed threats.

Time published the cash-stuffed-envelope story in December, 1994. Following complaints by Tyson for giving credibility to an unstable source, editors stated that the assertion was only a minor part of a lengthy "exposé." Oddly for a "minor" reference, the cash-stuffed envelope was the headline of a pre-publication news release. The Independent Counsel was quoted as confirming that a grand jury was gathering evidence related to the wacky tale. Smaltz said the allegation "had a ring of truth."

By his standards and those of other partisan Independent Counsels, the tooth fairy fable "had a ring of truth."

CHAPTER TWO

WITH MALICE

I thought my years of muckraking had immunized me from outwardly displaying incredulity. But that was before an encounter with Hickman Ewing, the top deputy to Whitewater Independent Counsel Kenneth Starr. We met for breakfast in 1994 at a Little Rock restaurant a few days after Hick joined Starr's Christian inquisition. Only minutes into the conversation, he made a statement that nearly caused me to fall face down in my platter of bacon and eggs.

"The only thing I know about Bill Clinton is what I saw in *The Clinton Chronicles*." Seeing my shocked expression, he quickly modified the comment. "I'm not saying I believe everything in the program. But where there is so much smoke, there must be fire. My job is to find the fire."

It was a stunning remark. On the basis of one of the most vicious propaganda videos ever produced about a President, Ewing presumed guilt. Perhaps he was joking and I missed the punch line. Or maybe he misspoke in trying to show impartiality. Regardless, the attitude is indigenous to many career prosecutors. They search for crimes to fit high-profile targets instead of finding malefactors known to have committed crimes.

The Denny's meeting took place four months after my CNN documentary suggesting there was nothing to the

Whitewater investigation. I had recovered from a bruised ego caused by the general indifference to my story. Hick was a close friend of a friend of mine, and I was attempting to exploit the connection. Developing him as a source would keep me abreast of new developments in an investigation that I expected to end in short order. Unfortunately, our mutual friend failed to forewarn me that Hick was a religious fundamentalist eager to embark on a moral crusade—a well-known fact in Memphis where for twenty years, he carried out God's commands as a prosecutor.

As a recovering Southern Baptist, part-time Presbyterian and believer in freedom of religion, I commend Bible-thumpers for their unquestioning faith. However, events in the first decade of the 21st Century suggest that religious fanaticism can bring down skyscrapers and kill people. It's a terrible analogy, but Whitewater devolved into a political jihad to bring down Bill Clinton. And Hickman Ewing was a foot soldier.

While U.S. Attorney for the Western District of Tennessee, he was well-known for putting corrupt politicians in jail. Armchair psychologists linked his aggressiveness to failures by his father, Hickman Senior. The well-respected high school football coach in Memphis became involved in politics and ended up in prison. Junior repeatedly denied a connection between daddy's sins and his own crusading zeal. But he never denied his born-again ardor for religious and conservative causes.

Indeed, Christian conservative groups honored him at a 1991 testimonial when he was replaced as U.S. Attorney. At the time, he told the Memphis *Commercial-Appeal* that he was considering a job with the Rutherford Institute, a right-wing legal group that regularly intervened in cases related to conservative issues. The job failed to materialize and Ewing opened a small law practice. In addition to legal work, he preached and devoted time to the Fellowship Evangelical Church, which he helped found.

Coincidentally—a curious coincidence—Rutherford assisted in a sexual harassment lawsuit filed by Paula Jones, a former Arkansas state employee, who claimed she was traumatized after Bill Clinton exposed his crooked penis to her in a Little Rock hotel room. The litigation emerged as a significant issue in the Whitewater investigation.

Despite Robert Fiske's swift progress in the early stages of the Whitewater investigation, he was replaced due to an alleged conflict of interest. His law firm had represented a large timber company that once sold property to Jim McDougal. Following Fiske's dismissal, Supreme Court Chief Justice William Rehnquist named a three-judge panel to find a replacement. The search committee was headed by U.S. District Court Judge David Sentelle—a protégé of Senator Jesse Helms.

Coincidentally, Judge Sentelle had lunch with his mentor before appointing Kenneth Starr as the new Independent Counsel. Sentelle later assured reporters that Whitewater—then dominating the news—never came

up. He said conversation was about old times and pros-
tate problems. Present at the lunch was Helm's North
Carolina Senate colleague, Lauch Faircloth. The right-
wing-to-the-extreme hog farmer would subsequently hire
smear artist David Bossie as an investigator for a Senate
committee investigating Whitewater. Watermelon-hater
Dan Burton also hired Bossie. Though circumstantial, the
symmetry gave weight to suspicions of a "vast right-wing
conspiracy."

Kenneth Starr's appointment was a blow to the mo-
rale of the Fiske staff. Some people quit and a new team
of morally upright prosecutors replaced them. Hickman
Ewing was the top of the recruit. Starr first interviewed him
at a McDonald's restaurant midway between Little Rock
and Memphis. By the time they finished their Big Macs and
fries, Hick was appointed to head the Little Rock office.

Had I known his religious beliefs in advance, it would
not have surprised me that he watched *The Clinton Chronicles*. Even so, relying on anything in the program defied
reason. In the first place, the DVD went far afield from
the purpose of appointing an Independent Counsel. The
investigation was supposed to focus on Bill and Hillary
Clinton's involvement in the Whitewater partnership, their
dealings with Jim McDougal's defunct Madison Guaranty,
and questions surrounding the suicide of Vince Foster.

The Clinton Chronicles was an idiot's guide to character assassination. It featured a cast of right-wing
characters who made the 2004 "Swift Boat" attacks on

Democratic Presidential candidate John Kerry's military record seem like a tribute. Vigorously promoted by the late Jerry Falwell, the so-called documentary was a forum for the crackpot fantasies of a former Arkansas segregationist judge, a low-ranking ex-Arkansas state employee, a loopy former congressman, and a hodgepodge of drooling characters unable to discern truth from fiction—as if they cared.

These were the kind of people who accused Tyson Foods of using its airplanes and trucks to haul cocaine around the country as if being billionaires was not enough for the Tyson family. The crazy allegation generated the funniest response to a question in the dozens of interviews that I conducted in reporting the madness of non-scandals that provided jobs for Ken Starr, Donald Smaltz and other Independent Counsels.

John Tyson—now Chairman of the Board of the giant food conglomerate—was surprisingly candid about what he called his "misspent youth." Asked about the company transporting dope on its planes, he laughingly said the story may be true, "but the only drugs would have been my personal stash." He has been clean and sober since 1990 and is an active member of a recovery group.

I know it's customary to say something nice about the dearly departed. But based on pre-Whitewater encounters with the Reverend Jerry Falwell—a topic for a later Chapter—I have to rely on the cliché, "He didn't seem to sweat a lot for a fat man." Watching the jowly TV preacher bear false witness for the benefit of his disbanded

Moral Majority and brainwashed Rush Limbaugh malcontents, I wondered what Jesus would do—WWJD? If Jerry arrived at his hoped for Heavenly home, an entry surely requiring generous dispensation, he probably knows what Jesus would not do. WJWND. He would not lend His name to smears by harebrained lunatics in $34.95 DVD's.

I was flabbergasted that "born again" Hick Ewing wasted eighty-three-minutes watching a compilation of gossip, distortions and outright fabrications—the antitheses of his Savior's teachings and the admonition about casting stones. *The Clinton Chronicles* was a bunch of crap. In Hick's defense, however, I had the advantage of knowing some of the starring characters, as well as details of allegations in the documentary. Indeed, my earlier exposés dealt with topics that came back to haunt me during the Whitewater sham.

In the fall of 1996, one of my ex's called to report that a private detective named Rex Armistead contacted her trying to find dirt on me. There was certainly plenty to be found. And my second wife—East Baton Rouge Parish Assistant District Attorney Patricia Byrd—knew where to look. Her knowledge of my misdeeds during our fifteen year relationship could easily have filled Armistead's notebook.

At a time when our romance was a step above casual, Patricia literally dragged me out of a New Orleans gutter, took me to a halfway house to be treated for DT's, gave me a place to live and even attended Alcoholics Anonymous meetings with me, although she didn't have a drink-ing problem. Nine months later in November, 1971, we were married. Too soon, according to the wisdom of many AA members. Still, we came within a hairbreadth of living happily ever after. During the marriage, I resurrected my broadcasting career, discovered a knack for muckraking, won big journalism awards in Louisiana, and collected big-ger prizes at television stations in Miami and Boston.

Returning to Louisiana nine years later, we were the parents of two adopted sons, and Patricia had a new Law Degree from Boston College. Our marriage—though shaky—almost survived the "too soon" caution flag waved by AA friends. Then I fell in love with my present wife. Other issues on both sides contributed to the divorce. None are worth dwelling on at this late date. Suffice to say that our 1986 split was nasty and bitter. Patricia saw the worst of my alcoholism and could tell hair-raising stories. However, she refused to share them with the detective. It was a gen-erous decision.

Rex Armistead really didn't need to waste her time to learn my transgressions. He could have asked me person-ally. Or taken notes at AA meetings. I held nothing back in sharing what ex-drunks call "our experience, strength and hope." Moreover, gory details of my personal life had been reported in books, magazines and newspapers. I made no effort to conceal my past. As a defendant in several libel lawsuits and a perceived adversary of over-reaching law enforcement agencies, I was accustomed to personal scrutiny. Nevertheless, Armistead's inquiry puzzled me. I left a message at his office, offering my muckraking skills in digging up dirt on me. He didn't respond.

I subsequently learned the detective was being paid by Richard Mellon Scaife, an eccentric Pennsylvania billionaire who bankrolled right-wing nuts in their efforts to discredit Bill Clinton. I also discovered that Armistead—a former director of the Mississippi Department of Safety criminal investigative division—was a longtime acquaintance of Hickman Ewing. They conferred during the Whitewater investigation, but I don't know if my sordid background was ever discussed.

The fruits of Armistead's snooping did reach another destination. According to an April, 1998 *Salon* magazine report, the information found its way into the files of Congressman Jim Leach's House Banking Committee. Under the headline, "Scaife Investigator Targeted CNN Reporter," freelance muckraker Murray Waas reported the visit to my former wife, as well as the detective's involvement in the "Arkansas Project, a four-year, $2.4 million campaign to investigate and discredit the President."

Having a private detective pry into my background was curious. As much as I would like to think otherwise, my CNN Whitewater documentary failed to have a significant impact. What made me more than a tiny pimple on a Sumo wrestler's butt in the eyes of Clinton critics were stories I reported about an international drug smuggler and his alleged association with a millionaire Little Rock business-man. Both men were attacked in *The Clinton Chronicles*, as well as in publications smearing the President.

The *Salon* exposé stated that "Armistead and two law firms received more than $250,000 from Scaife to look into allegations that President Clinton, while Governor of Arkansas, ordered state law enforcement authorities to protect the activities of a cocaine smuggling ring operating from a remote airport in the town of Mena, Arkansas."

Nobody knew better than I that the Mena claims were a fable kept alive for years by the *Wall Street Journal* op-ed page, and a collection of creepy journalists and Internet bloggers. The difference between them and me is that I had investigated the tales before they could find the town on a map. My first Mena story aired in 1984. And for the next ten years, I periodically chased down allegations that the tiny town was a hotspot of exotic goings-on involving drug smuggling, illegal weapons and secret CIA operations.

One of the characters caught up in Mena's *Loony Tunes* cartoons was a Little Rock investment banker named Dan Lasater. *The Clinton Chronicles* and other off-the-wall exposés portrayed him as a convicted dope dealer, money launderer, and a Bill Clinton confidante and financial backer. As a result of the alleged "close relationship," Governor Clinton purportedly signed a "Pardon" that cut short a Lasater prison sentence for drug dealing. His friend, Bill, also supposedly arranged for a Lasater-owned investment firm to collect millions in commissions from the sale of Arkansas bonds.

According to the lunatic fringe, Dan Lasater was akin to a corrupt "Leonard Zelig." But unlike the Woody Allen fictional movie character who turned up in real-life events, I reported that he was a real person in fictional events. Like their attacks on other "Friends of Bill," right-wing lunatics combined an ounce of truth with a ton of fiction.

Defending Lasater in a CNN story is a reflection of my AA belief in redemption—a trait unknown to Jerry Falwell and other religious zealots. The Arkansas millionaire was post-sin demonized in an array of forums — including Congress.

On June 9, 1994, for example, three Republican Congressmen led by watermelon assassin Dan Burton, went into near conniption fits during a slander extravaganza. Lucky for them, speeches on the floor of Congress are immune from lawsuits. In barely coherent remarks, U.S. Representatives Burton, Robert (B-1 Bomber) Dornan of California and Sam Johnson of Texas took turns viciously vilifying Lasater and Patsy Thomason, a woman who formerly worked for him. She was then the White House Director of Administration. In that capacity, she had access to a safe and keys in Vincent Foster's office and was among those summoned on the night of his suicide. Hence, she became a character in crazy conspiracy theories. In a guilty-until-proven-innocent speech, Dan Burton suggested she give up her White House job.

"If she is clean, if she is clear," he intoned. "Then, that is fine, and we will all apologize and she can go back to work at the White House." Ironically, Burton took an opposite view in 2008 in defending baseball star Roger Clemens. He claimed the athlete was being persecuted by Democrats for steroid use without a fair trial.

The Lasater allegations were not limited to maniacal politicians, *The Clinton Chronicles* and the right-wing media. Erroneous and exaggerated stories appeared in publications like the *Los Angeles Times* and *Newsweek*. He was portrayed as a big contributor to Clinton's gubernatorial campaigns. In return, he supposedly earned big bucks from state bond sales and also received a "Pardon" for drug crimes.

In reality, Lasater was a minor player in Arkansas politics. He contributed less than $10,000 to Bill Clinton's political coffers. An equal amount was raised at a campaign event sponsored by his company. He also made a plane available for three Clinton campaign trips. His firm did participate in bond sales, but it was never the lead underwriter. Commissions were relatively small. The so-called Pardon granted by Clinton only allowed him to possess hunting weapons. Since Lasater was convicted in federal court, the Governor needed concurrence from the feds to issue even a limited Pardon.

Indeed, the entrepreneur didn't need Bill Clinton to make money. He was a millionaire many times over before the age of thirty. Experience working at McDonald's as a teen-ager had inspired him to open his own hamburger stands. Profits helped him establish the Ponderosa Steak House chain. After selling the company, Lasater built the nation's most successful thoroughbred stable. His horses set a world record for the most wins in a season and he received three consecutive Eclipse Awards, the horseracing industry's most prestigious prize.

The Lasater link to the Governor had begun at a Hot Springs racetrack where he met Bill Clinton's mother, Virginia Kelly, a horse racing aficionado. He was also friendly with Clinton's brother, Roger. Overly so. They started snorting cocaine together, most of which was provided by Lasater. When Roger got in trouble with a dope dealer, Lasater loaned him money to pay the debt. And while Roger tried to stop snorting, the businessman gave him a job shoveling horse shit at his Florida racing stable. The attempt to stay clean and sober came too late. Roger was indicted on drug charges. And in a plea bargain deal, he squealed on his benefactor.

Dan Lasater's downfall was caused in large part by having too much money to blow—literally and figuratively. At Little Rock drugs, booze and babes parties, he gave friends pounds of cocaine. The fun and games ended with his arrest, a guilty plea, and a prison sentence for possessing and distributing drugs. He served six months in a federal prison before being assigned to a halfway house. While incarcerated, he found Jesus. People who know him say the jailhouse conversion was real and lasting.

When we met in 1994, Lasater was an active member of a large fundamentalist church and well-respected by church leaders and fellow congregants. Though not publicized at his insistence, he contributed generously to charitable causes in both time and money. His spiritual commitment and philanthropy flies in the face of the unforgiving attacks by the late Reverend Falwell and other "Christians," who either never read or forgot what they learned in the New Testament about redemption.

The Clinton Chronicles portrayed Lasater as just about the most corrupt guy in Arkansas. The *Los Angeles Times* and *Newsweek* described him as a "bond daddy," whose close ties to Bill Clinton got him a Pardon and earned big profits for his company. The stories didn't ring true. As far as I could tell from reading the articles, Lasater's company sold only a small number of Arkansas bonds. I knew from past experience that except for the lead underwriter, commissions from bond sales are comparatively small. I was also aware that Governors cannot Pardon federal crimes. So I began digging. My search for the truth about Lasater was not altogether altruistic.

CNN *Special Assignment* Executive Producer Pamela Hill had dropped hints that I might be sent to Los Angeles to do stories on the O.J. Simpson circus. I quickly conjured ways to avoid the assignment. O.J. fear prompted me to propose a project titled *Extremism Unchecked*. I promised Pam to report "never before disclosed material."

In an effort to find "never before disclosed material," I fired off a self-serving letter to Dan Lasater extolling my virtues as a fair-minded reporter. I figured that an exclusive interview with him could save me from O.J.

Lasater had been savaged unmercifully in *The Clinton Chronicles* and the target of inaccurate stories in the mainstream media. Hence, he refused interview requests. He believed that responding to the allegations only extended the misery. His media notoriety, combined with Starr's appointment as Independent Counsel and the arrival of Hickman Ewing in Little Rock, led him to believe he would be a high profile target. Convinced that his investment company's financial records were going to be subpoenaed, he spent hundreds of thousands of dollars on legal fees and related expenses to defend himself.

Included in my interview request was a videotape of the widely ignored Whitewater story I reported five months earlier. For good measure, I mentioned my experiences as an ex-drunk. I also journeyed through a valley in the shadow of disgrace.

Two weeks later, he agreed to discuss the possibility of an on-camera interview. I flew to Little Rock and again checked into the Capital Hotel. Accompanied by his lawyer, Lasater came to the hotel the same day. Following three hours of discussions, he was satisfied that I would treat him fairly.

First, I needed hard evidence to counter untruths about his activities. Lasater came prepared. He retrieved three large boxes of documents from his car. The records included documentation of all of his company's Arkansas bond sales, and a stack of correspondence between federal agencies and the Governor's office relating to the conditional Pardon signed by Bill Clinton. If I wanted anything else, he instructed his attorney to give me complete access to company records and personal material concerning allegations made against him.

Nothing I found over the next several weeks disputed Lasater's account of his company's dealings with the state, his campaign contributions, the circumstances of his arrest, and the propriety of the Pardon. I concluded that Lasater's notoriety was mainly due to cocaine-addled bragging about his supposed Clinton connection.

After convincing Pam that the current smear campaign was worth reporting, she assigned Washington based *Special Assignment* producer Matt Saal to again work with me. In addition to material Lasater made available, Matt and I gathered documents and interviewed people familiar with the "bond daddy." Wooten Epps, then head of the office that oversaw Arkansas bond sales, provided definitive proof that Lasater's role in state bond sales had been negligible. Epps was not personally acquainted with the "bond daddy." However, he said archival records disclosed minimal sales by Lasater's company.

Surprisingly, the most convincing evidence of a smear campaign was provided by Clinton critics. Desperation "dirty tricks" in a gubernatorial race years before were the genesis of rumors about the Bill Clinton-Dan Lasater connection. In last minute TV ads, strategists for Republican Frank White raised the issue. Describing Lasater as a major campaign contributor and close friend of Clinton, the political ads claimed that despite a record of cocaine dealing, the investment banker's company received lucrative state contracts. White and his campaign manager later expressed shame for the tactics.

Whitewater: With Malice aired December 4, 1994 in a Sunday prime time magazine show called *CNN Presents.* The segment failed to influence Clinton-haters. Just the opposite. Like the Whitewater documentary, the story raised the hackles of the far right and enhanced my standing as a Clinton apologist. I first came under attack by the *Clinton-Watch*—an arm of Willie Horton's public relations agency, *Citizens United.* The group's President, Floyd Brown, sent a newsletter to his right-tilted flock stating that my report "was one of the sorriest pieces of television journalism I have ever seen."

He cited my story as an example of Clinton ass-kissing. "The Clinton apologists in the liberal news media have proven time and time again that they will protect the President at any cost, no matter what it says about their journalistic integrity." I thought I heard echoes of Brown's criticism during the 2008 Presidential campaign when the media was accused of giving Barack Obama a free ride. The more things change, etc.

In August, 1995, another right-wing group operating under the misnomer of *Accuracy in Media* devoted five pages to dissecting the Lasater report. As evidence of my inaccuracies, *AIM* cited stories of Lasater wrongdoing that appeared in the *Los Angeles Times*—the very same article that prompted me to research the smears in the first place.

The *AIM* article advanced a theory of why I would do a favorable story on Dan Lasater's behalf. It cited my previous relationship with infamous international drug smuggler Barry Seal—one of the leading characters in *The Clinton Chronicles*.

In a concocted leap of logic, the faux documentary linked Barry Seal, Lasater and Bill Clinton to an exotic guns-for-drugs CIA operation at a small airport in Mena. I confess that *AIM* was correct in its supposition that my prior connection to the drug smuggler influenced a favorable Lasater report. But the reasoning was all wrong.

I was the only journalist who knew the real story of Barry Seal and Mena.

—

In October, 1984, I sat beside a cameraman at the window of a Miami hotel room watching four men in a parking lot four floors below. Adler Berriman (Barry) Seal was meeting with a tall, younger man sporting a bushy mustache and blondish hair. Two Hispanic men looked on, but said little. The blonde guy was an agent of the Drug

Enforcement Administration. The Latinos were Panamanian snitches.

The location of our vantage point for secretly videotaping the clandestine rendezvous was surrealistic—a
garishly decorated hotel suite with mirrored walls, a king-
sized waterbed, a columned Roman Tub, and a table-like
contraption similar to a gynecologist's workbench. Moans,
grunts and screams of "Oh, God. Oh, God," echoed in
the background. Despite the noise of a hardcore pornographic TV channel we should have turned off—or at least
muted—and the distractions of elaborate sexual accoutre-
ments, our attention remained focused on the meeting. It
was supposed to prove an outlandish story that Seal told
me a few days earlier. The grossly overweight pilot admitted smuggling tons of dope into the United States. But he
said that was before signing on as a super-spy for both the
DEA and CIA.

To corroborate his tale, I was unwittingly committing
a felony. A tiny transmitter and microphone were taped
beneath Seal's blue, salsa style shirt. The video was legal.
However, I learned after the fact that bugging conversations without the permission of all parties violated Florida
laws. I don't normally break laws, but the statutes had
changed since my television spying in Miami a decade before. The smart thing would have been to check the laws
beforehand. But this was a slapdash, spur of the moment
venture.

A day earlier, Seal convinced me to accompany him to South Florida to corroborate his alleged exploits as an undercover informant spying on Colombia's drug cartel and a bunch of characters with names like Escobar, Ledher and Ochoa.

My introduction to the world of Barry Seal occurred only two weeks before. At our first meeting, he didn't waste time with modesty. In a matter of minutes, he boasted of being the hero of an improbable undercover operation that linked Colombian cocaine barons to officials of Nicaragua's Sandinista government. He also bragged of being the nation's biggest cocaine smuggler, DEA's best ever informant, a former Green Beret and the airline industry's youngest 747 jumbo jet Captain.

By the time Seal finished reciting his adventures, I diagnosed him as a nut case. But listening to fairy tales is an occupational hazard of investigative reporters. Most times, I humored schizoid tipsters by asking a few perfunctory questions prior to telling them that I had to take an important phone call. Seal was more persevering. He insisted I come to his home to inspect material that would prove his story, as well as expose serious misconduct by Louisiana lawmen.

At the time, I was producing investigative documentaries for Baton Rouge ABC affiliate, WBRZ. After nine years in "big time television," I was back where I first established my muckraking bona fides. In gypsy-like travels as an investigative reporter in Miami, Boston and other venues,

I was accustomed to dealing with characters telling wild yarns. In this instance, Barry Seal's persistence wore me down. Since his address wasn't a mental hospital, I agreed to waste a couple of hours.

The first surprise was discovering that instead of an asylum, he lived in an architecturally distinctive half-million dollar home in an upscale neighborhood. A late model Mercedes 380 SL was parked in the driveway adjacent to an immaculately manicured lawn. The residence was considerably different than homes of most kooky tipsters—a few of whom lived in cardboard boxes under bridges.

Barry Seal was less imposing. He looked nothing like the braggart I envisioned during our phone conversation. An extra hundred pounds around the girth belied his claims of being a former Army Green Beret, which turned out to be an exaggeration of his Army Reserve duties. Nor could I imagine Barry's jumbo belly behind the controls of a jumbo jet. Moreover, his ingratiating personality convinced me that he was a first class con man. Remarkably though, the tales he told me were mostly true—and ultimately tragic. The 1984 meeting marked the beginning of a relationship that continued into Barry's afterlife, and eventually became a sidebar of the Whitewater investigation.

The enigmatic smuggler was murdered in Baton Rouge by Colombian hit-men eighteen months later and posthumously became an anti-hero of plots promulgated by right-wing zealots and semi-legitimate journalists.

As the legend grew, I was accused of covering up his Nicaraguan guns-for-drugs deals and concealing his alleged links to Dan Lasater, Bill Clinton and the CIA. Two documentaries I reported about Seal's life and death made me the target of intense criticism, a defendant in multimillion dollar libel lawsuits by cops and prosecutors, and the subject of the aforementioned investigation into my personal life by a private detective hired by Richard Mellon Scaife.

Barry Seal's gravesite must have quaked with laughter at the accumulation of fables surrounding his activities. He relished notoriety. The flamboyant pilot's need for attention is what got him killed. Unfortunately, I was an accomplice. He wanted to be a television star, and I agreed to put him in the spotlight. His braggadocio in our early meetings made the story irresistible. Seal's favorite word was "covert." He alluded to a long history of working for the CIA, though I found out that his spy interlude was brief.

Following our initial meeting, I began checking Barry's background. Some of the yarns were true. At the age of twenty-seven, he was a Trans World Airlines 747 Captain. His tenure ended abruptly because of a taste for adventure. He was fired in 1973 after being indicted in a plot to transport plastic explosives to Mexico.

His explanation to me was that the mission was part of a CIA plan to overthrow Castro's Cuba. In reality, it was an ill-conceived FBI sting operation designed to entrap an associate of New Orleans Mafia boss, Carlos Marcello. The conviction was overturned in May, 1976 because of FBI and prosecutorial misconduct in conducting the sting.

By then, Barry was in the aviation advertising business, flying small planes with streaming banners over football games and outdoor events. He also piloted helicopters, but not nearly as skillfully as fixed-wing aircraft. Once while transporting Santa Claus to a shopping center, his chopper hit a power line and thudded to the ground. "I felt sorry for kids who sat on Santa's lap," he told me. "We landed so hard, he shit in his pants."

The accident was about the only excitement in a mundane life of somebody who saw himself as a swashbuckling soldier of fortune. To supplement advertising income, Seal bought, sold and traded airplanes. The sideline introduced him to a network of aviation "consultants" who provided services to a booming industry. Drug trafficking.

The hippie generation had tempered society's attitude toward recreational drugs. Many middle-class and affluent Americans were experimenting with marijuana, cocaine, and other illegal drugs. To meet consumer demand, foreign suppliers recruited skilled pilots. Barry Seal found a new vocation. Six months after his explosives smuggling conviction was overturned, he hauled a load of dope into the United States. Oblivious to moral implications, he rationalized it was excitement, not greed, that attracted him to the business. Even so, he kept the money.

For a dope smuggler, Barry's lifestyle was not ostentatious. He spread the wealth by helping friends and contributing to community events like the Baton Rouge Symphony. His oddest philanthropy was supporting a former high school classmate's missionary work in Haiti. He gave his friend cash, taught him to fly and even helped him buy a plane to move around the country. The parson revealed the beneficence while delivering Barry's eulogy. Hiding good deeds contradicted a need for the spotlight.

Seeking attention was the storyline of Barry's life. He grew up in Baton Rouge and attended a high school that bordered the city's affluent Garden District. The all-white student body was a mix of kids from silk-stocking, blue collar and low income families. Neither scholar nor athlete, he found his niche at an airport near his daddy's gas station on the city's main boulevard. While still a teenager, he became a skilled pilot.

Barry's inordinate desire for recognition was evident at our first time meeting when he sat me down to view a videotape of a three-month old CNN news story, which disclosed that a pilot working as a DEA informant secretly snapped pictures of Colombian drug lords, Nicaraguan soldiers and a Sandinista official as they loaded 1500 pounds of cocaine onto a C-123 transport at a military airstrip outside Managua. Citing unnamed sources, the CNN report implied that the Communist regime of President Daniel Ortega was involved in international drug smuggling.

"I'm the pilot who snapped the pictures," Seal said after playing the video. "It's the biggest case in DEA's history. But Louisiana cops are fucking up the investigation."

"How so?" I asked.

"By investigating me."

Somehow, I kept a straight face listening to his non-stop monologue that ranged from grandiose to paranoid. He claimed the U.S. Attorney's office in Baton Rouge and the New Orleans federal Organized Crime Strike Force had put together a task force to build a case against him. He accused investigators of intimidating witnesses, planting evidence and encouraging perjury. As proof of persecution, Barry promised to make available corroborating witnesses, provide transcripts of secret Grand Jury testimony and give me copies of tape recorded conversations confirming his claims. He also said he would produce photographs of secret missions he undertook for the government.

I played along, telling him to show me his stuff. Sure enough, the next day he was on the phone making arrangements to deliver material. I was at home getting ready to attend my youngest son's junior high football game. Seal asked me to wait for him. When he arrived, I was in the carport preparing to leave. We spoke only briefly as he retrieved a stack of documents from the car trunk. The short conversation was a prelude to a peculiar event that would arouse my curiosity about Barry.

At the football stadium, I happened to run into the U.S. Attorney for the Middle District of Louisiana, a Ronald Reagan appointee named Stanford Bardwell. Seeing Bardwell was quite a coincidence since he was among the people that Barry criticized. I asked the prosecutor what he knew about the braggart. At the mention of Seal's name, the federal prosecutor visibly flinched. "I have nothing at all to say about him," he said before walking away.

The response surprised me. I wasn't Bardwell's biggest fan, but we had a cordial relationship. Like many U.S. Attorneys, he was a political appointee who had very little experience as a prosecutor. In private practice, Bardwell specialized in civil law. His odd reaction to my question suggested there must be something substantive to the self-professed drug trafficker's claims of being a VIP criminal.

An incident the following day added more intrigue to the Bardwell encounter. A newsroom receptionist handed me a cryptic phone message. "Does Mr. Seal know that Mr. Camp met with Mr. Bardwell? Someone on the side found it interesting."

The caller described himself as a "bystander." I suspected Seal of leaving the message. He probably arranged for someone to follow me to the football field. The note would add mystique to his tall tale. However, he acted genuinely surprised when I told him what happened. He blamed cops, saying they kept him under constant surveillance. I thought it unlikely that Seal would be followed to my home by agents, who then trailed me to a football game.

Despite my disbelief of Barry's ridiculous allegations of law enforcement misconduct, the material he gave me suggested overzealousness by local lawmen. Grand jury testimony, depositions, and related confidential documents disclosed a pattern of witness harassment and possible subordination of perjury. The documents prompted me to begin asking more questions about the pilot's background. But before I could get answers, Seal made an extraordinary proposal. He said DEA agents had summoned him to Miami for an urgent meeting with other informants. He invited me to fly with him in his Lear jet to videotape the meeting. The rendezvous, he said, would prove he was who he claimed to be. I had now truly reached the gates of a journalistic Land of Oz. Lear jets? Clandestine trysts with drug agents and informants?

Curiosity made the invitation difficult to turn down. However, traveling in Seal's plane while doing a story about him didn't meet traditional guidelines of ethical journalism. Not that there are hard and fast rules. Ethics are in the eyes of the beholder. My hard and fast rule is reporting the truth. I told Barry I would take a commercial flight and meet him in Miami. He said that was impractical. It was too late in the day to get a flight out of Louisiana. Leaving early the next morning would not give me enough time to handle the logistics necessary to record the meeting.

Facing a dilemma, I sought the advice of WBRZ News Director, John Spain. He was a former investigative reporter and knew that these kinds of ethical decisions were guided by experience, personal integrity and plain old gut feelings. After laying out Barry's story, he agreed it was worth pursuing—especially given Bardwell's strange reaction. I was given the go ahead. In order to maintain an arms-length relationship, the station could reimburse Seal the equivalent of round-trip airline tickets.

As we talked about Barry's strange tale, John's reporting instincts kicked in. He wanted a piece of the action. So I called to see if John could tag alone. No problem. But Seal declined the offer to pay for the trip, saying he didn't have an FAA passenger carrier permit. I thought he was joking. He hauls dope across America, yet worries about FAA rules. Hard to believe. But so was nearly everything else he told me.

Despite his refusal, we showed up at the airport with a check for four roundtrip airline tickets. The check was never cashed. Still, our consciences were clear. Traveling with John and me were cameraman Sailor Jackson and part-time newsroom employee, Chris Brezon, a thirty-three-year-old professional still photographer in his final year at LSU Journalism School. Sailor, his given name, was a talented young African-American cameraman who worked with me on previous documentaries.

Prior to departure, I contacted a close friend in Miami for help. Dave Choate was News Director of WSVN, the station where I collected two Peabody medallions eleven years earlier. He agreed to loan us the station's "snoop van," a non-descript vehicle with one-way glass that concealed the rear compartment. In the early 1970's, I spent many hours inside the van's forerunner spying on mobsters, corrupt politicians, and an array of scalawags. The station was then called WCKT.

It was a quick flight. The Lear landed at Fort Lauderdale International Airport, where Barry had been arrested a year earlier for smuggling Quaaludes into the country. The arrest raised the possibility of spending ten years in a federal penitentiary, inspiring him to change his job title from drug smuggler to DEA informant.

Barry's only prior jail time was in Honduras. Suspecting him of being a smuggler, cops searched Barry's plane for cocaine. But the dope had been stashed on a nearby island. Still, he was arrested him for possessing a 22-caliber pistol. A few days later, he was on the verge of being set free on the gun charge when a co-conspirator squealed.

Eight months in a Honduran jail was enough to put him in a deal-making mood after the Quaalude conviction. And Barry had a bargaining chip. He was then negotiating his biggest deal ever—3500 kilos of cocaine.

Colombian Cartel leaders knew Seal as "Ellis McKenzie," a pseudonym on his forged passport. They didn't notice news accounts of the smuggling trial of a man named Barry Seal. In the aftermath of his conviction, the drug pilot had much information to offer. But he had trouble finding a customer. South Florida drug agents shrugged off his overtures to be an informant. He also tried to call the office of a former high school classmate—none other than Baton Rouge U.S. Attorney Stanford Bardwell. The prosecutor refused to talk to him. Frustrated, he went straight to the top.

In February, 1984, Barry flew to Washington D.C. and knocked on the door of the Vice President's Drug Task

Force. He volunteered as an informant against the Medellín Cartel. Incredibly, bureaucrats in the high-profile drug fighting office had never heard of the cartel. Nor did they recognize names of major cocaine suppliers. They were smart enough, though, to refer him to a special Task Force in Miami. For those agents, it was like winning the national lottery of prize informants.

One of the lottery winners was now meeting with Barry as I sat next to a cameraman in a Miami hotel room. DEA agent Ernst (Jake) Jacobson was Seal's primary contact. He had arrived on schedule for the rendezvous with the two Latinos. We were well positioned. In addition to the WBRZ camera, we had found a bonus second camera inside WSVN's vehicle. It was parked only a few feet from where the men met. Although Chris Brezon made a living as a still photographer, he had used TV video equipment. We recorded the meeting from above. John and Sailor videotaped from the snoop van.

The drift of the conversation dealt with luring Pablo Escobar from his Colombian safe haven to Panama—a jurisdiction where he could be arrested by U.S. agents. As a neophyte in cocaine lore, I didn't know that Escobar was the cartel's big cheese. In fact, he was believed responsible for the April, 1984 assassination of Rodrigo Lara Bonilla, Colombia's crusading anti-drug Justice Minister.

Our undercover venture was going well until the four men started to enter Jacobson's car. Seal jumped back and ran inside the hotel. In a matter of seconds, he was banging on the door.

"Get this goddamned thing off me," he screamed while ripping at the transmitter we taped to his body. "There's a bug alarm in Jake's car. When it went off, I told them the noise was my beeper and I needed to take an important call."

I had heard an unusual sound on the videotape. However, the bug alarm story seemed far-fetched. I suspected there were conversations that Seal didn't want us to hear. Whatever his reason for removing the wire, he departed with Jake and the Panamanians. They were gone for about thirty minutes while we entertained ourselves by shooting video of the hotel room to show the boys back home. When Barry returned, we dropped off the van at WSVN and headed for Fort Lauderdale airport.

Before the trip home, I interviewed the drug smuggler inside the Lear. I didn't quite know what to make of him. Rather than accepting the reality that he cut a deal to stay out of jail, he saw himself as a soldier of fortune, who risked his life to help the DEA and CIA. I now believed parts of his story. But I was wary of doing a report that allowed him to malign Baton Rouge lawmen—some who were friends of mine.

By the same token, I had never worried about winning popularity contests with cops. And I didn't enhance my standing by reporting the Barry Seal saga. That's for sure.

CHAPTER THREE

GENESIS OF A MYTH

The Mena Intermountain Regional Airport in the west Arkansas foothills of the Ouachita Mountains seems an unlikely locale for spy stories and conspiracy tales. Before the arrival of Barry Seal, Mena was best known for its proximity to the Jot 'em Down Store in nearby Pine Ridge. The rural relic was made famous by Lum and Abner, popular 1940's radio characters. The Jot 'em Down Store was a fictional backdrop for dispensing homespun mountain observations about Washington politics and national affairs. It's too bad that Lum and Abner were not around when Mena gained mythical notoriety. The zany stories would have provided them months of material for comical commentary.

The yarn began in June, 1984, when a camouflage-painted C-123K piloted by Barry Seal landed at the airport with a full cargo of rumors and conjecture. Dubbed "The Fat Lady" in its Vietnam days, the retired military transport sat on a tarmac outside the hangar of an aircraft repair shop for six months before being sold. It left the ground twice, each time to circle the airport. But the simple presence of the mysterious plane triggered years of speculation that has never gone away. Examples:

...Mena was the home base of a major Nicaraguan Contra guns for drugs operation.

...Contra rebels were trained in the mountains around Mena.

...Bill Clinton, George Herbert Bush, Ronald Reagan (pick one) and the CIA

protected Barry Seal's drug smuggling operation.

...Bill Clinton and friends got cocaine as a reward for the cover-up.

...People on the verge of exposing the crimes were murder victims.

The dimwitted stories have continued for years, gaining considerable momentum when Bill Clinton was elected President. What made the Mena fable so astonishing was the willingness of supposedly intelligent people to believe the myth. Or worse yet, to exploit Mena for political gain.

In the summer of 1995, Iowa Congressman Jim Leach's House Banking Committee fired off letters to the Department of Justice, the CIA, the IRS and other agencies requesting thousands of documents relating to Mena airport, Barry Seal, and the rumors spread by the lunatic fringe. In back and forth correspondence—sometimes acrimonious—Leach tried to revive investigations that began ten years earlier at several levels of government, even though prior Congressional hearings, federal Grand Jury inquiries and other investigative entities had failed to produce a shred of evidence to support the myths. Regardless, the Leach committee labored on in a costly and counter-productive endeavor to find something that didn't exist. And never had.

Barry Seal was no "Friend of Bill," or any other President. Nor did he have ties to gun-runners. Mena never harbored Contra rebels or assorted spies. I don't belittle the Mena tales because of a Barry Seal denial. In fact, he often hinted to me that he was a CIA operative. Being a spy was more palatable than admitting he was an international drug smuggler who got caught and became an informant to avoid prison.

But as the only journalist to ever set foot inside the C-123, and the only reporter to travel with Barry Seal and his drug smuggling cohorts, I can report unequivocally that most of the Mena myths have little, if any, basis in fact. How do I know? Because many people with reasons to know told me so.

My list of sources includes former federal prosecutors in Miami, Las Vegas and Arkansas, DEA agents who worked closely with Seal, his defense lawyers in Florida and Louisiana, longtime co-pilots and crew members on his Central American smuggling trips, a former CIA operative, and trusted employees in Seal's smuggling operation. In addition to these denials, there is a mountain of documentary evidence disputing his alleged spy activities—DEA reports, transcripts of Congressional hearings, and hours of Seal's sworn testimony in trials in which he was the key witness against drug suppliers.

Compare my information to the claims of people who gave the Mena myth life. On the list are a former Polk County, Arkansas Sheriff, his deputies, a state cop assigned to Mena, an IRS agent stationed in Fort Smith, Arkansas, crazy reporters, and rumor-spreading blog believers. The mania began soon after the wheels of his C-123 touched down in Mena. But credible evidence never substantiated incredible stories. Still, it's a helluva story, stranger in many respects than the fiction surrounding Seal's exploits.

Three weeks after my Miami undercover video expedition, photographer Sailor Jackson and I went to Mena for phase two of Barry's show-and-tell. Wanting me to see the Fat Lady, he flew us to Arkansas in a twin engine propeller-driven Cessna Titan. I didn't bother to offer payment for the flight. I knew he would refuse. And besides, he had downgraded us from the Lear jet to a prop job.

Taking free flights did not play well for me in the future. Seal's largesse, combined with his overstated claims regarding our "close friendship," gave ammunition to Louisiana lawmen, journalists and screw-loose zealots who accused me of being bribed and manipulated by the smuggler. Indeed, Barry and I became friends. But an asterisk has to be attached to the term, "close friendship." Investigative reporting is a game of mutual manipulation. He was a source seeking to gain favor. I was a reporter gathering information. In a "friendly" way, we were conning each other.

In an often cited 1989 *New Yorker* article, essayist and author Janet Malcolm wrote, "Every journalist who is not too stupid or too full of himself to notice what is going on knows that what he does is morally indefensible. He is a kind of confidence man, preying on people's vanity, ignorance, or loneliness, gaining their trust and betraying them without remorse." That is a perfect description of investigative reporting.

There are no absolute rules in dealing with sources. Ethics are mostly situational. The result is varying degrees of compromise. My personal guidelines are don't lie, bribe or extort. Unless absolutely necessary. A joke, but not far from reality. In getting sources to talk, I have been guilty of downplaying the purpose of my inquiries, promising to keep names out of stories if people cooperate, and threatening to identify them if they didn't. I have a few regrets about my tactics. But not many.

I always kept Barry Seal in perspective. He was too forthcoming. As a rule, people don't disclose secrets and admit felony misdeeds in order to make the world a better place. A vital part of an investigative reporter's job is learning the motives of unsolicited confessions. In the end, what really counts is the truth, newsworthiness and importance of the information. Barry had a vested interest in talking to me.

If his yarn was true that Louisiana lawmen were jeopardizing an investigation of the world's biggest cocaine suppliers in their efforts to nail him, I had an interest in reporting that story. So, I simply listened to Barry and went with the flow—asking him at various junctures to produce the evidence, part of which was in Mena. Before the flight to Arkansas, I had not grasped the scope of the Nicaraguan sting operation.

Early news accounts—like the story on CNN—focused on allegations that the Sandinistas were implicated in the transshipment of cocaine to the United States. The most significant aspect of the investigation, perhaps, was buried in the CNN report and other early news accounts. Little was disclosed about the Medellín cartel's impact on U.S. drug trafficking and the Colombian organization.

Barry Seal had collected evidence to indict leaders of the biggest cocaine smuggling operation in the world. Yet, he said very little about the indictments in our initial conversations. He was mainly interested in playing the role of a fat James Bond. He wanted me to depict him as a CIA operative. To that end, he and two crew members donned brand new military fatigues in Mena to add an air of intrigue to our filming. Since we were playing television, I didn't object to the costumes.

Seal's co-pilot was Emil Camp, no relation to me. The coincidence would not be overlooked by conspiracy theorists. Emil later died after crashing into a mountain in a weather-related accident near Mena. He became the "spy who knew too much" in *Twilight Zone* stories perpetrated by the far right.

The Fat Lady's flight engineer was Peter Everson, a tight-lipped, bearded New Zealander. He had good reasons for being bashful around cameras. Peter worked for years as an informant for the DEA and Customs agents.

With the actors in place, Sailor Jackson and I spent the day and far into the night videotaping interviews with Seal, and doing the other stuff that goes into producing documentaries. Dressed as secret agent man, Barry was interviewed inside the C-123's cockpit and in the cargo compartment. In court testimony, affidavits, photographs, and in interviews with people on both sides of the law, I later confirmed his account of a remarkable undercover operation that almost ended within hours of getting started.

—

Five months before we met, Seal stared down a rain sodden grass airstrip in a remote area north of Medellín, Colombia trying to figure a way to stay alive. "We have a choice," he jokingly told co-pilot Emil Camp as they ran through a pre-flight checklist. "We can be killed in a plane crash or shot to death." Emil didn't find the gallows humor funny. The grim statement was prophetic on both counts. But not just yet. On this day—May 28, 1984—Seal was piloting a plane overloaded with 1500 kilos of cocaine. He knew his two-engine Lodestar couldn't get airborne before crashing into a forest at the end of the airstrip. But an attempt to clear the trees was better than being executed by a machine gun in the hands of an insane man sitting on horseback at the edge of the rain-saturated makeshift runway.

"I don't care what you say. You are going to load this airplane and get out of here, or I shoot you." The threat was made by Carlos Rivas Ledher, an undersized, thirty-five-year-old narco-trafficker. His small stature was at odds with a reputation of being one of the most vicious members of the Medellín cartel. Because of his temper and impulsiveness, Ledher had been demoted from a leadership position to countryside cocaine custodian.

Ignoring Barry's warning that the airstrip was too wet to get airborne, he ordered him to take off. Ledher and his partners were in near panic to move cocaine out of the country. Two months earlier, a National Police Anti-Narcotics Unit raided Colombia's biggest cocaine lab in Tranquilandia. Other raids followed. The cartel responded by assassinating drug fighting Justice Minister, Rodrigo Lara Bonilla. It was a grave miscalculation. The murder ignited a wave of public outrage.

Prior to Lara Bonilla's death, many Colombians tolerated the drug business, especially in rural areas where cocoa plants were harvested. Narco-traffickers helped the poor by contributing to worthy causes. Pablo Escobar, the most notorious cartel partner, was even elected to the legislature. He defended his business, arguing that the export of cocaine to the United States was no different than the importation of U.S. tobacco into Colombia. Escobar pointed out that cigarettes killed more people than cocaine. He had a point, except that one drug is legal, the other is not.

At any rate, the country's tolerance toward Medellín kingpins changed following Lara Bonilla's assassination. In the face of outrage, the cartel began retooling its delivery system—the source of ninety percent of the cocaine smuggled into North America.

To keep business perking along, a plan was devised to open processing laboratories in Bolivia and other South American countries. There was, however, a logistics problem. After taking off with nearly empty fuel tanks from remote jungle runways, airplanes used by smugglers didn't have the range to fly non-stop to the U.S. mainland. To solve the transportation quandary, an intermediate refueling stop was crucial. Nicaragua fit the bill.

As the new system was being implemented, the cartel moved its 3500 kilo cache to a location under the protection of Carlos Ledher. Panic had caused traffickers to let down their guard in recruiting "Ellis McKenzie." Barry figured if anyone came looking for him, they would realize they had the wrong guy. The real Ellis McKenzie was a tall, black Honduran — a Seal business partner.

Carlos Bustamonte, known in the drug trade as "Lito," hired Barry to move the drugs. Lito ran a luxury automobile dealership in South Miami that was a front for a money-laundering operation. As a go-between for several previous Medellín shipments, he was well acquainted with "Ellis McKenzie." Indeed, Lito became concerned when he failed to hear from the pilot for several weeks. He obviously didn't know about the Quaalude case. Seal called Lito following the trial looking for work. He was hired to move the huge cocaine load out of Columbia. It was his bargaining chip to avoid prison.

The Baton Rouge smuggler rarely met face-to-face with cartel leaders. Despite his reputation, Seal personally brought only a half-dozen shipments of drugs into the country. His genius was in meticulously planning flights. He paid pilots in his tight-knit organization to transport the cargo to U.S. drop-points in Louisiana and Florida. From there, he delivered the drugs to final destinations and collected the cash.

For this trip, the Medellín people wanted to meet McKenzie/Seal personally. So he flew to Colombia in the company of Felix Bates, an intermediary who acted as his translator. Barry spoke some Spanish, although not fluently. Bates escorted him to the elegant mountainside home of Jorge Ochoa for a meeting with the cartel leaders.

Present, according to subsequent court testimony, were Pablo Escobar, Pablo Correa and Jorge's brothers, Fabio and Juan David. A strategy was outlined to move the cocaine out of Columbia in two separate flights. Then Barry was told in hushed voices about Nicaragua's being a new transshipment point. He knew of no previous Nicaraguan involvement in the drug trade. Nor did the DEA. Or the CIA.

Three weeks after the Medellín meeting, Seal flew to Managua to meet Federico Vaughan, described to him as a high-level Sandinista official. In reality, Vaughan was a local fixer with friends in low places. He escorted Barry to the refueling site, a small military airport in nearby Los Braziles. The pilot was introduced to on-ground contacts and instructed how to get clearance to enter restricted Nicaraguan airspace.

If successful, the sting would be among the DEA's biggest ever cocaine cases. But the waterlogged airstrip was a setback. Barry knew it was impossible to get airborne. Carlos Ledher, fearful of the army's arriving at any moment, was in no mood to listen. Convincing the ill-tempered cocaine cowboy that the grass airstrip was too soggy for take-off was futile. Staring down the face of a machine gun, Barry decided to prove his point. And hope to survive.

"I'm going halfway down the strip at full throttle," he told Emil. "If we don't gain speed, I'll ground spin the son-of-a-bitch, so get ready to bail."

At the halfway point, the Lodestar didn't have enough speed for lift-off. Barry turned the plane sharply, crashing into foliage. He and Emil jumped out as fire spread through the fuselage. Despite the flames, Ledher ordered workers to unload the cargo. Two men were seriously burned when the aircraft exploded.

For the next five days, Barry and Emil stayed with the Colombian fruitcake. He dazzled them with stories of murdering people. It was the kind of conversation that sends chills up the spines of informants. When the airstrip finally dried, the cartel sent a Titan 404 to begin moving the cocaine. The plane was much smaller than the Lodestar.

It was capable of carrying 750 kilos if the fuel tanks were nearly empty. On June 3rd, Seal flew to Nicaragua for a fill-up. He landed at Los Braziles without incident.

Refueling, however, took longer than expected. It was nightfall at take-off, and he was flying in restricted air space without lights or clearance. Air controllers at Managua's Sandino International Airport could not identify the plane. Tracers were fired to illuminate the sky. One hit the Titan's left engine causing it to lose power. Seal was forced to land at Sandino. He and Emil were taken into custody.

They feared the worst. The DEA investigation was blown, the cartel's cocaine confiscated and the two smugglers faced long sentences in a Nicaraguan prison. But unexpectedly, an army sergeant Seal met at Los Braziles arrived to take charge of the cargo. The soldier assured him the cocaine was safe, and there was nothing to worry about. The following day, Federico Vaughan arranged for the pilot's release from jail.

A Managua newspaper reported the incident, explaining tracers were fired to guide a lost airplane. Despite fears that the investigation was compromised, the mishap turned out to be a boon for the undercover operation.

Pablo Escobar provided a plane for the return home. He wanted it flown to the states for maintenance. Given the ongoing problems, Escobar asked Barry to shop for a long range plane. Seal knew of just the aircraft. He had seen a C-123K transport advertised for sale in the April issue of *Trade-A-Plane*. The "Fat Lady" was owned by Harry

Doan, a New Smyrna Beach, Florida man rumored to have links to the CIA. Based on a future incident unrelated to Seal, the oversized airplane would become the basis of stories linking him to guns for drugs conspiracies involving Contra rebels.

Meanwhile, the acquisition of the Fat Lady excited Escobar and his Medellín pals. It could haul thousands of kilos of cocaine, as well as bring them equipment for the revamped trafficking operation. To fill the cartel's needs, Escobar gave Seal a $200,000 shopping list for everything from radio equipment to night vision goggles.

At this point in the sting, the CIA knew nothing about the operation. However, DEA officials in Washington notified the agency that a Nicaraguan government official was suspected of assisting cocaine traffickers. Intelligence officials asked to be part of the operation. This was the beginning of Barry's short-lived spook career. Prior to returning to Los Braziles, CIA technicians concealed two 35mm cameras in the Fat Lady, and gave Seal a small remote control to take pictures.

In the last week of June, he flew to Los Braziles in the C-123 with Emil and flight engineer Peter Everson to retrieve the cocaine. The cargo was stored in a warehouse near Sandino airport—every ounce intact. The drugs were hauled to Los Braziles airport and loaded through the rear cargo door by uniformed Nicaraguan soldiers and cartel leaders. The DEA had hit the jackpot. CIA-installed cameras captured images of Pablo

Escobar, Federico Vaughan, Gonzalo Rodriguez Gacha and others.

Shortly before dawn on June 26, Barry flew the Fat Lady to Homestead Air Force Base south of Miami, the DEA's designated location to begin the final stage of the sting. The cocaine was transferred to a rented Winnebago. "Ellis McKenzie" drove to a parking lot at a nearby mall to meet "Lito" Bustamonte, who recruited a driver to take charge of the cocaine. DEA agents and State Police followed the RV. A few miles away, an undercover agent intentionally crashed his car into the Winnebago. The Highway Patrol was called. When the driver failed to produce proper registration, the vehicle was searched and the cocaine seized.

Bustamonte was a short distance behind the Winne bago and suspected that the accident was staged—as did everyone else in the smuggling operation. Incredibly, Barry was not suspected of being part of the trap, possibly because he angrily accused others of squealing. In the days that followed, the RV driver was the only person arrested. Lito and his co-conspirators began to breath easy. It was a false sense of security. Secret indictments were kept under wraps while the investigation expanded.

Throughout, Pablo Escobar's confidence in "Ellis McKenzie" never wavered. To the contrary, he asked the trusted courier to return to Nicaragua in the C-123 with operational equipment and a load of personal toys like video recorders, bicycles, booze and cigarettes. Seal was also told to bring $1.5 million in cash to pay off the cartel's Sandinista friends. Lito provided the money.

DEA agents were unenthusiastic about Barry's leaving Miami with a box full of cash. What if he skipped the country? What if Escobar knew Seal was the informant? He would take the money, kill the pilot, and steal the Fat Lady. But potential gains outweighed dangers. The operation was now on the verge of ripping the underpinnings from the Medellín cartel. That is until Colonel Oliver North got wind of the investigation.

Learning about the pictures showing an alleged Sandinista official loading cocaine on an airplane bound for U.S. shores may have caused North to soil his drawers. As a national security advisor to the Reagan Administration, he was trying to raise money to support Nicaraguan Contra rebels. To hear him tell it, Daniel Ortega's ragtag army was poised to march through Central America and Mexico, cross the Rio Grande into Texas, and force U.S. citizens to address one another as comrade. In Spanish, no less.

To save the country from communism, North asked the DEA to shut down its Medellín undercover operation, give him the photographs to pass along to Congressmen, and have Barry Seal deliver Lito's $1.5 million to Contra rebels. As respectfully as possible, DEA officials refused the request. North was pissed. He reacted like a partisan jerk. According to Congressional testimony, he arranged for details of the sting to be prematurely publicized by the U.S. military's Latin America commander.

The *Washington Times*—a Reagan Administration propaganda arm—was the first to identify the C-123's pilot as a government informant. But not by name. The story irreparably damaged the narcotics investigation. Blaming the leak on the White House, Barry's DEA contact agent, Jake Jacobson, was furious. He called Seal to inform him that the case was falling apart. In the same phone conversation—secretly recorded by Seal—the agent tried to cut his losses. On the off-chance that Bustamonte had not heard the news, Jacobson asked his prize informant to set up a meeting.

Barry's attorney was present during the conversation and advised him against taking the risk. Nonetheless, he went ahead with the plan. As a result, three of six indicted defendants—Lito included—were arrested. Pablo Escobar, Federico Vaughan and Jorge Ochoa were beyond the reach of U.S. authorities.

A day after the July 18 *Washington Times* article, the DEA operation linking the Sandinista government to cocaine trafficking was front page news. The story, however, as overshadowed by another event. A mentally ill man armed with several weapons walked into a McDonald's franchise in the San Diego community of San Ysidro and opened fire, killing twenty-one people. A police sniper finally killed the gunman.

Barry Seal was not the kind of guy to play second fiddle to a massacre. He wanted the world to know he was the pilot involved in the sting. Seeing himself as a heroic undercover agent who risked his life to help bring down the Medellín Cartel, he wanted recognition. He also wanted to get Louisiana lawmen off his back.

Given his value as a witness, he couldn't understand why he was caught in the middle of a jurisdictional battle. So he came to me. The tug-of-war between Miami and Louisiana would form the basis of a one hour investigative documentary titled, *Uncle Sam Wants You.*

"Barry Seal is an enigma," I reported. "On one hand he has been working closely with federal drug agents and the Central Intelligence Agency. He is a key witness in one of the most significant drug investigations ever conducted in south Florida. But at the same time here in his hometown of Baton Rouge, the veteran pilot has been target of an intensive, and what he describes as an unfair investigation."

The November 20, 1984, my report opened with our undercover video of the rendezvous in a Miami hotel parking lot. It was a killer story—literally. Court testimony later revealed that a videotape of the documentary was delivered to Pablo Escobar.

"That's Ellis McKenzie," he reportedly said when the pilot's image appeared on screen. It took 16 months, but Barry Seal was a dead man.

Even with a death warrant out on him, the cocky informant continued to perform for the DEA. He was a point man in two other sting operations, resulting in twelve more indictments. The first case in Las Vegas, Nevada was the biggest cocaine bust in the state's history. In another

Seal sting, DEA agents secretly videotaped the payment of a $20,000 bribe to a top official of the Turks and Caicos Islands, a British colony 600 miles from Miami. The islands were a transshipment stopover for smugglers.

Criminal indictments are only as good as the final results. Seal compiled a perfect record as a witness. Nine convictions in Las Vegas, three in the Turks and Caicos trial and five in the Nicaraguan case. Following his testimony at the trials, all but one of seventeen defendants changed pleas from innocent to guilty. A jury deliberated less than an hour before convicting the lone holdout. Drug agents later described Seal in court testimony as "the most important witness in DEA history."

Regrettably, *Uncle Sam Wants You* contributed to the murder of the "most important witness." Barry Seal exposed his identity for all to see, including Colombian drug lords. And his arrogant criticisms of local lawmen so infuriated Baton Rouge cops and prosecutors that they vowed to get him—even though he was already got in Miami.

Documents that Seal gave me when we first met showed overzealousness on the part of his local pursuers. For instance, the U.S. Attorney's office in Baton Rouge made a deal with a near-do-well character named Kenneth Webb—former high school classmate that Barry paid to do odd jobs around the office. In return for informing on Seal, prosecutors promised to help Webb dispose of a flock of legal problems, including an auto theft charge. At best, he was a dubious witness.

Divorced and the father of a ten-year-old son living with him—sometimes in a car—Webb was a sad sack kind of guy with palsied hands and head jerks that suggested a perpetual hangover. Before becoming a mole, he had a history of mental instability and minor arrests. But upholding his end of the bargain, he told a federal grand jury that he delivered a shoe box filled with cocaine to Barry.

Then again, maybe it wasn't cocaine. Maybe it was a box containing sugar donuts. In an on-camera interview, he told me he fabricated the cocaine story because of intense pressure by drug agents. Webb's lawyer asked U.S. Attorney Stanford Bardwell to allow the unstable witness to correct perjured grand jury testimony. The request was denied.

It's understandable why cops wanted to bring Barry down. He went to extremes in ridiculing lawmen during our on-camera interview. "I'm not a drug smuggler," he stated. "I say prove it." The smirk on his face left little doubt about his guilt.

Most informants keep low profiles, especially those classified as endangered species. Not Barry. Despite credible information that a contract was out on him, he did just the opposite in building his image as a high profile adventurer.

"The cost of living an exciting life is high," he boasted in my report. "The exciting thing in life to me is to get into a life-threatening situation."

Barry's bluster notwithstanding, the local investigation produced results—albeit face-saving results for the smuggler. The night before *Uncle Sam Wants You* aired, he summoned me to his home. In contrast to past braggadocio, he was meek and apologetic in disclosing that he had agreed to plead guilty to a drug charge in Baton Rouge. I was given a copy of the agreement and asked to keep it quiet until an official announcement. He seemed confident that his Florida deal would keep him out of prison.

"As much cocaine as I've hauled into Louisiana, I don't know anything about this load," Seal said. He claimed that mounting legal expenses had caused him to accept the deal. The explanation was hard to believe. He seemed to be apologizing to me for the guilty plea, which was not particularly relevant to the issues raised in my documentary.

"It is not the purpose of this report to suggest Barry Seal is innocent, or for that matter guilty of anything other than those crimes for which he has already been convicted," I stated in the narration. "The targeting of individuals, the pressuring of witnesses and the abuse of the grand jury process raises questions about the integrity of our system of justice. And when such questions are raised—regardless of who asks them—they deserve to be answered."

U.S. Attorney Bardwell waited a month before trying to answer. In a law enforcement extravaganza, Barry Seal's guilty plea was made public. Standing beside Bardwell at the news conference were officials of the federal Organized Crime Strike Force in New Orleans, the FBI, the head of the Louisiana State Police, and local drug agents. Armed with a copy of the agreement Barry gave me, I asked Bardwell the obvious question. "Is there a plea bargain arrangement that guarantees Mr. Seal will not receive any time in excess to what he's been sentenced in Florida?"

"I'm not prepared to comment on that at this time." I continued to press and his response was the same to each of my questions. "No comment." I was not trying to embarrass Bardwell. But I believed the media was being misled. Instead of cracking a big narcotics case, Louisiana lawmen were jeopardizing a much bigger investigation.

As a fulltime digger of muck, I rarely attended news conferences. My interviews were usually one-on-one. Therefore, I was taken aback by the collective attitude of fellow reporters. They were clearly irritated when I kept challenging the forthrightness of the crème de la crème of Louisiana law enforcement. But faced with deadlines, general assignment reporters accepted the prosecutor's statement at face value—a shortcoming that plagues contemporary journalism everywhere in the country.

The plea bargain stated that Seal's Baton Rouge sentence would not exceed the pending sentence imposed in Florida. Based on what he called nods and winks by Miami DEA agents and prosecutors, Barry felt certain the reward for his undercover heroics in Colombia and Nicaragua would earn him a free pass. If so, the guilty plea was meaningless, but expensive. He relinquished ownership of two airplanes. He also agreed to a period of probation—a seemingly trivial footnote that turned out to be a deadly trap.

Shortly after the news conference, the drug pilot appeared before Federal District Court Judge Frank Polozola. The Judge apparently watched *Uncle Sam Wants You* and was quite upset by what he saw. He did not try to conceal his anger. Polozola made it clear that a day of reckoning would come when Seal's Florida case was concluded and a final sentence imposed.

Outside the courthouse, Stan Bardwell expressed confidence that Barry was going to prison as a result of the pending ten year sentence in Fort Lauderdale. But he admitted that he had not discussed the sentencing with anyone in Florida. "How could you possibly make that judgment if you haven't talked with the Judge?" I asked.

"Well, just based on prior experience. I just have a feeling that he's not in a position—he's got no reason to change it," Bardwell replied.

Minutes later, Barry Seal emerged from the courthouse. He was all smug smiles, saying he "reached exactly the type of settlement that I wanted to reach."

His Baton Rouge attorney was not so sure. Lewis Unglesby was among Louisiana's top criminal defense lawyers and savvy to the ways of federal judges. He believed his client had kicked a big gorilla in the balls with his statements on *Uncle Sam Wants You*. Barry's "catch me if you can" arrogance had alienated many people.

For the next few months, the cocky informant remained in protective custody while testifying at trials in Miami and Las Vegas. He also testified in Washington before the President's Commission on Organized Crime, giving details of the inner-workings of his operation and providing background on the Colombian cartel.

Except for telephone calls, there was very little contact with his wife, Deborah, and their two young children. She asked me a couple of times to come to their home to take Barry's calls. The conversations were mainly about his successes. He trusted me more than I trusted him. But I could not help but call him a friend.

Miami DEA agents were also intensely loyal. He delivered the biggest cases of their careers. Consequently, they were willing to go to bat for him in October, 1985, at final sentencing before federal Judge Norman Roettger in Fort Lauderdale. Agents testified about the risks Barry took in gathering evidence against the world's biggest cocaine traffickers. The judge was impressed.

"I think it is well known to all people in this district that promises of cooperation don't cut any ice with me at all….. but when a cooperating witness rises above the level that they have put their life in a position of peril, then I think they deserve to be suitably rewarded." The judge set aside Seal's ten year sentence.

Afterwards, agents and prosecutors tried to persuade Barry to immediately enter the Witness Protection Program. He acted unconcerned about stories that Colombians had vowed to kill him. For reasons I never understood, he could not accept the reality that the Medellín cartel wanted him dead. Standing next to him on a well-traveled Baton Rouge street, I once half-jokingly said I was uneasy in the company of a man with a contract on his life. He laughed, which brought to mind a comment he made in *Uncle Sam Wants You.* "The old saying, if you can't stand the heat, don't work in the kitchen. I can take the pressure. I'm not worried about the contract. If it comes, it comes."

Seal went to federal court in Baton Rouge on December 20, 1985. He felt confident that he was home free. But Judge Polozola had a surprise for him. Judges are often criticized for allowing personal prejudices to influence courtroom rulings. Polozola personified the reason for the criticism. Upset by the south Florida sentence reduction, he lashed out at the DEA informant.

"Drug dealers like Mr. Seal are the lowest, most despicable people I can think of," he declared. "People like you, Mr. Seal, ought to be in a federal penitentiary. You all ought to be there working at hard labor. Working in the hottest sun or the coldest day would be good enough for drug dealers like you."

The Judge imposed the penalties outlined in Barry's plea agreement on a drug conspiracy charge, and then he dropped a bombshell. The plea deal called for probation on a lesser charge of failing to properly report bank transactions. The provision gave Polozola a revenge mechanism. He ordered Seal to spend nights at a Salvation Army shelter during a six month probation period.

"And I can tell you right now, I don't care if it is the Drug Enforcement Administration, I don't care if it is the State Department, I don't care if it is the U.S. Attorney, I don't care who it is, you don't go any place, any place without getting my personal written approval in advance."

Attorney Lewis Unglesby was stunned. He begged the Judge to reconsider, pointing out the contract on his client's life. This angered Polozola even more. He stripped Barry of armed bodyguards, warning the pilot that he risked being considered a felon in possession of firearms.

"You take your chance, Mr. Seal. Take your chance. Have bodyguards with guns and take your chance....I'm giving you some fair warning that it could result in a probation revocation hearing. And then we'll have to determine whether that is or is not."

By now, Unglesby was steaming. "That's a double-cross by the government." Polozola was unmoved. He agreed to delay imposition of the sentence, pending an appeal. But it was clear that his mind was made up. "A judgment is a judgment, so you can do whatever you want to do," he told the attorney.

Unglesby and Seal's Miami attorney, Tom Sclafani, did everything they could to avoid having him report to the shelter on a predictable schedule. An attempt was made to get Barry back into the Witness Protection Program. Louisiana authorities initially agreed to relocate him to northern Florida near the Pensacola Naval Air Station, but reneged at the last minute on the pretext that Florida was a "drug state."

Seal returned to Polozola's courtroom on January 24, 1986—accompanied by Florida DEA agents, federal prosecutors from Miami and Las Vegas, and a representative of Scotland Yard. They pleaded with the judge to modify the sentence.

Jorge Ocho, the titular head of the Medellín cartel, was in custody in Spain awaiting extradition to the United States. Barry had become an even more valuable witness. He was the only eyewitness able to link Ochoa to U.S. cocaine trafficking.

Judge Polozola didn't care. He ordered Seal to report to the Salvation Army shelter immediately and begin serving the probation sentence. The colorful smuggler tried to put up a good front. He even brought a tambourine with him.

After checking into the facility, he called me on a regular basis offering new angles for stories about his trials and tribulations. I usually promised to follow-up, but never did. The story he really wanted me to do dealt with IRS seizures of his assets. He had testified in three trials that he grossed more than $50 million from drug smuggling. Little was said about overhead—like crashing uninsured Lockheed Lodestars in jungles, buying military transport planes, and paying pilots and other employees in his organization. Seal's yearly tax returns showed income in the mid-to-high six figures. IRS agents believed he was short-changing the government, though no money was ever found.

I had a final meeting with Barry on February 12, 1986. He came to WBRZ with the real Ellis McKenzie, a tall, muscular black Honduran. Earlier in the day, a private investigator working for Pablo Escobar's Miami lawyer asked me to arrange an introduction to Seal. The detective was a former Miami source that I owed a favor.

Like an idiot, I tried to barter a deal to fly to Colombia and interview Escobar. He promised to ask. In retrospect, I realize my request to travel to the jungles to meet the cocaine baron was dumb. What would I ask? "Hey, Pablo. Who did you kill today?"

Anyway, I called Seal. He contacted agents in Miami. They were curious why the detective wanted to meet him and told Barry to check it out. The meeting was rather humdrum. Barry was shown several of the photos he snapped in Nicaragua and asked to identify Escobar in the pictures. That was the extent of the discussion.

Before Seal departed, I asked his advice about interviewing Escobar. He said don't even consider meeting with the notorious trafficker. Before leaving, he bragged about treating his housemates to pizza. He had become the most popular guy at the shelter and invited me to come by some night with a photographer to do a feature story. I lied and said I would. The opportunity to attend Barry's pizza parties was short-lived.

During WBRZ's February 19, 1986, evening newscast, I stood at a picture window in John Spain's office overlooking the newsroom. Suddenly, everyone was facing me. The Assignment Editor came running toward the office.

"There's been a shooting in the parking lot at the Salvation Army." He didn't have to say anything else.

"Jesus fucking Christ, they got him," I responded. Not very classy, but my reaction at the moment. Alone and stripped of bodyguards, Barry arrived on-time for his 6:00 p.m. check-in as directed by Judge Polozola. Before he could get out of the car, a man stepped from the shadows and fired a dozen shots from a MAC-10 equipped with a silencer. The flamboyant pilot-turned smuggler-turned informant died instantly.

Three Colombians—a gang that could shoot straight, but couldn't plan straight—left a trail of blunders. Witnesses saw them in a stolen car casing the shelter a few hours before the shooting. The getaway car was stashed a mile away in an empty lot—a bingo parlor parking lot that opened at nightfall. By the time Barry was murdered, cars of bingo players filled the lot. A security guard was on duty. Seeing the men switch vehicles and race away, he jotted down the license tag number.

FBI agents traced the car to a rental agency at New Orleans airport. One of the suspects arrived while agents waited for an arrest warrant. He fled before they could take him into custody, hailed a cab, handed the driver a wad of cash and asked to be taken to Alabama. The suspect couldn't catch a break. After an all points bulletin was issued, he was captured in rural Mississippi when the taxi hit a deer, and state police were summoned. He led FBI agents to the other Colombians, who were hiding in New Orleans. They were all convicted and sentenced to life terms in prison.

U.S. Attorney Bardwell held a news conference the day after Seal's murder. He tried to justify decisions that cost DEA its most important witness during a critical phase of the Medellín cartel case. I asked if he was trying to teach Seal a lesson.

"Sure. Not to get killed, but certainly to impose some punishment for his crimes," he uncomfortably replied. The implacability of Louisiana authorities seemed incomprehensible. Vengeance not only cost Seal his life, but also deprived the DEA of a vital witness in pending trials and ended any chance of extraditing leaders of the Colombian cocaine cartel.

"They had a chance to stop people that were the biggest people there were. And they knew they were the biggest people," said Seal's attorney, Lewis Unglesby. "Instead, they were able to prove the point that Barry Seal was going to report to the Salvation Army and do probation like they wanted it."

I hesitated about attending the funeral. Why reenforce suspicions that I was too close to the drug smuggler? But after living for so long with my reputation—first as a drunk and later as a "derelict gunslinger"—it was too late to worry about criticism. So I paid last respects to a guy whose life was not well-lived until his final years.

Others in Baton Rouge apparently shared my view that Barry genuinely tried to redeem himself. Nearly every seat in the funeral chapel was filled. Despite his nefarious occupation, friendships ran a gamut from janitors to judges, all of whom shared memories that were atypical of portrayals associated with a drug smuggler. Notably missing from the funeral were the federal drug enforcement agents whose careers he advanced. They were ordered to stay home or be fired.

Deborah Seal and the couple's children, nine and six years old, stood next to the open casket when I entered the chapel. As I walked forward to offer condolences, Deborah saw me and began sobbing, "You are the only one who believed him."

Embracing her, I saw the tortured looks on the faces of Barry's heartbroken children with tears streaming down their cheeks. Placed beside the body were crayon printed notes. "We love you, daddy." Seeing their despair, I nearly drew blood biting my lip. Breaking down at a drug smuggler's funeral was not an appropriate reaction in the macho business of muckraking.

Barry Seal's life was over. But he would live on in infamy.

CHAPTER FOUR

DANCING ON BARRY'S GRAVE

Twenty-six days after Barry Seal's funeral, he was raised from the dead by President Ronald Reagan. In a nationally televised speech aimed at influencing Congressional approval of a $100-million aid package for Contra rebels, the President displayed one of Barry's Nicaraguan undercover photographs. The picture showed close-ups of Seal, Federico Vaughan and Pablo Escobar as they loaded cocaine onto the C-123 transport. Citing Vaughan's link to the Colombian cartel, Reagan said the snapshot was proof that "top Nicaraguan Government officials are deeply involved in drug trafficking." Barry was at last getting the kind of attention he craved.

Drug Enforcement Administration officials disputed the President's portrayal two days later, describing Vaughan as a corrupt bureaucrat, who held a low-ranking position in Nicaragua's Interior Ministry. But truth was not a high priority in the Administration's effort to assist the Contras. Even as Reagan spoke, funds were illegally being funneled to rebels—money that was generated from the secret sale of arms to Iran. A month before his speech, the President had authorized the CIA's participation in a scheme that led to the Iran-Contra investigation in which eleven Administration officials were convicted.

As a result of a confluence of loosely connected episodes, Barry Seal's undercover work made him a tangential character in the scandal. He was an anti-hero of Right-wing and liberal loonies in a milieu that created the Mena myth, and gave credence to conspiracy fables linking the drug smuggler/turned informant to the CIA, three Presidents, and Arkansas businessman Dan Lasater— among others. In Baton Rouge, I had been far removed from this world of international intrigue.

Indeed, a few days after Reagan's speech I delivered what I thought was my finale in reporting the life, adventures and death of Barry Seal. I traced the gaffes of Louisiana drug agents, U.S. Attorney Stanford Bardwell, federal Judge Frank Polozola and U.S. Attorney General Edwin Meese. Strangely, Meese had failed to intervene in the turf battle that made Seal easy prey for the hit men. I should have called my documentary, *I Can't Believe So Many People Were So Damned Stupid*. Instead, it was titled *Murder of a Witness*. Under any name, though, the theme was the same. How could this happen?

"Barry Seal, without question, was the most important federal witness in the country," said former Assistant U.S. Attorney Donald Campbell, the lead prosecutor in the Las Vegas case in which Seal testified. "He could give more information, supply more intelligence, get more convictions than any other living human being."

Edwin Meese's explanation of the turf battle between Miami and Baton Rouge law enforcement agencies was a bunch of mumbo jumbo. "There is obviously an investigation ongoing at the present time of the crime that's involved. And there were some other questions asked as to some of the administrative aspects of it, and we will be looking into that." If an investigation took place, the results were never publicly revealed.

My opening narration of *Murder of a Witness* gave a personal perspective on Barry Seal. "I did not, nor do I now see him as some sort of folk hero. His involvement in drug smuggling was despicable and inexcusable….however, he was given an unusual opportunity to make reparations for his mistakes. And according to many high-ranking law enforcement people, he made his amends to society with tremendous courage."

Fifty-five minutes later, I delivered what could be interpreted as an apology for the incompetence of Louisiana officials. "The U.S. Attorney and a federal Judge in Baton Rouge were left to make decisions that apparently went far beyond their backgrounds and experiences. Baton Rouge has never been known as a center of international drug trafficking. Colombian hit men coming here would not seem a reality. It is, instead, something akin to a scene from *Miami Vice*. Attempting to ascertain who is to blame for the blunders leading to the murder of a witness as significant as Barry Seal is not nearly as important as taking steps to ensure other government witnesses are not placed in similar jeopardy."

Stanford Bardwell resigned as U.S. Attorney three weeks later. He said the resignation had nothing to do with the Barry Seal fiasco. Judge Polozola reportedly told WBRZ lawyers that *Murder of a Witness* hindered his chances of being appointed to the Fifth Circuit Court of Appeals in New Orleans. If true, my career had real purpose.

I certainly regret the fact that *Uncle Sam Wants You* played a role in getting Barry killed. Otherwise, damn the critics who accused me of defending a cocaine smuggler. They must have watched a different *Uncle Sam Wants You*. I clearly stated that "Seal's involvement with Colombian cocaine traffickers" was the leverage he used to cut a deal with DEA agents. I reported that his sole reason for becoming an informant was to avoid ten years in the penitentiary. In any event, his smuggling activities were secondary to exposing law enforcement turf battles and abuses.

As expected, the exposé set off a storm of criticism, as well as litigation. Two drug agents and an assistant U.S. Attorney filed slander suits. Both cases were dismissed before going to trial. Other detractors—among them the head of the state police—wrote letters of protest to WBRZ and to newspapers. It was not a first for me. Alienating lawmen by exposing examples of win-at-any-cost justice was a curse on my career.

A United States Attorney in Boston once accused me of being a "tool of organized crime" because I questioned prosecutorial tactics in pursuit of a notorious art thief named Myles Connor. He was accused of double murder in a case in which he had no motive, and evidence was so thin that prosecutors offered get-out-of-prison-free cards to the worst kinds of vicious criminals. "Sure, I've beaten, robbed, maimed and killed," they testified. "But I would never tell a lie." Connor was eventually acquitted.

The U.S. prosecutor's portrayal of me occurred after I committed the unpardonable transgression of ambushing FBI agent John Connolly to question him about an attempt to recruit a prison escapee as an informant in order to frame a public official. Connolly refused to comment and hightailed it down the street like a fleeing Mafia figure. Twenty-two years later, my suspicions about the agent's misconduct were confirmed on a much bigger scale. In May, 2002, he was convicted and sentenced to ten years in federal prison in the worst informant scandal in FBI history.

Connolly's corrupt legacy didn't end there. In November 2008, he was convicted of Second Degree murder in a mob hit of former World Jai Alai President, John B. Callahan whose body was found in a car trunk at Miami International Airport. Both Connolly convictions related to his friendship with James (Whitey) Bulger, a gang leader in the South Boston Irish neighborhood where Connolly grew up. Bulger paid bribes to the agent for leaking information of ongoing FBI investigations and identifying cooperating witnesses. The gangster – brother of one of Massachusetts most powerful politicians—fled Boston in 1994 when Connolly tipped him of a pending indictment. He remains on the FBI's Ten Most Wanted List. The 2006 Academy Award winning movie, *The Departed*, was inspired by the relationship between the agent and Bulger.

John Connolly was a protégé of another rogue FBI agent, Paul Rico. He helped frame four innocent men in a 1967 mob murder. It turned out that a Rico informant was the actual triggerman. Even though the agent and other lawmen knew the snitch was lying, he was the principal witness against the men. Rico's misconduct remained a secret for almost three decades. Meantime, two innocent defendants died in prison, and the others served more than thirty years. Ironically, the prosecutor in the case was the U.S. Attorney who called me a "tool of organized crime." The truth of the frame-up finally emerged in August, 2007, when a federal Judge ordered the government to pay $101-million in damages to the wrongly convicted men and/or their surviving families.

Following his FBI retirement, Paul Rico became head of security for World Jai Alai. In the course of the Connolly investigation, Rico was linked to the murder of another executive of the pari-mutuel company. A year before John Callahan was killed, Roger Wheeler was shot to death in the parking lot of an exclusive Tulsa, Oklahoma golf club. Whitey Bulger associate, John Martorano, admitted pulling the trigger. Former FBI agent Rico allegedly arranged the contract killing. The Connolly mentor died in January, 2004 at the age of 78 before his case went to trial.

My estrangement from lawmen extended beyond the FBI. Local cops in Miami were rip-shit when I testified under subpoena as a defense witness on behalf of so-called Mafia boss, Anthony (Tumac) Accetturo. The hoodlum was being railroaded on a bogus charge of battery on a police officer. My cameraman had filmed the alleged incident as we followed Accetturo from a grand jury room in a Fort Lauderdale courthouse. The video showed the mobster's arm lightly brushing against a police photographer as he reached for an elevator button. My testimony and the film resulted in an acquittal.

"You report bullshit about me, but you're still a fair guy," Tumac said outside the courtroom. "Anytime you need a favor, just call Tony." It was a gracious offer, but I've never wanted anyone whacked.

The probity of defending characters like Accetturo, Connor and Barry Seal invited criticism. It was easy to say they got what they deserved—even if falsely convicted of crimes. But that is shortcut justice. And unnecessary. As usually happens, they were later convicted on legitimate charges. Tumac and Myles Connor went to prison, assuaging my unease in reversing the roles of good guys and bad guys. Barry paid a higher price.

The case of the four innocent men framed by Paul Rico still bothers me because it exposed my personal prejudices in pre-judging people by ethnicity. In October, 1980, I received a letter from Boston attorney John Cavicchi asking me to look into the case. He enclosed a 1970 polygraph examination and several affidavits disclosing that Rico's informant, Joseph Barboza, AKA "The Animal", had recanted his court testimony three years after the men went to prison. For a contemptible reason, I failed to follow up on the story. The names of the defendants ended in vowels, so I wrote them off as Italian gangsters trying to worm their way out of jail. Writing a story may not have made a difference at the time, but I would feel better knowing I tried to help them.

As far as Barry Seal's death, I rationalize that if not me, somebody would have reported his story. However, I know that my true motive for putting his face on television was self-interest. The swashbuckling soldier-of-fortune made good TV. Unfortunately, that is how too many news decisions are made.

In addition to helping kill Barry, my report contributed to the Mena myth. I had allowed him to drop hints of multiple covert missions, though it was pretty obvious early in the production of my program that his CIA connections were mainly imagined. During the first Mena trip, I stood alongside the Fat Lady listening to my namesake, Emil Camp, recount how CIA technicians installed cameras in the plane. He was like a little boy telling of his first trip to the circus. Emil's thrill over a routine task by CIA mechanics suggested to me that spying was a brand new experience. No doubt, the Nicaraguan sting operation was his first and only spy adventure.

Stories of spying added intrigue to my documentary. Therefore, when Barry and his crew donned military fatigues in Mena, I went along with the ruse—hypocritically choosing style over substance. I say hypocritical because similar television compromises have been a major complaint of mine for years.

Uncle Sam Wants You was not the first, nor would it be last time that I walked a journalism tightrope in order to keep exposés interesting and entertaining. My justification was if nobody watched, I wasted air time. However, the melodramatic elements of my shows were tame by today's standards. A weak defense for sure.

Hints of spy missions were an inside joke perpetuated by Seal's smuggling team, and his friends at Mena airport. People outside the circle didn't get the joke. Unaware of the punch line, two investigators in particular—Arkansas State Policeman Russell Welch and IRS agent Bill Duncan—made second careers of gathering information about the drug smuggler and his associates.

Like Barry's antics in Louisiana, he baited the two lawmen. He never made a genuine effort to disabuse them of suspicions that he was a frequent flyer of drugs into Mena Intermountain Regional Airport, and a frequent flyer of guns leaving the airfield. His denials of being a guns-for-drugs smuggler left the impression that he was lying. As a result, Trooper Welch and Agent Duncan became key sources of many stories written by conspiracy-minded reporters.

In truth, Mena was a maintenance depot for Seal's operation—never a smuggling destination. His planes were serviced by Rich Mountain Aviation, a company that specialized in aircraft fabrication and modifications. Airplanes used by smugglers required increased loading capacity and extra fuel tanks, called bladders. Rich Mountain was one of two companies in the Southeast with the expertise to do that kind of work.

The business was owned by Fred Hampton. A partner, Joe Evans, previously worked for Seal in Baton Rouge. Hampton and Evans either knew, or should have known, about Barry's smuggling activities. They apparently took the position of don't ask, don't tell by accepting his explanation of doing covert work for the government.

The blasé attitude came back to haunt them. In November, 1984, the FBI planted dope residue in a confiscated plane. An undercover agent flew it to Mena and taxied to the tarmac adjacent to the Rich Mountain hangar. Acting as if he were dropping off a car for new tires, the agent placed an order with an employee for a fuel bladder. He said he would return in a couple of days to get the aircraft. He strongly suggested that the plane would be used for drug smuggling. It was very strange. But there was a purpose.

Almost before the agent was out of sight, the local Sheriff conducted a raid. The FBI had tipped him that a stolen plane containing marijuana was parked outside Rich Mountain Aviation to have bladders installed. The

Sheriff seized the aircraft, and immediately called local reporters to announce he had uncovered a big drug operation.

How big? There were a few marijuana seeds in the plane. How about the bladder work? Actually, it is the responsibility of aircraft owners, not aviation mechanics, to get FAA approval for modifications. The work is not illegal, per se. Therefore, no crime had been committed. The attempted "sting" was a case of Department of Justice agencies stumbling over each other.

Fred Hampton was so outraged that he filed a libel lawsuit against the Sheriff. In pre-trial pleadings, the FBI agent/pilot admitted the charade in an affidavit. He said the plan was to gather evidence about Hampton's company and its links to Barry Seal. Following the odd episode, Hampton no longer took chances. He asked for and received documentation from the DEA stating that Rich Mountain was readying aircraft "in connection with an official investigation"—another hole in the Mena myth.

Two months after the FBI's *Three Stooges* sting—February, 1985—Emil Camp was killed while flying in bad weather. He had taken a plane to Little Rock for an FAA inspection. The crash caused speculation that he was killed by the CIA, or somebody wanting to keep him quiet. The reality was that Emil didn't have an instrument rating. He became disoriented in low hanging clouds south of Mena and ran into a mountain.

"We can get killed in a plane crash or be shot to death" was Barry Seal's joking remark when forced at the barrel of a machine gun to take off on a soggy grass runway in Colombia. Half of his grim joke had come to pass. And exactly one year after Emil's crash, Seal was murdered. The deaths were pivotal in the fabric of the Mena myth.

A former Army criminal investigator named Eugene Wheaton was among the first to link Mena to wild and crazy conspiracies. Learning of Seal's assassination, he deduced that Mena was a CIA base linked to the Iran-Contra arms scandal. Wheaton shared his epiphany with a left-wing do-gooder legal group called the Christic Institute. Relying in large part on the information, Christic lawyer Daniel Sheehan filed a racketeering lawsuit in federal court in Miami against thirty defendants with alleged CIA ties. They were accused of murder and mayhem, drug smuggling and gun-running.

Sheehan asked for $23-million in damages. What he got was a $955,000 judgment against the Christic Institute for filing a frivolous lawsuit "based on unsubstantiated rumor and speculation from unidentified sources with no first hand knowledge." The sanction bankrupted his organization. But many so-called journalists believed the Christic allegations—several of which involved Barry Seal and his presence in Mena. What evolved was a remarkable case of the left-wing joining forces with characters that Hillary Clinton accused of participating in a "vast right-wing conspiracy."

Any uncertainties about Mena's being a spy base were expunged in October, 1986, when the C-123 transport once owned by Seal crashed in Nicaragua. Unlike the DEA sting, the Fat Lady went down on an authentic spy mission while delivering supplies to Contra rebels. Two crewmen died in the crash. But in defiance of a CIA policy designed to conceal traces of U.S. involvement in this type of mission, pilot Eugene Hasenfus wore a parachute and bailed out. Captured by Sandinista troops, he ended up in prison.

Barry Seal's prior ownership of the C-123 added an exclamation point to suspicions about activities of the fat pilot and his Fat Lady. In the aftermath of the Hasenfus crash, reporters started showing up in Baton Rouge to interview me. I was perceived as an expert on Barry and his Mena operations. Some journalists, however, considered me as the defender of an unredeemed cocaine smuggler, an enemy of law enforcement, and a protector of CIA secrets. Good and bad, I enjoyed the attention.

I was interviewed by ABC's *20/20* and also quoted extensively in a series of *Miami Herald* articles reported by Jeff Leen. He and *Herald* reporter Guy Gugliotta later co-authored *Kings of Cocaine*, a comprehensive account of the Medellín cartel, and Barry Seal's role as an undercover informant. Although ghoulish, I picked up a couple of thousand dollars as a consultant for the movie, *Double-Crossed: The Barry Seal Story*. Dennis Hopper's performance captured much of Seal's personality. Some scenes were downright eerie, a near duplication of video we shot in producing

Uncle Sam Wants You. The film, however, went overboard in trying to redeem Barry. He was not nearly as altruistic in becoming an informant as Hollywood depicted.

By 1988, the Mena rumors were out of control. Few people were around to dispute the outrageous assertions. Barry and Emil Camp were dead. Peter Everson was doing undercover work for government agencies. The denials by Fred Hampton, Joe Evans, and other Rich Mountain Aviation people were disregarded. The most knowledgeable insider still alive was Barry's ex-brother-in-law, William Bottoms.

Known in drug circles as "Billy Bob" and "Bare Bottoms," the former Coast Guard pilot retired from drug smuggling after his slate was wiped clean in return for testifying alongside Barry in Las Vegas. Following the trial, Bill worked undercover for U.S. Customs agents on cases unrelated to Barry. As rumors multiplied, he tried to set the record straight, even flying to Mena to meet reporters responsible for spreading the tales. Nobody listened to anything that failed to conform to outlandish conjecture.

The most incredible Mena yarn was the allegation that Nicaraguan rebels were trained in the nearby mountains. Residents in the sparsely populated area had never seen any sign of gun-toting Latinos. That made no difference. Like UFO believers, conspiracy theorists accepted as fact the fantasy that Contra troops were running to and fro through Arkansas hills and dales.

The fable stemmed in part from a small landing strip on property owned by Bill Bottoms, Fred Hampton and Joe Evans. They built the short runway for trips to a fishing and hunting recreational area near the tiny township of Nella. The lunatic fringe was certain the runway had more nefarious purposes.

I make no pretense of knowing the inner-workings of the CIA and its support of the Contras. But as a willing student, I made trips to Arkansas and points beyond to learn about Contra troops lurking in the mountains. If they existed, the rebels were trained in tactics of invisibility. At least to local residents.

The "secret" airstrip was a glorified cow pasture. Weeds were up to my shins. Only a brave and highly skilled pilot would try to land there in a Piper Cub carrying passengers. I asked people on adjacent property how many Contra rebels were roving around the area. They just laughed. These mountain folk knew how to keep secrets.

Before leaving Arkansas, I went to Fort Smith to interview U.S. Attorney Michael Fitzhugh. His office investigated Mena activities based on information provided to him by IRS agent Bill Duncan. A federal grand jury failed to find evidence to warrant an indictment. How about those Contra rebels being trained near Nella? Fitzhugh laughed.

I next traveled to Miami where Barry Seal testified in two trials. Federal prosecutor Dick Gregorie handled both cases. He spent days preparing Seal as a witness. Surely he knew about Barry's CIA activities. He also laughed.

From Miami, I headed to Las Vegas. Seal was the chief witness in Nevada's biggest ever drug trial. The case was prosecuted by Assistant U.S. Attorney Donald Campbell. Like Gregorie, he spent many hours debriefing Barry. Maybe he knew something about the drug pilot's CIA connections. Campbell joined the laugh fest.

After striking out in the interviews, I looked for clues in hundreds of pages of Seal's sworn testimony in Miami and Las Vegas. Barry was asked repeatedly about his alleged CIA connections and allegations that he transported guns to Contras. Under oath, he was cross examined by defense lawyers who specialized in destroying prosecution witnesses. He denied ties to the CIA or any involvement in gun-running.

He could have lied. But only if he was a complete idiot. Dick Gregorie, Donald Campbell, and everybody else involved in the drug cases put Seal on notice that if he so much as shaded the truth, his plea bargain would be voided and he would go to prison for a minimum of ten years. Since freedom was Barry's sole reason for becoming a DEA informant, it is hard to believe he would risk being caught in a lie. He was no fool.

In efforts to impeach Barry as a witness, defense lawyers played portions of my documentary to prove he was a liar. Reading those portions of his testimony, I admit to a nervous stomach. What if he claimed to have suckered me into doing the story? Fortunately, I was able to breath easy. Barry defended his statements in *Uncle Sam Wants You*. He reiterated the belief that Louisiana authorities resorted to illegal tactics in an effort to get him—the central point of my program.

After reading Seal's trial testimony, making trips to Mena, Miami and Las Vegas, and doing nearly a dozen on-camera interviews, I produced a series of reports titled *The Mena Myth*. The "exposé" received little attention outside Baton Rouge. Or for that matter, in Baton Rouge. Still, I mistakenly believed the tales would soon fade away.

Not quite. Beyond my borders, an extraordinary political phenomenon continued to evolve. Liberal-leaning alternative publications regularly carried stories linking Mena to drugs-for-guns schemes. The Administrations of Ronald Reagan and George Herbert Bush were accused of covering up the Mena mystery. The accusations were also spread as part of a "vast left-wing conspiracy"—a hodgepodge of ultra-liberal radicals obsessed with the Iran-Contra affair. And when Bill Clinton was elected President, the Mena Myth became the property of right-wing extremists who gave more bizarre spins to the fable.

In 1989, I left the environs of Barry Seal's gravesite to become CNN's Senior Investigative Correspondent in a newly-formed highfalutin' muckraking unit. I was followed there by Barry's ghost. Even before the Presidential election, far-right promoters of anti-Clinton propaganda added fanciful yarns to Barry's Mena activities, which I tried to ignore since I knew better. But I started paying attention when the Reverend Jerry Falwell began promoting *The Circle of Power* and its evil twin, *The Clinton Chronicles*.

In tandem, an incestuous ensemble of alleged journalists gave momentum to the myth by corroborating one another in books, magazines and tabloid newspapers. In 1994, a character named Terry Reed published *Compromised: Clinton, Bush and the CIA*. He offered 543 pages of "first hand recollections" about working as a CIA operative with Barry Seal and other drug pilots. Reed was Mena's most secret spy. Nobody recalled ever seeing him prior to the epic memoir.

In an on-camera interview for a CNN segment, I surprised Reed by bringing him face-to-face with Rich Mountain Aviation partner, Joe Evans—one of the ostensible Mena co-conspirators named in the book. Evans stood next to the camera in the line of vision of Reed, who failed to show a flicker of recognition until I introduced them.

The "CIA pilot" was not the least bit embarrassed when Evans said, "I've never seen you in my life." Following the interview, he inscribed *Compromised* with a message for me. "May this book lead to a _full_ understanding of what happened at Mena." The book is the most voluminous collection of Mena bullshit. It is so off-the-wall that the right-wing publication, *Accuracy In Media*, discredited Reed's fantasies.

In 1996, a writer named Roger Morris jumped on the "_full_ understanding" bandwagon in a book titled, *Partners in Power.* Described on the dust cover as a prize-winning historian, Morris cited Terry Reed as a Seal associate.

But the strangest anecdote in the "prize-winning historian's" book told a tale attributed to former Arkansas State Trooper, L.D. Brown—a disgruntled ex-Clinton bodyguard, who was one of the sources named in the *American Spectator's* "Bill's babes" article. Brown was a spy wannabe. To that end, he claimed that Governor Clinton arranged for him to accompany Barry Seal on a CIA mission to Honduras in the C-123.

To his utter shock, Brown said he discovered it was a drugs-for-guns flight. But he was not nearly as shocked as I was. October 23, 1984, was cited as the date of Brown's trip—the same day I was in Mena inside the C-123 transport with Barry.

Sober then for a dozen years, I'm sure I would have noticed guns being loaded on the plane and our junket to Central America. The date of my Mena visit is documented by interview material, as well as an IRS record of a $10,000 cash withdrawal by Seal from his Capital Bank checking account prior to our flight from Baton Rouge.

In Mena, I witnessed a cash payment—amount unknown—to Fred Hampton for work by Rich Mountain Aviation. Barry also spent $1,200 to buy fuel for the Fat Lady as we prepared to get video of a flight. He taxied to an airport gas pump and said, "Fill it up," just like going to his daddy's ESSO station in the days of full service, except the attendant didn't clean the windshield. Sitting behind

Barry, I watched as he peeled off twelve $100 bills. Before buying fuel, he had revved the engines for half an hour or more to flush condensation that had built up in the tanks during the hot summer months—an indication that the Fat Lady must have sat idle since the Nicaragua sting operation.

Although the short flight was for the benefit of our camera, events of the day may explain the reason Trooper Brown selected the date for his fantasy trip to Honduras. He had access to surveillance reports disclosing that Barry and two crew members were running around the airport in military fatigues. However, the plane only circled the airport. It was a final flight before being sold. Maybe L.D. Brown's guns-for-drugs CIA excursion to Honduras was in a different C-123 with a different Barry Seal.

Whatever the case, Brown's fable was reported as fact in the Roger Morris book, as well as the *American Spectator* and other publications that tilted to the far right. The phantom flight had yet another shocking twist. According to Trooper Brown, he reported what he had seen to the Governor, who purportedly told him not to get his jockey shorts in a wad. Clinton was quoted as saying the cocaine was "Lasater's deal"—a strange and wondrous story— though totally false. Under "Clinton Rules," that made no difference.

Partners in Crime author Roger Morris was "Partners in Sloppy Journalism" with Sally Denton, another believer of Mena fairy tales. They co-authored newspaper and magazine articles about Seal, the CIA and Mena, then co-whined when the mainstream media disregarded their "reporting."

Another competitor in the Mena fiction contest was British tabloid reporter, Ambrose Evans-Pritchard. His name could have been further hyphenated to Ambrose-Evans-*Reed*-Pritchard. He wrote the 1997 book, *The Secret Life of Bill Clinton*, as well as articles in newspapers and magazines in which he cited Terry Reed as a source.

I hope the fact that Evans-Pritchard and Morris took cheap shots at me hasn't influenced my opinion of their works. In a letter to the *New York Observer,* Morris complained about an unfavorable book review that quoted me as disputing his account of events related to Barry Seal. Morris described me as an "obscure" reporter lacking journalism credentials. Considering my four Peabody medallions and numerous other journalism prizes, I thought I had escaped obscurity.

By and large, the mainstream news media steered clear of the nuttiest Mena stories. A notable exception was the op-ed page of the *Wall Street Journal*, though it barely qualified as mainstream. Columns by Micah Morrison repeated Mena rumors, quoting Arkansas state cop Russell Welch and IRS agent Bill Duncan as sources.

One of the nation's last great muckrakers, Jack Anderson, also touched on Mena in a couple of columns. His stories about Mena and Barry Seal were ambiguous.

To my amazement, highly-respected CBS News correspondent Bill Plante gave credence to the myth. In the early stages of the Whitewater investigation, he reported an *Eye on America* segment that stated without qualification that "Barry Seal's organization helped Contras smuggle tons of cocaine and laundered drug profits through Arkansas." Interviewed for the report were Russell Welch and Bill Duncan. More astonishing was the appearance of Terry Reed. Referring to the cow pasture-like airstrip north of Mena, Reed told Plante it was used to "train Contra pilots."

"I was involved in the flight-training aspects of upgrading the Nicaraguan freedom fighters to make them capable of flying combat aircraft," Reed said, claiming to have been hired by Barry Seal. I presume that Bill Plante never saw the Nella training ground. One thing is certain, combat aircraft other than helicopters could not land or take off from the short runway.

Remarkably, Plante credited Oliver North with helping the DEA in Barry Seal's Nicaraguan undercover mission when, in fact, it was North who wrecked the investigation. It was puzzling how a veteran correspondent could be so badly snookered. He had been given background dispelling the Mena Myth by then U.S. Attorney Mike Fitzhugh. According to the prosecutor, Plante's report totally ignored his explanation. Instead, Fitzhugh was accused of failing to pursue cases related to Seal and Mena. In reality, he repeatedly investigated evidence provided by IRS agent Duncan and State Trooper Welch, but never found anything more substantive than rumors.

Four months after Bill Plante gave legitimacy to the crazy stories, I relied on my Baton Rouge reporting experience to reveal the real facts in a CNN segment. The late Tip O'Neil — former Speaker of the U.S. House of Representatives — said "all politics is local." Investigative reporting is also local, whether it is unearthed in Baghdad, Baton Rouge or Washington D.C.

I was fortunate to learn the craft in Baton Rouge, Louisiana.

CHAPTER FIVE

A ROGUE GOVERNOR AND A HORNY PREACHER

On nights when the skies are clear, Louisiana's Capitol city could be mistaken for a giant metropolis. Dazzling lights sparkle beneath puffy clouds stretching endlessly along the banks of the Mississippi River. But come daybreak, the billows are revealed to be residue rising from smokestacks. The twinkling skyline transforms into a mixture of oil and chemical refineries that are the backbone of the state's economy.

Baton Rouge's nighttime illusion is as deceptive as Louisiana politicians who have occupied cells in federal penitentiaries and in the state's notorious Angola prison. Like the stifling humidity of summers that begin early and end late, a history of corruption hovers over Louisiana's towering thirty-four-story Capitol building. Prior to relinquishing its corruption title to Illinois, sticky-fingered government officials and free-range rogues roamed Capitol corridors for decades, giving Louisiana a reputation as America's northernmost "Banana Republic."

Working for a Baton Rouge radio station in 1972, I launched my muckraking career by uncovering a bribery scheme resulting in the indictments of bankers and a state official. The exposé sprung me to major market television in Miami and thence to Boston. A decade later at the age of forty-seven, I returned to the place where I started.

I brought home with me a collection of journalism prizes.

Television careers are measured by the size of viewing audiences. Miami was the nation's fifteenth largest market and Boston ranked number five. At number ninety-one, Baton Rouge was way down the list. Moving downward was a difficult decision—professionally and personally.

I was returning to the scene of painful memories in a place where I made my final descent into the depths of alcoholic degradation. My first wife and our four children still lived in Louisiana. Tragically, my 28-year-old son, Michael, was awaiting trial in a New Orleans jail for a vicious crime that would eventually result in a life sentence.

Sober for nearly a dozen years, I had not yet bridged a father/son gap that had been strained between us since his childhood. As a result of my career travels and his constant moves across the country, Mike remained a stranger. Although I couldn't admit it then—even to myself—I wanted to avoid the parental humiliation of being in close proximity to my son's tragic situation. I now had a second wife, two adopted sons and in my mind, professional and personal respectability.

Moreover, I worried that after years of neglecting the children of my first marriage, they would resent the attention I gave to a new family. A gratifying reward of sobriety had been developing better relationships with my children. Separated by many miles, the distance helped them forgive my past failures. Now what?

Professionally, my return home seemed at first to be a horrible mistake. In the final week of October—three months following my homecoming—I sat in a small conference room with five people watching a videotape of my first exposé as muckraker in residence for WBRZ, Baton Rouge's ABC affiliate. As final credits rolled, I waited for accolades. There was dead silence. Douglas Manship, the President of the station's parent company, was at a loss for words. He paced the room before facing me.

"Goddamn, John, I didn't bring you back to lose my TV station."

"Oh, shit." I thought. Doug was patriarch of a family-owned, mini-media conglomerate that consisted of WBRZ, a television station in Texas, Baton Rouge's daily newspaper, and three radio stations, including WJBO where I was introduced to muckraking ten years before. His ancestors acquired the family's first Baton Rouge newspaper in 1909. As the company grew, descendants wended upwardly through the ranks as a matter of entitlement. Doug was the latest to head the company in the line of succession. He was the newspaper's Executive Publisher. Two sons and a daughter worked in various capacities for the newspaper. A third son, thirty-five-year-old Richard was WBRZ's General Manager.

My early tenure as News Director of WJBO radio and as host of a popular daily talk show had been interrupted in 1971 when I decided that work interfered with my drinking. So I quit. Or maybe I was fired. No matter. In exile, I discovered that being sober was better than being drunk. Rehired a year later, I stumbled into my career as a "prize-winning" muckraker.

By the time I returned to Baton Rouge in 1982, I proudly displayed two Peabody medallions and a bunch of other broadcast journalism awards. WBRZ was truly fortunate to have someone of my ilk. At least, that was the impression I tried to convey. In truth, I was lucky to have a job. An investigative reporting tsunami that swept across the nation following the Watergate scandal had slowed to a trickle in the wake of corporate takeovers. Looming starvation was my primary motivation for returning to Baton Rouge.

But my memory of Doug Manship's journalistic courage was also an influencing factor. As a budding muckraker for WJBO, I was encouraged by Doug to dig deep into stories that were seldom reported on radio. He never so much as flinched at the prospect of controversy. Threats and intimidation suggested to him that I was on the trail of something worthwhile.

My 1972 exposé of a bank bribery scheme involved cronies of U.S. Senator Russell Long. Snooping into affairs of his friends caused the powerful lawmaker to bitterly complain to Doug. I only learned of the intervention months later when we successfully defended a multi-million dollar lawsuit stemming from the story.

Besides courage, Doug Manship taught me that journalists have an obligation to report stories without consideration of outside perceptions. Days before an election early in my investigative reporting career, I uncovered damaging information about our Congressman, who was a cinch to be re-elected regardless of what we disclosed. Realizing the exposé could be perceived as election eve politics, I suggested we delay it until after the election. Doug set me straight in a hurry.

"I don't care if people consider the timing political. We don't withhold information from voters. They can make their own judgments about the man's character."

I had not seen Doug in the decade since departing for "big time TV." And he was not in a welcoming mood in the conference room prior to reviewing my first WBRZ exposé. The "boss," as he was addressed by most employees, barely acknowledged my presence before watching the documentary. The lack of hugs and kisses didn't bother me nearly as much as his reaction.

Potential litigation seemed foremost in his mind—uncharacteristic of the man who once stood so solidly behind my stories. He had good reasons to be apprehensive. Titled *Keys to the Vault*, the thirty minute documentary ran a high risk of lawsuits. It would also alienate one of WBRZ's biggest advertisers. The report revealed that American Bank—then Louisiana's biggest state-chartered financial institution—was in turmoil because of insider loans.

The bank's biggest loss involved a failed Alabama real estate development. The loan had been facilitated by American Bank's chief legal counsel, who happened to have an ownership interest in the property. The lawyer's name had popped up unexpectedly in my research of a controversial insurance firm that was then the target of a high profile federal grand jury investigation. The company was formed for the sole purpose of selling supplemental retirement policies to state employees.

Louisiana's rascal in residence, Edwin Edwards, facilitated approval of the tax-sheltered plan in the final days of the second of his four terms as Governor. He also arranged for salesmen to pitch the policies to state employees during working hours. Before his election to a first term in 1972, we were fairly friendly. That quickly ended when he learned I was gathering information about his secret links to the insurance deal. He had agreed to an on-camera interview, characterizing it as "rolling in garbage."

"What happened while you were away from Louisiana," he asked. "You were once a good reporter."

Stories about complex political deals using the word "insurance" are mind-numbing to television newsroom producers. "Who the hell is going to understand this story?" they ask. Sometimes, nobody—a major shortcoming of my career. As a documents guy, I accumulated stacks of paper in the same manner as reclusive eccentrics found dead next to meowing cats in trash-filled apartments. Because documents are boring, TV reporters avoid following paper trails in musty file rooms.

Keys to the Vault was overloaded with documents. But the tale had an intriguing twist. The insurance company President, Kenneth Womack Sr., had mysteriously disappeared from his apartment with the morning coffee still perking.

For a year, FBI agents had conducted an ineffectual nationwide search for the executive. They may have been victims of a legend about the eccentricities of the late FBI Director, J. Edgar Hoover. As the story goes, Hoover visited a New Orleans racetrack on a steaming hot day in the 1950's. An inveterate horseracing aficionado, he wore a dark suit, tightly knotted tie and high heels (a cheap joke reflecting my deejay dreams). Anyway, he wilted in the heat and left the track before the bell sounded for the final race. Thereafter, errant agents were punished by reassignment to Louisiana—Hoover's version of Hades. Consequently, FBI investigations became the province of bungling lawmen.

The anecdote may be apocryphal. However, it was told to me by an agent reassigned to Baton Rouge after he was caught assisting a Pennsylvania Sheriff install an illegal wiretap during a robbery investigation. When the device was discovered by an innocent suspect, the sheriff blamed the agent. Illegal wiretaps were not considered a big deal during the Hoover era. Getting caught was a grave sin. My agent acquaintance said he was sentenced to finish his career in close proximity to alligators and snakes that populate Louisiana's Atchafalaya swamp.

The search for Ken Womack gave the Hoover tale credibility. The missing executive's estranged wife, Annette, told FBI agents that her runaway husband was almost certainly living with a girlfriend in New Jersey. But even with the correct address, they couldn't find him. In the FBI's one time visit to the woman's apartment, Womack hid in the closet. She denied knowing his whereabouts, and agents went on their merry way.

In another ludicrous turn while the FBI was cold on Womack's trail, he checked into a Veterans Administration Hospital in Philadelphia under his own name after being diagnosed with cancer. Agents apparently failed to check Veterans and Social Security registries. Only after he died in the VA hospital did they learn he was hiding in plain sight. His wife, by then divorced from Ken, informed the FBI of his death. The girlfriend had contacted a Womack relative, who notified his former spouse.

Like most multifaceted investigative reporting projects, *Keys to the Vault* unfolded in bits and pieces. The Edwin Edward's investigation and Ken Womack's sudden departure were big news when I arrived in Baton Rouge. My research began with a bit of serendipity at the insurance company's abandoned offices.

The new tenant pointed to piles of paper left behind after an FBI search. Like a dumpster diver, I dug through old computer printouts covered with incomprehensible numbers. One document caught my eye. It was a partnership agreement between Womack and a controversial businessman. His dealings with Edwin Edwards had been part of an earlier federal investigation. Also listed as a partner was American Bank's legal counsel. He had never been publicly linked to the firm.

To follow up on the partnership, I contacted the bank's former President. He reportedly resigned because of clashes with the lawyer. He was unaware of the partnership, though not surprised. He showed me a federal examination report that sharply criticized the attorney's ties to dubious insider deals, including a Talladega, Alabama real-estate and golf course development called Point Aquarius.

Though much bigger than Whitewater Estates, the project was remarkably similar to Bill Clinton's investment. Both seemed sure things—at least until deregulation of the S&L industry sent interest rates skyrocketing and second home financing plummeting. The transactions were an excellent primer for my Whitewater stories a dozen years later.

The American Bank audit was a road map to a trove of material in government agencies and courthouses in Talladega, Montgomery, Birmingham and Pensacola, Florida. The documents disclosed other shenanigans by the bank's legal counsel and his partners. Hard evidence notwithstanding, Doug Manship questioned whether my exposé was worth the expense of potential litigation and the loss of advertising revenue.

"Are we going to be sued?" he asked the two lawyers in our conference room.

"Probably," said libel expert Frank Middleton. He had defended me in lawsuits stemming from my radio bribery story years earlier. Frank and another lawyer had approved the *Keys to the Vault* script. They were seeing the video for the first time.

"Will we win?" Doug wanted to know.

"John says the story is solid and we feel comfortable with his back-up material. However, nobody can predict what a jury will do."

"When is the thing supposed to air?" Doug asked his son, Richard.

"Tuesday night. Bank executives saw the on-air promos and notified us they will cancel all advertising if the program runs."

"Jesus Christ," Doug exclaimed. "Four days away and I'm just now finding out that we're ruining a man's reputation, losing a big advertiser and we're going to be sued. The guy will own the television station."

Across the room, News Director John Spain squirmed uneasily. He had convinced me to come home with a speech using the cliché that Doug and Richard wanted us to "kick ass and take names." Right now, Doug Manship seemed ready to kick our butts.

John was thirteen years younger than I. But he was old enough to have seen me at my worst. Or so he claimed in a 1989 magazine interview describing an encounter in the late sixties while he was a student at LSU. Driving home late one night, he said a scruffy- looking drunk waved him down. "He didn't know me, but I recognized who it was because this was a guy I admired. It was John Camp, who was a great radio reporter at the time. We talked, and I took him home." It's possible. Like many events in my boozing days, I don't recall the incident. Regardless, "great radio reporter" was a nice touch.

Before becoming WBRZ's News Director, John had a flair for investigative reporting and occasionally tracked me down in Miami and Boston for background on stories that I reported in Baton Rouge. We developed a nice rapport, mainly because he let me pose as a hotshot, big time newsman. When John called me in Boston with a job offer, he didn't know I was collecting unemployment checks. Even so, I thought he was deranged to think that I would return to a burg like Baton Rouge. I don't know what I was thinking. He offered more money than my salary at a major station in Boston. He also promised resources and freedom to do stories without time constraints or deadlines. Although skeptical, sanity prevailed over ego and I accepted the offer.

John and I were opposites in style and personality. He could be very charming, but had an explosive temper if things went wrong. I was an easygoing con man, rarely given to tantrums. He dressed in tailored suits, freshly pressed shirts and expensive neckties. I favored the reporter's uniform of blue blazer, khaki slacks, button-down oxford shirt and loosened K-Mart tie. John swaggered through the newsroom. I slouched.

Despite differences, we were unified in plans "to clean up River City." However, our grandiose vision seemed doomed as we listened to Doug Manship's rant. The boss didn't act like the same guy I considered a journalism hero.

In my radio days, he put his media monopoly on the line by letting me do high risk stories. I wondered if age had diminished his dedication. After mumbling a stream of profanities following his viewing of *Keys to the Vault*, he delayed a final decision. He wanted to see the documentary again in the privacy of his home.

"I want you with me," Doug told the attorneys. "Maybe we can figure out what to do with this damn thing."

I didn't pack my bags. Nevertheless, I was more than a little concerned about our plan to "clean up River City." My future remained in suspense until late the next day when Attorney Bill Wilson called with the verdict. He now handled most of WBRZ's First Amendment issues as a prelude to Frank Middleton's retirement. "We've looked at the program several times," Bill said. "You need to make some changes."

"What kind of changes?" I asked, bracing myself for a technical nightmare that extensive re-editing would encompass. But more humiliating was the prospect of replacing the heavily promoted hot scoop with a rerun of *Hollywood Squares*.

"First, take out the line about the guy's Silver Star in Korea. Also drop the reference to his chairmanship of Billy Graham's Baton Rouge crusade," he said. I was puzzled. Those were highlights of the man's life. "Doug believes the information only makes him look like a hypocrite. Hypocrisy is not illegal." Good point.

"What else?"

"That's it. Doug thinks it's an excellent story. Next time, give him more notice when you're putting his TV station at risk." Happily, the boss had not changed after all.

Keys to the Vault would receive a DuPont Columbia award, the first of two dozen major national prizes given WBRZ during my seven years at the station. I had found an investigative reporter's dream job. John Spain gave me whatever time and resources necessary to work on projects. And not once did he, Doug, or Richard Manship deny me anything essential to advancing a story. Nor did they ever try to steer me away from exposés because of legal jeopardy, outside pressures, politics, or personal interest. And the Manship family had a strong personal interest when I exposed property tax inequities in Baton Rouge. I identified WBRZ as a prime beneficiary of the Tax Assessor's largesse. I heard no complaints from above.

Nor did the station shy away from controversy. Time and again, we were a target of vitriolic attacks because of my investigations. Everybody simply shrugged. Very few television stations in the country, if any, would give thumbs-up on stories that lawyers said were absolutely certain to result in lawsuits. Fortunately, we never lost.

WBRZ did something else remarkable. In an era when important news stories were being condensed to two minutes or less, my investigative documentaries were aired in prime time without commercial breaks.

Although *Keys to the Vault* ran a half-hour, many other reports were fifty-eight minutes—uninterrupted by commercials or station promos. I joked that the Baton Rouge Water Company could measure our ratings by the number of toilets flushing at the conclusion of the shows.

The station exemplified the inherent advantages of local ownership of radio and television stations. The bureaucracy was streamlined, and the editorial decisions were far more gutsy than in corporate environments that now dominate the broadcasting industry.

Keys to the Vault didn't cause people to take to the streets demanding reforms. But for me, the exposé symbolized WBRZ's commitment to investigative reporting. The bank lawyer avoided indictment. I've purposely left out his name. He later redeemed himself by performing many good deeds in the community. He's now dead and there's no need to embarrass his do-gooder family. From Edwin Edwards's standpoint, my revelations were no more than an annoyance, although the story prompted him to label me a "derelict gunslinger." But neither my report nor the related grand jury probe interfered with his re-election to two more terms as Governor.

As one of the most colorful politicians in state history—and the nation's—his audacity kept voters entertained. Edwards once boasted that the only way he could lose an election was "to get caught in bed with a dead girl. Or a live boy." In his final winning campaign, he faced former Nazi and Ku Klux Klan leader, David Duke. Preferring colorful rascals to hate-mongers, bumper stickers urged voters to "Elect the Crook." The "crook" returned to office for a final hurrah.

Edwards' political philosophy of beneficently rewarding friends with the spoils of victory made him fair game for reporters and prosecutors. He was twice acquitted of bribery charges in 1985 and 1986 before finally stepping too far across the line separating patronage from corruption.

In 2002—four years after leaving office and twenty years following my documentary, he was convicted of taking bribes in return for riverboat gambling licenses. At the age of seventy, he was sentenced to ten years in prison.

There are important personal sidebars to *Keys to the Vault*. In 1986, I married the widow of missing insurance executive Ken Womack. Annette is my third, present and hopefully, final spouse. We were introduced at a meeting of a not-so-secret Twelve Step society. She was eighteen months sober at the time and less than thrilled to meet an "old-timer" whose day job was raking muck. Though my investigation of her estranged husband had not yet begun, she suspected me of infiltrating her sacred refuge to get leads on his whereabouts—an understandable concern. Reporters had staked out her home to get information. And she sure as hell didn't want a career muckraker hanging around the one place where the brewing scandal was a non-issue.

Ken had skipped town leaving behind Annette, three children and his mother—a diabetic amputee who lived with the family. He never contacted them. Despite all the publicity, the grand jury failed to uncover evidence that Ken committed any crimes. He was simply a scared, borderline alcoholic, who believed that running away was the only option he had in dealing with the pressure of a politically-charged investigation. Given my battles with alcoholism, I understood his decision. It was an exit that I once tried.

The vanishing act took a heavy toll on Ken's family. Burdened with $3-million in debts he accumulated, they were evicted from a heavily mortgaged home, Annette's automobile repossessed, and she was harassed by bill collectors. Even with a Masters Degree in English Literature, finding a job was tough for someone out of the workplace for twenty years while raising children. She moved the family to a small apartment, returned to college and obtained a postgraduate degree in social work and has since built a career as a psychotherapist.

Keys to the Vault overlapped Annette's many personal crises. Because of our Alcoholics Anonymous connection, I avoided asking her help in researching the story. As a result, her suspicion of me gradually diminished. We became friends, good friends, closer friends and eventually married. All is well that ends well.

There is another personal disclosure related to *Keys to the Vault* that involves my second wife, Patricia. Before we started dating, she had a longstanding relationship with a law partner of the American Bank attorney at the center of my exposé. In fact, Patricia and I spent weekends at the law firm's lake cabin. The past romance had no relevance to my reporting. I regularly ran into my past in Baton Rouge—sometimes painfully so.

To my knowledge, Doug Manship never previewed another documentary of mine after *Keys to the Vault*. Nor do I know of instances in which he criticized my exposés. For that matter, I don't remember getting compliments from the boss. His silence may have been my greatest praise. He expected no less than what we accomplished.

Except for trips on the company airplane to collect journalism prizes, I rarely saw Doug. In the rarified air of muckraking nirvana, a routine part of the job was accepting awards. Nearly all my documentaries won prizes. Indeed, I attended so many presentation ceremonies that I became the first in my family to own a tuxedo instead of renting.

—

As much as I would like to take full credit for my prize-winning ways, I was in a special place at a special time. Not only at WBRZ, but in a city and state where I could pick and choose from a buffet of scandals and intriguing charlatans. The most colorful was a horny holy man who would have a profound impact on my career.

If there is such a thing as muckraking karma, my destiny was to encounter Brother Jimmy Lee Swaggart. Again and again. Like couples who marry, divorce and remarry, we had a long and volatile love-hate relationship. To use a word associated with fundamentalist religions, I was "saved" by the preacher. Not my soul. But my career. I was in danger of descending into an abyss of apathy before America's most infamous whoremonger raised me from the tomb of the unknown journalist. Jimmy and I met five years before he tripped over his dick, causing a $150-million a year spiritual empire to come tumbling down.

Though not banned in the Roman Catholic stronghold of Boston, his popularity there was negligible. I was vaguely aware that rock and roll icon Jerry Lee Lewis had a well-known evangelist cousin living in Baton Rouge. However, I barely recognized Jimmy Swaggart's name prior to returning to Louisiana. He had begun his television preaching in 1973, the year I left for Miami.

In the early days of his televangelism, Brother Jimmy taped his syndicated shows at WBRZ's studios, and when I arrived station employees had many tales to tell about the preacher's uncanny ability to spontaneously unleash buckets of tears. Bob Courtney—a former radio colleague and close friend—was WBRZ's Assistant News Director. He described the evangelist as the most preternatural performer he had ever seen.

Bob traveled with Jimmy in 1981 while producing a series of stories about the rapidly expanding ministry, which was then emerging as one of Baton Rouge's biggest employers—albeit low income jobs. Recounting his Swaggart experience, Bob cited an on-camera interview which captured the essence of the evangelist's theatrical talents.

With tears streaming down his cheeks, Jimmy told of a sinner—a prostitute, ironically—who was on the verge of committing suicide. But while watching Swaggart's TV show, she committed her life to Christ instead. Unfortunately, the cameraman interrupted Swaggart in mid-sob to change videotape at the most dramatic moment in the story. Bob feared that he had lost a great sound-bite. However, when the interview resumed several minutes later, he said Jimmy picked up at the exact point where he left off. Without missing a beat, he turned on the tears as if he possessed a weeping faucet.

Bob's series of reports—*Profit or Prophet*—was not an in-depth investigation. What he observed, though, convinced him that it would be worthwhile for me to dig into the organization's finances and fundraising tactics. I was busy on another project and didn't have much interest in the story. But converging events soon roused my curiosity.

First, a sad-faced truck driver showed up at my office complaining that Brother Jimmy unfairly fired him and his wife. The man drove one of the eighteen-wheeler rigs that transported television production equipment, gospel recordings and a variety of religious merchandise to Swaggart's twice-monthly crusades. The couple had relocated in Baton Rouge from the Midwest for the specific purpose of becoming helpmates of Jimmy and Jesus. She worked in a warehouse that processed the ministry's huge mail-order business. However, she was labeled a trouble-maker after complaining of sexual harassment by a super-visor, and the couple was fired.

The distraught man showed me a copy of a termination letter from Brother Jimmy stating in effect, "I love you, but don't let the door hit you in the ass." The dismissal didn't qualify as an investigative story. But it was interesting that Swaggart converts had traveled from faraway places to work for minimum wages.

Not long after the trucker's visit, an unhappy mid-level manager at the ministry came to see me. He also bitched about Jimmy's arbitrary and unchristian-like treatment. To prove the point, he gave me a stack of internal memo-randa. The documents suggested that the ministry's top three executive's—Jimmy, his wife Frances and their son, Donnie, were overbearing micro-managers consumed with minutiae.

A story of internal whining didn't grab me. But I knew better than to look gift sources in the mouths. I started contacting other disaffected former employees. The com-plaints were much the same—people disillusioned by the perceived arrogance of Brother Jimmy and his family. Still, nobody provided me with a "smoking Bible."

Not surprising since I didn't know enough about television ministries to ask more than superficial questions.

I was looking for an Elmer Gantry angle. Did he steal money? No. Does he screw around with women, or for that matter, little boys? Never—an answer that later had to be amended. How about booze and drugs? Oh, no. Then why do I care? Well, he is duplicitous and dictatorial. So?

In the absence of egregious misdeeds, I was ready to say "Amen." Then I met a man who gave me a crash course in televangelism. George Jernigan was the ministry's former Director of Finance. Jimmy fired him for being an advocate of truth-in-begging. Like many other employees, Jernigan joined the ministry because of an abiding belief in Jimmy Swaggart's good works. Having previously worked for squirrelly Pat Robertson, Jernigan was savvy about the inner workings of TV ministries.

Jimmy and Pat proselytized similar Pentecostal doctrines. But Robertson's whining casket salesman voice was the antithesis of Brother Swaggart's sobbing come-to-Jesus-or-else rhetoric. Pat was an entrepreneur who became a religious celebrity. Jimmy was a religious celebrity who became a moneychanger.

A ninth grade drop-out, Swaggart was the son of a reformed bootlegger. College-educated Robertson was the son of a U.S. Senator. The differing backgrounds reflected in the manner in which the two not-for-profit organizations were operated. Robertson had efficient accounting controls. Jimmy's ministry was a mom, pop, and son operation.

George Jernigan wasn't the kind of guy to maliciously spread gossip. Tall and slender with a rounded beard sans mustache, his posture and deliberate manner gave him the appearance of a stern Amish farmer. He remained almost reverentially subdued in criticizing his former employer, once interrupting my questioning to pray for guidance before answering. God must have been pissed at Jimmy. After prayerful meditation, Jernigan told me of the ministry's extravagant spending, and explained how contributions of jewelry and other goods were converted for personal use by the Swaggart family. His biggest criticism was directed at a fundraising gimmick called the "Children's Fund."

"I'm not asking you to face the heartbreak I feel when I pick up a dying child in my arms in one of the poor Third World countries overseas, realizing that our help came too late to save his or her life," Swaggart sniveled while showing pictures of emaciated children staring forlornly into the camera.

Feeding starving children was certainly a righteous cause—except contributions didn't go directly to a Children's Fund. Jernigan said the money was diverted into the general fund. Only pennies on the dollar went to feed children. As the ministry's chief finance executive, he complained to Swaggart about the misrepresentations. It was "Goodbye, George." Brother Jimmy didn't tolerate criticism.

A sense of omnipotence has caused the downfall of several big time television preachers. As messengers of God, many celebrity pastors believe they are above accountability. Billy Graham is an exception. He was surrounded by people who saved him from himself. According to Rice University sociologist William Martin, author of *Prophet With Honor*, longtime advisors like Cliff Barrow were never hesitant in confronting Graham if he lost sight of the primary purpose of his mission. Martin's book was the first and most definitive biography written with Graham's cooperation.

Swaggart acted as if he was exempt from reality checks. Not long after firing George Jernigan, the televangelist let loose an outburst of arrogance during a tape recorded staff meeting that personified the danger of an out-of-control ego. He angrily told employees that he didn't need smarty-pants accountants telling him how to run the ministry, which was then collecting $40-million a year.

"Some of the Brothers here have questioned my judgment," he began. "Let me set the record straight. I have forgotten more about administration and organization and business than most of you will ever learn. I know what I'm doing. I probably know what I'm doing more than any man you've ever laid eyes on in your life. Don't ever think I don't know what I'm doing. Somebody talks about the chain of command. You're looking at the command and you're looking at the whole chain, every single link in it."

The harangue was very much at odds with the genial, self-effacing country revivalist who charmed the hell out of me when we first met.

CHAPTER SIX

"ONE OF THE FINEST INVESTIGATIVE REPORTERS IN THE WORLD"

On a dank Sunday night in March, 1983, I stood on a rain-dampened tarmac outside a hangar at Baton Rouge's Ryan Airport and impulsively embraced Brother Swaggart. We had just returned from a ministry crusade in Hampton, Virginia. After learning that I was working on a documentary about his organization, he invited me to travel with him to see his good works first-hand. Watching the televangelist in action was a one-of-a-kind experience. He was unlike any preacher I had seen before.

His three day crusade in Hampton was comparable to a rock concert. At each service, he filled the 10,000 seat Coliseum to capacity with true-believers, near-believers, and curiosity seekers. And whatever money they put in collection plates was a bargain. Jimmy provided both entertainment and spiritual nourishment. At the conclusion of sermons when the first chords of *Softly and Tenderly, Jesus is Calling* sounded, scores of people solemnly marched forward to dedicate and rededicate their lives to the Lord.

Following Sunday's final service, I half expected to hear an Elvis-like "Jimmy has left the building" announcement as he made a quick getaway in a limousine parked inside the coliseum. Within an hour, we were airborne on his private plane, chomping on Wendy's hamburgers that were picked up on the way to the airport. I was impressed. Embarrassingly so.

"I've really enjoyed being with you," I mumbled after landing in Baton Rouge. Impulsively, I gave the former holy-roller tent preacher a big hug. My face flushed as I recalled acting like a star-struck high school girl. I was not the hugging type. But Jimmy succeeded in making me his friend—the whole point of inviting me to tag along.

"John, I'm just so very happy you could travel with us," he said after my rapturous display of affection. "We live in a glass house and I want you to look closely at what we do. I don't expect a puff piece, but be fair in what you report."

"Of course I'll be fair," I said, reciting the investigative reporter's mantra.

I already knew my definition of fairness was considerably different than his. Prior to the Hampton trip, I spent weeks gathering information about ministry finances. I found evidence of extravagant spending, fundraising misrepresentations and spiritual manipulation of well-heeled converts. Nothing in Hampton changed my mind about the tax exempt organization's abuses in collecting and spending tens-of-millions of dollars in the name of God. So I drove away from the airport with mixed emotions. Despite my awkward suck-up to Swaggart, I knew he wouldn't like my reporting. An understatement.

Observing the preacher had been akin to walking through a carnival house of mirrors and seeing his many changing images. Like an actor in a repertory company,

Jimmy switched characters in an instant from fiery evangelist to hard-nosed businessman to talented musician and entertainer. In interviews and informal chats, he was ingratiating, easygoing, and self-effacing—the quintessential "good old boy." But he had a disconcerting habit of continually using the phrase, "To be honest with you." It implied he was not forthcoming in previous statements.

I sensed something else odd in being around Jimmy. I felt a peculiar kinship. I attributed it to a similarity in our backgrounds. We were the same age and both of us grew up in semi-dysfunctional Southern families. Moreover, we became seventeen-year-old husbands and daddies while our high school classmates were still attending proms. And like the preacher, I was a role player — as an investigative reporter, and in my personal life. Still, I couldn't quite identify what it was in Jimmy that caused my odd affinity. Five years later, though, I learned we had something in common that I could not have imagined. By then, he had ascended to the top of television's religious huckster heap.

Before the fall, Brother Swaggart was beyond compare in the business of assembly line soul-saving and money-collecting. He displayed traces of Elmer Gantry. Unlike Sinclair Lewis' fictional clergyman, Swaggart truly believed that he heard God's call. The Lord's voice would later be drowned out by a cash register after he became trapped in an unending cycle of having to raise money to go on television to raise money to stay on television. The dilemma is indigenous to big TV ministries.

Jimmy was "saved" in a tiny Assembly of God church in Ferriday, Louisiana—the same church where his mamma, daddy, cousins, and other family members had their spiritual roots. He started preaching as a teenager, passing up an opportunity to get a lot richer, a lot quicker as a secular performer. First cousin Jerry Lee Lewis issued a tempting call radically different from God's summons. The rock-and-roll icon wanted Jimmy Lee to follow him to *Sun Records* in Memphis. The legendary recording studio launched "The Killer's" career, as well as the careers of Elvis, Johnny Cash and several other star-bound entertainers.

Jimmy Lee's piano style was nearly identical to that of Jerry Lee and another cousin—country singer Mickey Lee Gilley. They each learned to play on the same keyboard in the living room of Jerry Lee's home. Their distinctive style was called "Sam's walking left hand," named after an elderly Black handyman who taught them the method. It was a hybrid blend of honky-tonk, country, gospel and blues made famous by Mississippi Delta performers who frequented roadside taverns and nightclubs around Ferriday and in the nearby riverboat town of Natchez, Mississippi.

In the mid-1950's, the three cousins left Ferriday heading in different directions. Jerry Lee and Mickey Lee strayed from the strictures of the church, getting rich off the Devil's music. Jimmy Lee became a struggling itinerant preacher. He drove Louisiana's blacktop back roads, evangelizing under tents, on street corners and in tiny country churches. His income came from the "love offerings" of small congregations.

While Jimmy Lee struggled, Jerry Lee climbed to the top of the music charts. His wild escapades made him the bad boy of rock and roll. Cousin Jimmy soon began using Jerry Lee as an example of the evils of a Godless lifestyle. The rock star seemed unfazed. In fact, he was extraordinarily generous with his pious relative. After learning that the revivalist was driving an old jalopy that scarcely made it from one town to the next, Jerry Lee bought Jimmy a brand new Oldsmobile. And anytime the preacher was in desperate financial straits, he could depend on his sinner cousin for help.

Many folks attended Jimmy's revivals just to hear about Jerry Lee's sins. Besides family gossip, curiosity seekers heard a firebrand style of preaching and a unique brand of gospel music. Congregations soon grew. Swaggart began to fill large auditoriums and arenas instead of just tiny churches. The fortunes of the cousins were changing.

When I accompanied the televangelist in 1983 to Hampton, he was traveling to crusades in a customized seventeen-passenger ministry plane and shopping for a bigger, faster and more luxurious aircraft. He was well on his way to becoming the nation's most watched TV clergyman. In contrast, Jerry Lee had fallen on hard times. He was lurching from one performance to the next, wounded in body and soul by his excesses. Jimmy Lee was proving to Jerry Lee that God's way was the right way. The preacher's crusades were attracting much bigger crowds than his cousin's rock shows. And no wonder.

The televangelist's performances were daunting. Open floppy Bible in hand, he marched, darted and prowled across makeshift altars with the grace of a professional athlete. He raged against promiscuous sex, alcohol, illegal drugs, pornography and homosexuality. Whether in Bible Belt churches of the deep South and Midwest, or in New York City's Madison Square Garden, he attracted overflow congregations with a mesmerizing message of sin and salvation, right and wrong, and Heaven and Hell.

Jimmy Swaggart was a modern-day Billy Sunday, the born-again former major league baseball player and turn-of-the-century revivalist who danced across altars, railed against whiskey, led temperance raids on barrooms, and became a leader in the prohibition movement sixty years earlier. The Louisiana evangelist displayed the same flair for emotionally manipulating audiences. His sermons were pure art.

Bending deeply at the waist and speaking in a near whisper that sounded like a deep growl, the impassioned evangelist pointed his weapon-like finger at flinching worshippers and television viewers, threatening sinners with eternal damnation in the burning coals of Hell if they didn't repent. Jerking upright from a twisted crouch, he pointed heavenward shouting, "Glory, Glory, Glory," as he sobbed for unsaved souls, who had not yet found Jesus.

Pausing only to peek at his gold Rolex to ensure the sermon was on schedule, the evangelist attacked heathen politicians, Godless Supreme Court Justices, the satanic news media and religious denominations that deviated from his homegrown theology. He came down especially hard on the Roman Catholic Church, describing it as "a false cult."

Saving Catholics from the Pope and priests, he explained, was a "burden" God had placed on him. In an ironic criticism, Jimmy noted that priesthood celibacy resulted in "innumerable sordid, tragic, and sometimes vile scandals." Also high on his list of sinners, were do-gooder "secular humanists"—a phrase he spit out like an obscenity in describing people, who offered worldly solutions to quandaries he deemed spiritual.

By the time Brother Jimmy finished maligning secular humanists, Catholics and others failing to pass his entrance exams to Heaven, members of his congregations were worked into such an emotional lather that they appeared poised to dash from the arenas and kick the atheistic asses of the Lord's hell-bound enemies. Better yet, they were willing to pay to get the job done. He was a master at shouting "Hellfire" in a crowded church, causing panic-stricken sinners to extinguish flames with buckets of money.

Swaggart's carefully choreographed crusades were actually made-for-television productions in which he took command of the minds, hearts and wallets of frenzied followers. They were his co-stars. Audiences laughed when he laughed and cried when he cried. Every inflection of his voice, catch in his throat or tremulous sob stirred a reaction. Throughout sermons, congregants passionately prayed aloud and spoke in unknown tongues, a gibberish that is peculiar to Pentecostals.

Unlike other holy-dollar TV competitors, Swaggart seldom mounted a politically populist soapbox. He didn't try to form right-wing organizations like the late Jerry Falwell, whose toad-like countenance suggested "You're going to Hell and I'm glad." Nor did he campaign for candidates in the manner of Pat Robertson—the weasel-like TV magnate whose smug manner announces "I've got the answers and you never will." Jimmy was inimitable.

After being so overwhelmed on our return to Baton Rouge that I nearly planted a kiss on his lips, the friendship of convenience quickly deteriorated. In a series of interviews, I asked questions that produced embarrassing answers about Swaggart's fundraising misrepresentations, salaries paid to him and his family, and the Ministry's profligate spending. It was soon apparent to him that my documentary was going to be anything but a "puff" piece. To blunt the impact, he made a preemptive strike. At a Wednesday night service a week before the program, he warned followers of an apocalyptic assault on the ministry by a heathen reporter.

"This man who is supposed to do this thing about our organization told me, 'I'm not evangelical. I don't believe in being born again. I don't believe in any of this stuff.'"

Then, in a raspy voice that got louder with each syllable, he addressed me directly. "You talk about fairness and honesty. You don't even know what fairness and honesty is. You don't believe in God. You don't believe in the Bible. You don't believe in the Word of God. You don't believe in nothing. Professing to be wise, you're a fool."

It was a strong first hint that Swaggart was a pathological liar. Indeed, his first question to me heading to Virginia related to my spiritual background. I told him I was a retired wino who sneaked into a Presbyterian church on a semi-regular basis. He seemed happy that I wasn't a full-fledged pagan. Or so it seemed. The assault on my ways—holy and unholy—indicated he didn't like Presbyterians, or ex-drunks, or he was a liar.

Titled *Give Me That Big Time Religion*, my one-hour WBRZ documentary aired in prime time in May, 1983. It earned me a third George Foster Peabody medallion. "The program may well have been the most comprehensive report on big time evangelism ever done by a local television station," the Peabody panel stated.

After seeing *Give That Big Time Religion*, many reporters have asked how I gained access to the inner sanctums of Swaggart's organization—one of the reasons it received so many accolades. First, I told the truth about my intentions. Second, I used blackmail. Actually, I prefer the word, "leverage."

I knew a secret about Jimmy. Compared to future revelations, it was a minor transgression. The mini-scandal involved a brief romance between a Swaggart family member and a musician in the televangelist's back-up ensemble. Names are not now important. Anyway, ministry officials were more concerned about Jimmy's overreaction than the fling itself. He threatened to do bodily harm to a guitar player caught strumming in all the wrong places. "Tell that no good husband of yours, if he's in town tomorrow, I'll kill him," he was quoted as telling the straying musician's wife.

I discovered details of the episode in a lawsuit evicting the couple from a ministry financed home. I had no intention of reporting the affair and assured Jimmy's apostles that I didn't plan to report his fit of pique. Maybe the word "plan" caused their discomfort. Anytime I encountered obstacles, I only needed to remind them of my fairness in not reporting details of the lawsuit. My magnanimity removed the barriers.

It was a chickenshit tactic. But I never lied. Ministry officials knew I was searching for warts and blemishes. Moreover, my blackmail stratagem was genteel considering Swaggart's methods of snatching Social Security checks from the purses of little old ladies, manipulating wealthy widows to sign over fortunes, and using the plight of starving children to gain access to bank accounts of guilt-laden TV viewers.

A California heiress named Zoe Vance was Swaggart's most generous benefactor. She died in 1981, leaving millions to the ministry. Before going to her reward, she showered the organization with $3-million in cash and gifts. More was at stake in her Will—a bequest of an $800,000 La Jolla, California oceanfront home, an apartment complex, stocks and bonds, and royalties from gas wells earning $100,000 a month.

Affluent relatives didn't need the money. Nevertheless, they challenged Ms. Vance's Will as a matter of principle, accusing the ministry of "preying upon her loneliness and illness." The "preying" was outlined in documents disclosing that after serenading Ms. Vance with a private organ recital, Jimmy baptized her in the Pacific Ocean outside her home. The obviously ill woman was later put on public display. Calling her "Aunt Zoe" during a televised crusade, Swaggart summoned the patron to the altar. Shedding invisible tears, he sobbingly prayed for Aunt Zoe's miraculous healing.

The lawsuit was eventually settled after the ministry agreed to abide by strict guidelines in spending the windfall. In fairness, it should be pointed out that Ms. Vance seemed perfectly content with the bang she got for her bucks. A longtime business associate told me that her personality completely changed. "She seemed more interested in things, more alive," he said. "I think that she probably enjoyed life more."

Because of Swaggart's positive impact on people like Ms. Vance, I had unsettling moments during my research. I worried about undermining the beliefs of his followers. Jimmy's brand of religion was different from my beliefs.

So was the doctrine of snake-handling fundamentalists in the mountains of West Virginia and Tennessee. But in Alcoholics Anonymous I had learned lessons of tolerance in spiritual matters—a clichéd attitude of "different strokes for different folks."

Nevertheless, I relied on the ministry's former Director of Spiritual Counseling to assuage my concerns over informing Swaggart followers of his abuses. Noble Scroggins responded to letters from Swaggart viewers asking for spiritual guidance. Like fired Comptroller George Jernigan, Scroggins previously worked for other evangelists, including Billy Graham. Scroggins said he joined Brother Jimmy as a true believer in the ministry's work. But his opinion changed as a result of a letter from an elderly Texas woman, who wrote that she and her sisters were struggling to survive on Social Security.

The sisters were contributors to fundraising appeals to feed starving children. But facing hard times, they were unable to fulfill pledges. The letter asked if it would be sinful to commit suicide so that proceeds of their life insurance policies could go to the Children's Fund. Scroggins said he literally ran to Jimmy's office, expecting the preacher to immediately call the deluded woman. Instead, the letter was casually set aside. Jimmy promised to deal with it later. Scroggins resigned shortly thereafter. The anecdote disabused me of any misgivings in exposing the ministry's fundraising misrepresentations. I was doing God's work—a fantasy intrinsic to muckrakers.

My investigation began in late 1982 when the organization's annual revenues were about $40-million. Five years later when Jimmy got caught peeking at the privates of a prostitute, income was about $150-million.

Operating like a secular mail order business, the ministry sold Jimmy Swaggart Bibles, books, religious study guides and a full line of other spiritual accessories—all displaying his signature, which made it easy for St. Peter to identify Swaggarites as they arrived at the Pearly Gates. But in the television competition for holy dollars, Jimmy's popularity as a musician gave him a huge advantage over religious hucksters. He was among the nation's leading Gospel performers. Jimmy Swaggart albums were heavily promoted at crusades, on TV programs and seven radio stations owned by the ministry.

"I have sold more long play albums than any Gospel singer on the face of the earth has ever sold in the history of gospel music," he boasted to me. Gold and Platinum records were on a wall outside his office. They were counterfeits. The Recording Artists Industry Association never so honored him. Why he displayed counterfeit plaques is puzzling. He really didn't need bogus awards to prove his popularity.

My junket to Hampton, Virginia was proof to me of Jimmy's stature as a full-fledged religious superstar. He attracted a demographic jumble—young and old of all colors, ethnicity and socio-economic backgrounds. Fashions ranged from Goodwill to Armani. He even had groupies, mostly middle-aged believers. They followed him to crusades across the country. His celebrity status was obvious when mingling with crowds. While he was shaking hands and giving brotherly hugs to fans, Bibles and music albums were thrust in his hands for autographs. Admirers wanted pictures with him. The sick and lame sought to have his hands laid on them in hope of miraculous healings.

The ministry's merchandising methods would be adopted by other celebrity preachers, but none before or since reached his revenue heights. When we first met, new headquarters were under construction in Baton Rouge on a sprawling $100-million campus featuring an arena-like tabernacle, television production studios, a mail-order warehouse and a maze of administrative offices. A monthly magazine, *The Evangelist*, reached nearly a million followers. Also in the final planning stages were primary and secondary schools, a Bible college, recreation amenities and retirement condominiums.

The televangelist's wife, Frances, spearheaded much of the expansion. The daughter of a part-time Pentecostal preacher, she was born in the tiny community of Wisner not far from Ferriday. At age fifteen, she dropped out of school to marry seventeen-year-old Jimmy. She became a semi-celebrity, although some employees called her "the Dragon Lady." They claimed she made decisions based on whims.

Son, Donnie, was third in the chain of command. His adolescent appearance and tentative manner was the antithesis of daddy's outgoing personality. An only child, he had traveled the revival circuit with his parents when they stayed in cheap motels or spare bedrooms of church parsonages. Before the family settled in Baton Rouge, he was home-schooled by momma. She relied on a correspondence program as a teaching tool. Until Junior High, Donnie's nomadic life caused his public school attendance to be intermittent.

From the day we met, he and his mother opposed giving photographer Sailor Jackson and me unrestricted access to the ministry. In the final days of our production, their disquiet intensified—in large part because of an interview with Frances in which I asked about a $16,000 desk in her office. A ministry bookkeeper gave me an invoice showing the cost of the desk. Still, Frances hotly denied the extravagance. I feared she was going to chase us away before a final interview with Jimmy. They finally decided to go forward if ministry cameras were allowed to tape the interview to ensure it was edited in proper context. The context of *Give Me That Big Time Religion* was lack of oversight.

"Hundreds of billions of dollars come into television ministries which are nearly all tax-exempt," I reported. "There is almost no official monitoring of these organizations. The IRS doesn't have the manpower to closely scrutinize the electronic churches. A Congressional proposal for tighter controls was abandoned several years ago."

The documentary included four separate Swaggart in-terviews. I show one in particular to journalism classes to emphasize the importance of preparation. There were no nasty exchanges—just calm questions and answers that exposed Jimmy's tendency to dance around the truth.

"What is your salary?" I asked.

"You know, it's around thirty thousand dollars, but that's not quite correct."

"I was told $5700 a month," I prompted. Sizeable at the time, but not a huge sum for the head of a $40-million company. His wife and son collected bigger paychecks.

"Well, that's not my salary. I get a check for $5700 a month. I turn right around and write the organization a check for $3500 right away, every month, and give it right back to them. That $3500 was set up by the CPA's and the attorneys. It has to do with a parsonage allowance," he explained.

"A big percentage of the $3500 is to repay money bor-rowed from the ministry," I interjected. Jimmy amended his answer.

"That is correct. That's what I was about to say. I bor-rowed some money from the organization a couple of years ago. I don't know what the interest rate is."

"Fourteen percent," I prompted.

"Fourteen percent. You know more about it that I do, John," He said, realizing that I knew the answers to ques-tions that I asked.

Except for his salary—revealed to me by George Jerni-gan, I found the information that formed the basis of my questions in court documents and publicly available IRS filings. Uncertain of what I knew, Jimmy decided truth was his best defense. That let me go fishing.

The most prevalent rumor concerned the Swaggart family's raids on the ministry mailroom and freeloading off followers. Rather than deny the truth, he recited a list of lavish gifts from converts. He removed a $10,000 gold Rolex watch from his wrist and dangled it before the camera. He said it came from a California jeweler who "probably paid wholesale." The shoes and suit he wore for the interview were also gifts.

"Frances has had some stuff given to her, some jewelry given her. What she has been given, I don't really know. But she has been given some clothes. She was given a coat the other day, a mink coat, I think it was, by a very wealthy lady. She has been given several rings, to be honest with you."

Highly agitated, Frances interrupted. "Jimmy, I don't like this. Now this is just ridiculous." He waved her away.

"It's all right, forget that. It's no problem at all." But it was a problem for a preacher who frequently pointed to an old Volkswagen in his driveway as a symbol of the family's modest lifestyle. Instead, he drove a Lincoln Town Car donated by a Chattanooga businessman. Jimmy's admissions and his wife's belligerent evasiveness were examples of a pattern of deceit that permeated the organization.

Based on what I saw and heard, I made an amazing prophecy as we were leaving the ministry. "This guy wants to be caught in his lies. He is going to self-destruct one day," I told Sailor Jackson. He laughed, saying I was crazy. Five years later, the photographer recalled my prediction and was ready for me to give him stock market tips.

As I anticipated, Brother Jimmy overreacted to our documentary. He attacked me, the station and the news media in general. Full page ads in local newspapers suggested that my report was a plot by Satan to destroy the ministry. He even purchased a full hour on a competing station in Baton Rouge to air a ministry-produced program under the traditional title, *Give Me That Old Time Religion*, which gave me sweaty palms. Aware that ministry cameras recorded my final Swaggart interview, I had been very judicious in writing and editing. However, investigative reporting is subjective—my version of truth. Factually, he found little to complain about other than the fact that the documentary was wrong, wrong, wrong. Specific wrongness was unclear. Regardless, he saw a fundraising opportunity. WBRZ could make amends by sending him a donation. We passed.

Give Me That Big Time Religion was my breakthrough documentary. The saga of Jimmy Lee Swaggart and Jerry Lee Lewis epitomized good versus evil. Keyboard dissolves showed the similarity in piano styles, and the differences in venues—a pulpit and a honky-tonk. Following a performance in Baton Rouge, Jerry Lee praised his cousin in a poignant interview and expressed unease over his own spiritual flaws.

"I would hate to know that I was going to Hell. Because if I miss Heaven, I know I have missed the call. And I never could picture Jesus Christ singing, *A Whole Lot of Shaking Going On*. And this worries me."

"Jerry Lee has had a lot of hard times," Jimmy Lee said in our on-camera interview. "But I hold him in high regard. He bought me a new Oldsmobile, a 1958, when the car I had was falling to pieces. And I will love him because of his kindness, period, from now on out."

Twenty-plus years after *Give Me That Big Time Religion*, televangelism remains fertile ground for digging. Abuses continue to be rampant. But lawmakers shy away from investigating electronic churches and money-grubbing preachers.

"Congress shall make no law respecting an establishment of religion" are the first words of the U.S. Constitution. Hence, very few politicians are willing to question the misuse of God's money. An exception is GOP Senator Charles Grassley of Iowa. In 2007, he requested financial data from six televangelists whose lifestyles emulate oil rich potentates. Among the preachers was faith healer Benny Hinn, whose money-machine is a topic of another chapter.

In Swaggart's zeal to be TV's most-watched parson, his ministry evolved into an elephantine financial pyramid. To feed its voracious appetite, a variety of fundraising schemes were concocted. Urgent appeals told of emergencies that threatened to put Jesus out of business.

Unwittingly, the International Assemblies of God Church aided in the deceit. The parent church gave Swaggart leeway in taking credit in television appeals as a sole support of foreign missions that were, in fact, only partly funded by the Baton Rouge ministry. In effect, Jimmy paid a fee to take full credit for the Assemblies good works.

And what about sex? I didn't dwell on the issue. My main focus was the size of Jimmy's bank account, rather than the size of his libido. Besides, insiders were absolutely certain that he was free of fleshly blemishes. In the absence of titillation, most journalists—television and print—ignored the multi-billion dollar tax exempt business. I had the story all to myself. But not the whole story as I learned five years later.

Give Me That Old Time Religion purported to tell all there was to know about television's most colorful evangelist. However, I failed to notice a delicate condition that made Brother Jimmy's name synonymous with hypocrisy.

Worse, I ignored the results of a peter-meter test I devised several years earlier that should have tipped me off about Jimmy's hanky-panky. My analysis involved gauging the extent of a preacher's facial scrunch during prayers. I came up with the test while attending a quasi holy-roller church in Massachusetts at the urging of my second wife, who was searching for something akin to her Baptist roots. Presbyterian inhibitions caused me to fidget during the preacher's long prayer interludes. When he commanded that every head be bowed and every eye closed, I peeked.

As the intense pastor droned on with supplications that I feared might last until judgment day, I noticed his little moon-face all scrunched up like a ball of twine. He seemed in pain from indigestion. Or from transgressions he couldn't bear to think about. Not long afterwards, he ran off with the family babysitter. Jimmy scrunched even more.

Five years after my documentary—February, 21, 1988—Swaggart's confession to weakness of the flesh was a tele-vised spectacle that is etched in the memories of millions of people. "I have sinned against you, my Lord," he wailed, eyes closed, body racked by convulsive sobs as a torrent of tears flooded his tortured face. "And I would ask that Your precious blood would wash away and cleanse every stain until it is in the seas of God's forgetfulness, never to be re-membered against me anymore."

I watched the Shakespearean-like soliloquy in disbelief. As the reporter claiming to know more about Swaggart than any journalist on earth, I had completely missed his hooker habit. I assured everyone that he would never get caught in a sleazy sex scandal like fellow TV preacher, Jim Bakker. Only months before, Bakker confessed to a brief liaison with a part-time church secretary and amateur masseuse.

Displaying a paucity of Christian love and mercy for a fellow Assembly of God pastor, Swaggart launched un-relenting attacks on the Reverend Bakker. Therefore, it seemed like poetic justice when Jimmy got caught. For religious cynics and stand-up comics, the Baton Rouge evangelist's pecker problem seemed too good to be true.

But what about me? As an unofficial biographer and self-proclaimed Jimmy Swaggart authority, I had dazzled visiting reporters with accounts of my alleged expertise. As I sat polishing my journalism medallions and trophies, I dished out caustic comments to writers dispatched to Baton Rouge by newspapers, magazines and books. I appeared on TV and radio programs and offered insights to any and all groups wanting to hear the inside scoop about the televangelist. Indeed, many journalists wrongly assumed I was the sheet-sniffing muckraker who discovered Jimmy's proclivity for hired paramours.

The credit goes not to me, nor to any reporter. He was caught red-handed—literally, since masturbation was his gig—by a revenge-seeking part-time sheriff's deputy whose TV preaching daddy had been labeled an adulterer by Swaggart. Hearing rumors of Jimmy's forays into non-preacherly neighborhoods, the distraught son used police surveillance skills to catch him consorting with a twenty-dollar whore outside a seedy rent-by-the-hour New Orleans area motel room. The part-time cop snapped photographs before summoning poppa to the scene for a televangelist to televangelist showdown. "What's happening, brother?" the deputy's daddy asked.

Jimmy wept.

The impromptu photo session in December, 1987 didn't become public for three months. ABC's *Nightline* broke the story after receiving a tip that officials of the International Assemblies of God Church were investigating Swaggart's peccadilloes. Network producers called me—the alleged expert—to find out what I knew about the preacher's predicament. I thought they were joking. It couldn't be. But it was.

Nightline aired the story two days before Jimmy's Sunday morning confession. I was a guest on the program. But lacking carnal knowledge of the televangelist, the only commentary I could offer was, "Surprise, surprise, surprise."

Two days later, a near stampede clamored to get inside his 7000-seat Family Worship Center. Many hadn't darkened religious doorways for years. This was a mea culpa Super Bowl. Sadly for me, penis naiveté had jeopardized my status as a leading Swaggart authority. But on confession day, Jimmy rejuvenated my reputation. Moments before admitting sins against God, family and his dedicated followers, he paused to speak to his "old nemesis," as he described me.

"I love you, John. And in spite of our differences, I think you are one of the finest investigative reporters in the world. And I mean that." It was an astonishing statement before a packed house and a national television audience that eventually watched his syndicated program.

Produced like a Broadway show, the surrealistic extravaganza featured a musical overture by the church orchestra, stirring hymns by a blue-robed gospel trio, and the music of a 150-member choir standing on a four-tiered semi-circular platform stretching the width of the crimson carpeted altar. As prelude to the main event, the ministry's featured vocalist moved the congregation to tears with an inspiring *a cappella* hymn. Then came the main event.

"Brother Swaggart has made a detailed confession of his moral failure," an Assemblies of God Church official said in introductory remarks. "But no spiritual purpose would be served by answering questions about specific details." This was upsetting to churchgoers, who were only there to hear the nitty-gritty of his erotic adventures. But they would not leave disappointed.

When Jimmy finally moved to the pulpit, he was greeted with thunderous applause. Retreating from previous attacks on heathen reporters—me in particular— he conceded that newspapers and television newscasts treated him fairly in disclosing rumors of his sexual misconduct. He singled out *Nightline*, saying the program had "even shown compassion." Following the "I love you, John" riff, Swaggart gave a performance that left the audience sobbing in the aisles.

Brother Jimmy's histrionics were so masterful that feelings of outrage and disgust were temporarily transformed into sympathy and forgiveness. "I don't plan to whitewash my sin," he began, acknowledging in the abstract that he had committed sordid transgressions. "I would like to make it worse than it actually is."

Actually, it doesn't get much worse for a world re-nowned preacher than getting caught with a whore in the middle of the day. Despite the absence of specifics, he strongly hinted that his iniquities went beyond misde-meanor trespasses. "I do not call it a mistake, a mendacity. I call it sin," he cried, disabusing converts of the hope that his hobnobbing with hookers was not the same as Jesus walking among sinners.

His tacit admission of wrongdoing set off a wave of distress. Ministry cameras recorded close-up images of the agonized tears of heartbroken congregants. Using pro-duction techniques that made Swaggart crusades so pop-ular, anguished followers were cast as supporting actors for his televised confession. It was a hideous exploitation of emotions—an act designed to gain sympathy for the evangelist and salvage his religious empire. To that end, he performed magnificently. Mournful moans and sobs rever-berated through the sanctuary, interrupted incongruously by intervals of applause that began with a smattering of handclaps and steadily intensified to booming standing ovations.

Jimmy's humiliated wife, Frances, didn't join in. She sat motionless, a Valium-like expression concealing the mortification she must have felt. "God never gave a man a better helpmate and companion to stand beside him," he sniveled while addressing his wife. "I have sinned against you. Forgive me." A barely discernible nod suggested that a marital pardon would be a long time in coming.

Donnie sat beside his mother, tightly clutching the hand of his wife, Debbie. A preacher's daughter from rural Mississippi, she appeared ready to flee the church and catch the next bus home. "I have sinned against you," Swaggart sobbed to the couple. Donnie was more forgiving than momma. His features were twisted in despair as he mouthed the words, "I love you," over and over to his disgraced daddy.

Heaving with sobs, the evangelist paraphrased King David's entreaties for God's mercy and absolution in the 51st Psalm. And as he became progressively overwrought, wails and moans by spiritual brothers and sisters resonated through the cavernous church. The cheeks of the most cynical witnesses were dampened. The performance ended with Swaggart's announcement of penance. He planned to leave the pulpit for a period of one year to rehabilitate his genitalia.

That was the signal for Jimmy's dispassionate wife and distraught son to come forward in dramatic fashion and lovingly embrace him. Acolytes sitting with the family joined in a gang-hug. They were followed by scores of "Swaggarites" who marched from pews to form a giant huddle encircling him. They forgave the televangelist his trespasses as he had never before forgiven those who trespassed against him. The tearful performance seemed to have miraculously salvaged the future of his organization.

It sure plucked my heart strings. Until the bizarre confession, I didn't realize Brother Jimmy considered me a world class investigative reporter. Nor did I know he loved me. For four years, he did a good job of concealing his true feelings. Presumably, terms like "snake" and "reprobate" were meant as expressions of love—sort of like the pet names that are part of intimate rapport between couples.

In hiding his love and respect for my muckraking skills, he apparently fantasized about bizarre encounters between us. In his monthly magazine, *The Evangelist*, Jimmy once quoted me as saying, "I think you're stealing money."

I (Swaggart) replied with a question: "Why would I want to steal money from the Ministry? I sell more records than anyone has ever sold in gospel music – if I desired more money, all I would have to do would be to receive a small royalty from the sale of each record, which is perfectly legal." I then asked him another question: "Do you know why you think I'm stealing money? Because if you were in my shoes, you would steal every dollar you could get your hands on, wouldn't you?" He (me) looked out the window for a few moments, turned back to me and said, "Yes, I would." (Swaggart) That's the type of man we're dealing with.

Nothing remotely resembling the dialogue ever occurred, nor could anything I said have been construed in such a manner. But he could not help himself. The article confirmed my suspicion that Swaggart was a pathological liar.

I didn't expect his love for me to last very long. And I was right. There was a motive behind his affection. I was a one man focus group in measuring the impact of Swaggart's confession. The same afternoon, ministry lawyer William Treeby called to get my reaction to the performance. I said it was great, especially the part about me being "one of the finest investigative reporters in the world." In fact, I thought Jimmy deserved an award for *Best Performance by a Disgraced Preacher*. The anus-constricted attorney didn't appreciate my humor.

Son of a Texas Pentecostal preacher, Treeby grew up in a my-way-to-Heaven or your-way-to-Hell environment. Surprisingly, he remained in sin city after graduating from Tulane Law School in New Orleans and eventually became a partner in a big silk-stocking firm. We were never friendly. Hence, I was taken aback that he cared even a tad about what I thought. Perhaps he and Jimmy figured if I could be persuaded of the evangelist's contrition, anybody could. I tried to sound compassionate, saying something to the effect that I hoped the preacher would get help.

"What kind of help are you talking about?" Treeby asked.

"Psychiatric counseling."

"We don't believe in that stuff," he snapped.

Convinced the Lord would relieve him of the compulsion, Swaggart compressed his one-year rehabilitation into three months. He returned to the pulpit after holy dollars dwindled to a trickle, which was unfortunate for him.

God needed more than three months to deal with the parson's private parts. *The Secret Sex Life of Brother Jimmy Lee Swaggart* went into reruns a several months later when he was caught with another bargain basement hooker—this time in Palm Springs, California. Followers were less forgiving the second time around.

In the months that followed, revenue plummeted from millions to thousands and he faded from the TV screen. As this is written more than two decades after the sexual escapades, Brother Jimmy keeps preaching on religious-programmed radio stations—several of which are owned by the ministry. His television programs are carried on a few cable outlets and satellite networks. A small congregation attends Sunday services at Swaggart's Baton Rouge edifice.

In my heart of hearts, I wish he had stayed whore-free. He contributed to the spiritual growth of many people who found Jesus inside TV sets. Sadly, many were converts of fragile faith—more captivated by the man than the Word he preached. They were the real victims of the sex scandal.

I also felt sorry for Jimmy—the kind of compassion I feel for patients in mental hospitals. Based on the absurdity of his sex junkets, he seemed a candidate for the nut house. The televangelist was among the nation's most easily recognized TV preachers. His crusades were on stations in nearly every American city. A nightly Bible study program saturated cable systems, his picture appeared in national publications, and he was a frequent guest on network news and public affairs shows. Yet, he prowled a seamy red light district in broad daylight. I found it incomprehensible that he allowed his unmanageable organ to become a weapon of mass destruction of the ministry.

Then I discovered the reason for his behavior in an extraordinary pamphlet he authored in 1981. The thin publication was taken out of circulation almost immediately. It deals with sexual addiction. Titled *that THING*, the booklet portrays in detail the agony of a man obsessed with pornography and masturbation—the same compulsions Swaggart confessed to leaders of the International Assemblies of God Church. He admitted that the problem had plagued him since adolescence.

In *that THING*, Jimmy writes in the third person of uncontrolled sexual urges that he ascribes to a young man who supposedly came to him seeking spiritual counseling. "I know its evil, it's wicked, it's dirty. I've promised God a thousand times I would quit and broke these promises a thousand times. I'm thinking seriously of killing myself."

The specificity of direct quotes in the twenty-five-page volume, combined with Swaggart's nearly identical confession to church elders, suggests the statements of his young visitor are an account of Jimmy's innermost thoughts. If so, *that THING* explains the seemingly inexplicable. He was a sex addict unable to resist deep-seated impulses.

"Weakness overcomes me and I go right back to it again. I can't cast this sick thing out of my life."

Bill Clinton and other philandering politicians could have written the same words in explaining the insanity of their sexual antics. Addiction comes in several forms.

I certainly understood *that THING* because it was no different than "my Thing." I had made many remorseful "never again" pledges after drunken binges. And like Jimmy's alter ego, "I broke these promises a thousand times."

No wonder I felt a strange kinship with Jimmy. It takes one to know one.

CHAPTER SEVEN

FATEFUL ENCOUNTERS

Sixteen years before Brother Jimmy Lee Swaggart got his comeuppance, I reached the nadir of my drunken degradation on a New Orleans curbside a few miles from the motel where he and a street-walker companion were caught on candid camera.

My life-altering bender began at the Baton Rouge Press Club, a midnight spa for reporters who put the morning newspaper to bed. The club was often my last stop before putting me to bed. From there, I could stagger four blocks to a dingy downtown studio apartment conveniently located next door to the radio station that tolerated me as its News Director and the host of a daily talk show. On nights of really heavy-duty frolicking, I went directly to the station and slept on a couch outside the newsroom. The Farm Editor woke me up in time for my early morning newscast.

I altered this routine on February 1, 1971.

Standing unsteadily before club members, I declared my intentions to abandon my job, family and all pretenses of respectability. I was going to New York City's Greenwich Village to start a Bohemian life as a writer. The announcement was greeted with an apathetic "good riddance." After waving goodbye to drinking companions, I stopped at the apartment to load a few possessions into a sputtering

Austin-Healy Sprite convertible. But prior to leaving town, I felt compelled to deliver a pair of valedictories.

The first farewell was to my estranged wife. I had deserted her and our four children nine months earlier in favor of booze. Glenda Adams was my high school sweetheart, and the first girl to help steam the backseat windows of daddy's 1951 Ford. Our passion eventually resulted in a hurried marriage. We were seventeen years old.

Despite the circumstances, Glenda and I stayed together for eighteen years. Whether by coincidence or perverted cruelty, my unwelcome drunken appearance at her door took place the week of our wedding anniversary. I celebrated with a diatribe, accusing her of causing my sorry condition. If she were more accepting of the emotional abuse and shame I heaped on the family with my drinking, carousing and adulterous behavior, I wouldn't be leaving on this dipsomaniacal voyage.

The outburst was followed by a crying jag. I pleaded for forgiveness, pledging to be a good husband and father in the future. She was unmoved by promises that earned me past reprieves. When she refused to let me come home, I reacted in alcoholic fashion.

"Fuck you. I didn't want to return anyway." Our three daughters sat crying at the top of the stairs, listening to my insanity. Not the sort of childhood memory to cherish.

After emotionally bashing the family, I took care of a second piece of business. I called my soon-to-be ex-boss, Roger Davison—a former disc jockey known as "Ravin'

Dave." I told him to cram the radio station WJBO up his rear orifice. I informed him that I wouldn't be doing newscasts that day, or performing my other duties. Ever again.

I was doing Dave a favor. For four years, the station was the venue for a multitude of my stupid stunts. Rarely was I held accountable—at least until I dragged him out of bed with this early morning telephone call. His previous lapses in judgment had given me a false sense of security. Sure I imbibed a bit. But that was a reporter's job. An important person like me needed to get out and mingle with equally important people.

I could easily afford to support my booze addiction. As a minor news celebrity for a prestigious radio station in the Capitol city, I had no ethical qualms about mooching drinks on a nightly basis at taverns and clubs frequented by politicians, government officials, and other movers and shakers. Flaunting what I believed to be my broadcasting influence, I specialized in freeloading. My beat included lavish parties sponsored by lobbyists trying to win the friendship of legislators and bureaucrats. And reporters. So I was among the first to arrive and the last to leave. Or to be carried out. Free drinks, food and entertainment were my just desserts for gracing the soirees.

In addition to drowning my journalistic integrity in liquor, I had an inordinate talent for consistently embarrassing my employers. There were publicized trips to jail, fistfights with reporters, a drunken shoving match with the Lieutenant Governor and an assortment of other indiscretions. But I was "just having fun."

Morning-after stories of my "fun" were supplemented by on-air gaffes—like being relieved in mid-sentence during a newscast because my drunken narration sounded as if I were speaking in unknown tongues. The relief newscaster was a heavily-accented Australian. The sudden change must have startled listeners.

The audience was also privy to other spine-tingling radio moments such as the day I signed off in the middle of my talk show because of the onset of DT's. I interrupted the guest to say, "That's all folks," and walked out of the studio. A befuddled disc jockey rushed into the studio and started playing records while the guest sat with a puzzled look on his face. No explanation was given for the show's abrupt conclusion.

In a state of panic caused by delirium tremens, I drove to a hospital emergency room to remedy a blood-alcohol imbalance. Admitted as an in-patient for treatment of "exhaustion," doctors poked, prodded and forced tubes into my body to find the cause of my fatigue. Despite the circumstances of my arrival, the word "alcoholism" was never uttered. The diagnosis was unnecessary. I knew what ailed me.

If I had lingering doubts, the crazy episode in front of my wife and children, and the wake-up call to "Ravin' Dave" again confirmed the condition. Though drinking took a horrible toll on everybody around me, a built-in denial mechanism had allowed me to disregard the chaos. Not this time. Following the Press Club bon voyage, I revised my itinerary. Instead of going to Greenwich Village, thirst caused me to detour to New Orleans. Seventy-two-hours later, I was perched on a curbside near Jimmy Swaggart's unhappy whore-hunting grounds. Sobriety was only a couple of beers away.

As epiphanies go, mine was ugly. I retain mental snapshots of the final frenzied bender. Unlike previous binges, I didn't have a blackout—the momentary amnesia that erases memories of drunken humiliations. Wearing a cheap, soiled brown suit and a drool-stained blue shirt, I lurched along saloon-lined streets. I was filthy and unshaven. And somewhere along the way, I lost a contact lens. But impaired vision didn't prevent me from seeing the horror of my circumstances. It was like an out-of-body experience.

I was kicked out of one Bourbon Street tavern after another for being too drunk, a state of intoxication nearly impossible to achieve in Louisiana's Mecca for inebriates. In one seedy bar, I was knocked down and mugged. My response was to scream obscenities at the bartender and bystanders, who did nothing to stop the robbery. Thrown out, I continued the harangue until a couple of young street people interceded. Fearing I was about to get killed, they promised to share a bottle of wine if I calmed down.

I countered with an offer to supply refreshments. First though, I needed to replenish my money supply. I invited them to join me for dinner and drinks at Antoine's, the famed New Orleans eatery noted for its old South formality. The restaurant was owned by the family of Louisiana Attorney General William Guste, a frequent guest on my radio show. I knew he would be happy to reciprocate my broadcasting hospitality. However, when I arrived at the elegant café with disheveled caretakers, a horrified maitre-d' denied us entrance.

Insulted by his rudeness toward a patron of my prominence, I demanded he contact my "dear friend," the Attorney General. He would vouch for my respectability. And by the way, be sure to get check cashing approval. To avoid an even worse scene in front of diners, we were hustled into a backroom while he reluctantly made the call. My pal, Billy, was on the phone minutes later.

"I'm sorry to bother you, but I find myself in New Orleans a little short of funds and I need to cash a small check." Uncertain what was going on, Louisiana's top law enforcement official vouched for what turned out to be a bouncing piece of paper. He told the maitre-d' to cash the check, keep us out of sight, feed us and get us out of there.

Fed and flush, I invested in a couple of gallons of cheap wine. The goodies were hauled to a rundown two-room crash pad occupied by a dozen or so "flower children." For the remainder of the night, we sipped wine, discussed the meaning of life, the futility of war, the horrors of racism, and formulated plans to overthrow our oppressive government. By early morning, I passed out on the floor next to a little band of aspiring revolutionaries scattered about the room naked and in various stages of undress.

Regaining consciousness in late afternoon, I helped finish the wine as we resumed our discourse on the disgraceful state of the world. But the onset of D.T.'s disrupted my plans to lead the revolution. Unsure how to deal with a palsied and disoriented drunk, my new friends dug the telephone number of a Baton Rouge girlfriend from my pocket and alerted her of my condition.

Patricia Byrd Green and I began a casual romance a few weeks after I left my family. The affair would lead to the altar. Though I departed town without saying goodbye, she made a seventy-mile dash through the fog-shrouded Mississippi River flood basin that separates the two cities. Arriving in the French Quarter, she drove for an hour up and down narrow streets before finding me. I was stooped over on a curbside like the hunchback of skid row, my feet and soul firmly planted at the lowest point of my life.

To ward off an attack by snakes, bugs and beasts, we went to the emergency room of the mammoth New Orleans Charity Hospital. Directed to the rear of a long line of more deserving patients, I opted for alternative medicine. We bought a six pack of beer to stabilize me while driving to a glorified flophouse in Baton Rouge called Recovery House. I was treated there once before for D.T.'s. The ramshackle two-story wood frame residence was a privately operated detoxification place that served paraldehyde, a potent cocktail that fends off alcohol-induced convulsions and hallucinations. The foul tasting, gag-inducing concoction was served by an ex-drunk named Bill Jumper.

Recovery House visitors were mostly like me—scared drunks needing quick relief from self-inflicted pain. Because of a large number of non-paying visitors, Bill scrambled to keep the primitive treatment facility open by selling used books and hand-me-down clothing. Like the Attorney General, he had also been a guest on my radio show. So I felt no scruples in taking chemical payola. Setting my beer can on the front porch, I braced myself for a taste of paraldehyde. It was the turning point of my life.

After Bill served me a dose of the potion, I quickly fell into a deep slumber. A dozen hours later, I awoke from the coma and shuffled downstairs to the kitchen. I hadn't eaten since the Antoine's backroom banquet. A sandwich and tea helped me regain consciousness. Still dazed, I sat at a dining table with Bill and two other drunks, the only other Recovery House residents. In a game of "can you top my misery," each of us told woeful tales of despair.

Bill was not a gung-ho recruiter for Alcoholics Anonymous. As far as I know, he didn't hold grudges against the Twelve Step program. However, he had devised his own Six Step formula. It was basically a condensed version of AA's principles. I don't recall his reasoning. Perhaps he thought the method would get clients sober twice as fast. Regardless, after we wrapped up the dining table anguish contest late in the afternoon of February 4, 1971,

Bill suggested we follow an AA custom of reciting the *Lord's Prayer*.

Religion and spiritual stuff made me uncomfortable, especially praying aloud. But what the hell. Bill was giving me a freebie. So I prayed along with the other guys. And something happened for which I have no rational explanation. At the darkest moment of my alcoholic descent, I was flooded with a sensation of well-being unlike anything I had ever experienced. Maybe it was a delayed rush from the paraldehyde. Or perhaps the kind of born-again experience folks feel when they suddenly find Jesus. Whatever the cause, I felt my life was going to change. And from that hour forward, it did. The desire to drink left me. But with a lot of help from friends. I decided to go for the full Twelve Steps.

Despite an aversion to things spiritual, my perceived epiphany had been preceded by an uncharacteristic search for a lightning bolt ethereal remedy for my misery. I even attended a Billy Graham crusade at Louisiana State University's Tiger Stadium. By my reckoning, if anybody could produce a miracle, it was Billy Graham.

On opening night of the revival, I waited for God to set things right in my life. It was a perfect setting. Thunderstorms threatened the stadium and lightning bolts flashed in the distance. None hit me. At least, not then. That's because I didn't have a desire to be weaned from the bottle. All I wanted was to make my problems go away, and recapture the sense of well-being I felt as a teenager after my first sips of the tonic.

The day after my puzzling flash of solace at Recovery House, I checked out and confronted a do-or-die alcoholic crossroads. There were plenty of excuses to drink. I had lost my family. "Ravin' Dave" fired me. I was broke, deeply in debt, behind in child support, bad checks were out, and I was being evicted from my apartment for non-payment of rent. Based on my history, the odds of a profound and lasting change were slim. But somehow, I didn't get drunk.

My family was skeptical. Glenda wished me luck, especially in finding work so I could pay child support. Justifiably, she expected reruns of past failed promises. My parents sent me a curious note, apologizing for making me crazy. They volunteered to avoid all contact if it would help restore me to sanity. At the age of thirty-five, I was starting from ground zero in terms of decency and responsibility.

A difficult road lay ahead. Yet, I felt strangely sanguine about the future. The day after leaving the halfway house, I showed up at an AA meeting wearing a raggedy, blue polyester jumpsuit. Most of my clothing had been stuffed in the car that I abandoned in New Orleans. Having seen me come through a revolving door in the past, the small Baton Rouge AA fellowship didn't expect me to hang around very long. Yet, they had not given up on me. No matter how many times a drunk stumbles into meetings, he or she is always enthusiastically embraced.

Patricia was my chief adherent. Her support was a matter of hope rather than belief. After hauling me from New Orleans to Recovery House, she had a vested interest in my success. She was an amateur drinker, but attended meetings with me nearly every night. AA helped her deal with non-booze problems. Like me, for example. Since we were not married, she felt more comfortable in AA meetings than in Alanon.

The first tangible evidence that AA produces miracles was finding my lost car in the French Quarter. My clothes and all else in the unlocked convertible remained intact, a commentary perhaps on the quality of my possessions. Despite being parked for a week in a restricted zone, there were no tickets on the windshield—a mini-miracle in itself.

The lost car was only one of several immediate dilemmas. But I found a solution to each. Following my eviction from the apartment, Patricia let me move in with her. Glenda cut me slack in paying child support. Bad checks were covered by WJBO's severance pay. And creditors held off for awhile when I explained my dire circumstances.

It seemed that my broadcasting career was over. Prospective employers in Louisiana knew enough about my drinking episodes to give me the brush-off. "We'll call you if something becomes available." Unable to find a broadcasting job in the state and lacking bus fare to leave Louisiana, I was ready to answer convenience store "Help Wanted" signs when serendipity intervened.

I received a call from Lew Carter, General Manager of WXOK, Baton Rouge's "urban" radio station, which targeted African-American listeners. Its programming was dominated by rhythm and blues, funky disc jockeys and loud commercials. WXOK was part of a white-owned network of stations in several Southern cities.

The exploitative trash-for-cash format had prompted the Federal Communications Commission to order the company to add local news and public service programming, or risk losing lucrative broadcasting licenses. I was not Lew's first choice to meet the FCC mandate. He tried to recruit a young black man named Bill Taylor whom I hired and trained as a newsman before my inglorious departure from WJBO.

Bill didn't want to leave the city's most prestigious station for an uncertain future at WXOK. However, he mentioned my plight to Lew. Since experienced African-American radio reporters were then in short supply, I was contacted as a last resort.

"Can I trust you to stay sober?" Lew asked.

"Absolutely."

What else was I going to say? It was my only opportunity to remain in the news business. Hiring a barely sober white boy to run a news department for black folks was a big gamble, though not altogether dumb. My WJBO talk show had been a dim beacon of reasonableness during Baton Rouge's racially volatile era of school desegregation, civil rights demonstrations and reactionary responses to changing times in Dixie.

As a white manager of a soul station, Lew was something of an enigma himself. An aficionado of jazz, he was a tweedy country club kind of guy. His easygoing personality was the polar opposite of WXOK's frenetic programming. However, he comfortably bridged the gap between the city's elite and WXOK's jive-talking African-American disc jockeys. He also seemed at ease with a white trash recovering alcoholic. Happily, I was back in the radio business.

On my first day at the station, Lew led me to a vacant room and asked for a list of equipment needed to get a news department up and running. Within a week, I delivered regularly scheduled newscasts as WXOK's only white on-air employee. I can't say that I acquired soul. But I learned a lot about the absence of black perspective in the mainstream media. Unless a story had an obvious race angle, reporters rarely contacted African-Americans for comment. I was guilty of the same oversight at WJBO. I regularly interviewed black guests on my talk show. But seldom did I seek their comments when reporting stories that affected all citizens, irrespective of color.

Like a majority of native born Southerners, I grew up in a family that used the "N" word. My parents denied being bigots. They just wanted "blacks to stay in their place." I have a lasting memory of daddy's reaction following my encounter with baseball star, Jackie Robinson.

I was thirteen years old and working as "roof boy" for the minor league Mobile Bears, retrieving foul balls that landed on top of the grandstand. A screen at the rear of the roof prevented them from going into the parking lot. Before and after games, I ran errands for players. I was paid fifty cents a night, plus tips, to watch baseball games and hang around professional athletes. It was great.

On trips north from Florida spring training in those days, major league teams played exhibition games in the cities of minor league farm clubs. The Bears were affiliated with the old Brooklyn Dodgers. When the team bus arrived at Mobile's Hartwell Field in 1949, I helped the Major League's first black player carry his equipment bag to the clubhouse. Daddy was not impressed.

"Hey, Marie," he called to mother. "Come and listen to Johnny brag about carrying a nigger's suitcase." It was supposed to be a joke—a symptom of culturally ingrained Southern prejudices. In dad's defense, when I took up the civil rights banner years later, he bragged to friends about my support of the cause.

My so-called "enlightened" racial attitudes were probably formed in the military. In Okinawa in 1954, I was the first airman in my barracks to choose a black roommate.

It didn't take me long at WXOK to realize that my "enlightened" understanding of discrimination was superficial at best. I had never been the victim of blatant bigotry. Nor had I experienced the humiliation of being turned away from a segregated school, public facility, or denied a job because of my skin color. I came close—an experience that was more comical than sinister.

I had an ongoing dialogue with a black-owned syndicated news service that provided the station with national material for newscasts. In turn, we fed Louisiana stories to the network. The state was then a civil rights hotspot and there were plenty of stories to pass along. Indeed, my feeds became so frequent that the New York based company made a job overture.

"You realize I'm white," I asked the recruiter. There was a long pause. I heard him take a deep breath. "Yes, of course," he said unconvincingly. "We'll be getting back to you real soon." I'm still waiting.

Sadly, many young blacks faced the same wait from white-owned companies. Also disheartening was the ignorance and bigotry of friends. My barber once asked if the body odor of co-workers bothered me. Such misconceptions were deep-rooted in Baton Rouge and most parts of the South. Working at WXOK taught me lessons that I could only learn in predominately African-American surroundings.

I was later able to empathize with a black high school girl, whom I interviewed while producing a documentary on poverty in Baton Rouge. Breaking into tears, she told of missing the senior prom at her integrated school because her mother couldn't afford a nice dress. In the same program, a teen-aged boy said his most memorable meals were leftovers momma brought home from her job as a maid at an LSU sorority house.

More tragic were the struggles of poor and elderly blacks in getting medical care. "I don't know how I gonna breathe if the welfare don't get me my medicine," an asthmatic woman cried in the documentary. Six hours after the interview, she died of heart failure while waiting for a welfare worker to deliver the prescription.

Despite my self-proclaimed empathy for those deprived of the American dream, I was a phony. My outsized ego was severely damaged by the tumble from News Director, ace reporter and talk show host at Baton Rouge's leading radio station to my job as WXOK's token white boy. But instead of feeling gratitude for a career reprieve, I began fabricating an excuse for my presence at the station. I would tell former colleagues that the job was an assertion of my commitment to civil rights—foisting myself off as a self-sacrificing Peace Corps journalist.

The opportunity to promulgate the fiction presented itself at an NAACP news conference. For the first time since my failed attempt to succeed as a skid row bum I was about to come face-to-face with reporters that I had avoided since my day of reckoning. The prospect of seeing them at a Baton Rouge hotel was so unnerving that I sat in the parking lot for several minutes summoning up the courage to go inside. Entering the lobby, I immediately ran into Louisiana's Associated Press bureau chief, Charles Layton. He greeted me with a smile and a handshake.

"Where have you been, John?" he asked. "I haven't seen you for awhile." My answer was so stunning I thought it was the voice of another person.

"WJBO fired me for being a drunk," I blurted out. "I'm working at WXOK, trying to get things back together." Had I actually made this humbling admission to someone? I could not believe my own words. Charlie took the sting out of my confession.

"That's great. I knew you were having problems. I hope things work out." It was no big deal to him. Like most Baton Rouge reporters, he knew about my drinking.

Acknowledging my alcoholism outside of AA meetings was an important step in maintaining sobriety. Disclosing my membership violates AA's tradition of anonymity in print and broadcasting. Personal anonymity reminds us that no matter how long we have been sober or how important we think our standing, we are no different than the odorous drunk who staggers into a meeting for the first time needing help.

I breach the tradition because it's nonsensical to use semantics in describing how I evolved as a reporter. My sobriety and career are interwoven. And therein lies the most gratifying exposé of my career—a story that never got on the air.

In my 1971 no-booze fervor, I tried to drag winos off the street to go to meetings. As an unofficial AA recruiter, I picked up two guys named Tony and Bob at a halfway house operated by Baton Rouge's federal anti-poverty agency. On the way to a meeting, they said all the food in the facility had been stolen and asked me to buy them hamburgers. They said the theft was not unusual. Thieves had also absconded with medications, television sets and everything else of value.

Skeptical about the complaints of two street drunks, I did some research. A quick inventory and check of records revealed that the problems were worse than Tony and Bob indicated. Besides the pilfering, there was no discernible treatment program, nor any oversight by the agency running the halfway house.

Armed with these facts, I wrote an exposé. But before airing the story, I contacted the agency head, Charles Tapp. He pleaded ignorance of the boondoggle and asked me to delay the story until an in-house investigation. We were longtime acquaintances and I trusted him to do the right thing. It didn't take long for Charlie to confirm the problems. The next day, he conceded that the grant money was being thrown away. He admitted that his staff was unqualified to run Baton's Rouge's only publicly funded program for indigent alcoholics. Fearful of losing federal grants, Charlie made a proposition I couldn't resist. His agency would bankroll a new halfway house if I recruited ex-drunks and civic leaders to run the program.

I sought the help of Eugene Snelling, head of Baton Rouge's Alcoholism Council. He was a good friend and among those who helped save me from myself. In August

1971, we put together a group of folks from inside and outside the recovery community to form a not-for-profit corporation. In a matter of weeks, Baton Rouge's first authentic treatment center for indigent alcoholics was opened.

It was named in honor of Pat O'Brien, a legendary Louisiana crusader on behalf of drunks. O'Brien House is now among the leading halfway houses in the nation—a multimillion dollar residential facility that has given hope of a better life to thousands of homeless drunkards and drug addicts. I was Chairman of the initial Board of Directors.

I don't want to overstate my role. The biggest contribution that I made was to my ego, which badly needed a boost. Tony and Bob were responsible for establishing the facility. They were the first clients. It is their legacy, though neither achieved long-term sobriety. The fact that it survived my short-term involvement is evidence that there is a God. I didn't know what the hell I was doing.

At the same time O'Brien House opened, I inadvertently returned to the boozing playground that greased the sliding-board to my bottom. A telephone call from former drinking pals dragged me out of bed one night. They wanted permission to submit my name as a candidate for President of the Baton Rouge Press Club. It was an odd request. I had only been in the club a couple of times for weekly newsmaker luncheons. However, the nominating committee assured me that my candidacy was a mere formality.

A Shreveport Capitol Correspondent was the chosen one. But to appear fair-minded, members needed a second name on the ballot. Half asleep, I agreed to be a straw candidate. A month later, I got another midnight call.

"Congratulations, you've been elected Press Club President." I was now President of an after-hours drinking spa for reporters and Chairman of the Board of a safe haven for drunks. Fortunately, I was attending AA meetings almost every night, which kept me away from my Press Club constituency.

I was still dealing with anxieties on the home front. After eight months of "living in sin," Patricia uttered the "M" word. We had a relatively stable relationship that I wanted to keep simple. However, I didn't have the courage to tell her of my misgivings about getting married. Nor did I reveal my ambiguous feelings toward Glenda. In the back of my mind, I believed everything was going to be hunky-dory. I had my fun. Soon, we were going to get back together again. Had I been true to myself and to Patricia, I would have delayed traipsing down the aisle until I resolved the uncertainties.

But we sealed the deal in November, nine months after I stopped drinking. Decisions of such magnitude require more sobriety. My dishonesty and cowardice came back to haunt us. Meantime, good things were happening.

—

A month after the wedding, I received a surprise call from "Ravin' Dave" Davison. He had recovered from being told to stick WJBO up his ass. Hearing rumors that I was so-ber, he beckoned his penitent newsman home. My old job as News Director and talk show host were filled by some-one else and Dave wasn't sure what to do with me.

I dreaded telling Lew Carter. He had saved me from a convenience store career. But he was a classy guy—happy to have facilitated my journalism rebirth. WXOK's news department was in shape to be taken over by someone else. Among those following in my footsteps was a young LSU journalism graduate named Melvin (Kip) Holden. He moved from WXOK to television to politics, serving as a state Senator before his election in 2004 as the first black Mayor-President of East Baton Rouge Parish. His election would have been unimaginable three decades earlier in the racially divided Parish.

Dangerous racial conflict plagued Louisiana through-out the sixties and early seventies. The most tragic incident took place during my first week back at WJBO. On Janu-ary 10, 1972, I was sitting in my old seat as substitute talk show host for my successor when a disc jockey handed me a note stating, "The Mayor and the Governor have declared a state of emergency for East Baton Rouge Parish and imposed a curfew."

I had no idea what was going on and immediately went to a commercial break. The deejay said he took the message on the station's red emergency phone. Minutes later, I learned that gunfire had erupted in a black business district near downtown Baton Rouge. The incident had followed a confrontation involving Black Muslims, city policemen and sheriff's deputies.

Five people were killed and dozens injured in the shootout, including a TV anchorman, who was beaten so badly he became incapacitated for life. The disturbance started after Muslims blocked a main thoroughfare and refused a police order to move. It was unclear who fired the first shots, but two deputies and three Muslims were killed. Newsman Bob Johnson, an anchor for my future employer, WBRZ, was nearly kicked to death. He suffered brain damage and has been in a nursing home since.

Race relations deteriorated even further ten months later in a stand-off between lawmen and black students on the campus of Southern University—then the nation's largest historically black college. Two students were killed when a sheriff's deputy fired into the crowd of demonstrators outside the school administration building. The trigger-happy deputy was never identified.

Against this backdrop of racial discord and violence, WJBO emerged as one of the South's premier radio newsrooms. Our four member staff was a mix of complementing personalities. Phil Oakley, a rotund veteran reporter with an ego to match his size—and mine—succeeded me as News Director. We clashed in my first days back. I thought I was still in charge. In heated discussions, he disabused me of the notion. Thereafter, I kept my nose out of the news directing business. He became a great friend.

Our tight knit group included two younger WJBO reporters. Bob Courtney—six-foot-three, heavyset and with
a stentorian baritone voice. He was an aggressive and
smart newsman whose musical talents once earned him
an audition at New York City's famed Julliard School of
Arts. Moving from WJBO to television, he became Baton
Rouge's leading governmental reporter before leaving to
serve as Louisiana's Undersecretary of State. He later started
a political consulting business.

Robert Collins was our pony-tailed hippie reporter.
Despite long hair and 1970's bell-bottomed jeans, he was
the most conservative and inhibited member of our rau-
cous staff. When a television offer came along, he quickly
grabbed hair shears, bought a blue blazer and became a
successful on-air correspondent. In the mid-1980's, Robert
graduated from law school and subsequently served as an
administrative judge for the state.

I was the final member of the fabulous four, a deposed
News Director looking for a new niche. I didn't challenge
Phil for the talk show. I occasionally sat in as substitute
host, but three years of interviewing hundreds of guests
was enough for me.

My new title was Director of Special Projects and I went
in search of projects that I deemed special. In the first few
weeks, I produced thirty-minute radio documentaries
about prison reform, deficiencies in Louisiana's mental
health hospital system and the aforementioned report on

poverty in Baton Rouge, which challenged the myth of "welfare Cadillac mothers."

My muckraking career began by accident. And almost went bust on my first venture. I devoted a lot of time to my first "investigation" and found nothing worth reporting. The target was a Louisiana "think tank" that received millions of dollars in government grants. A credible source suggested the not-for-profit company wasted vast sums of money on unfinished projects, exorbitant salaries and unnecessary expenses. I got blurred vision from reviewing the firm's state contracts and internal documents. My research produced only nitpicking missteps, making me wonder if I missed bigger issues as a result of inexperience. I could write a story, but disclosing a few minor expense account discrepancies didn't seem fair.

I reluctantly gave the bad news to Phil, expecting him to suggest that I quit searching for scandals and begin contributing more to the station's daily newscasts. He only shrugged and told me to find another story. His mild reaction had a lasting impact. Learning to abandon a project that didn't pan out was a valuable lesson.

As simple as it seems, abandoning a story after days and/or weeks of research is one of the most difficult decisions facing investigative reporters. There is always a temptation to justify the effort by turning trivialities into exposés. The early lesson helped me avoid the pitfall of trying to fit a round peg into a square hole, even when authoritative sources told me it would fit. Failure to abide by this simple rule is one of contemporary journalism's greatest shortcomings. Trifling mistakes and misspeaks are regularly blown out of proportion—especially by twenty-four-hour news channels.

Following the setback, I soon found a worthwhile story in a nondescript state agency that kept its files under lock and key in an office one-hundred-fifty miles north of Baton Rouge. The same source who sent me on the futile expedition at the research institute pointed me in the direction of Louisiana's Advisory Council for Vocational and Technical Education. I showed up unannounced and asked to inspect the agency's financial records. The politically-connected Director was absent from the no-show job.

I informed his secretary that state law required her to open public records for my inspection, or risk going to jail. An exaggeration, but I was new to muckraking. She unlocked the file cabinets and told me to let her know if I needed any help. Without much effort, I found dozens of documents revealing under-handed political machinations by the Director, wasteful spending and inflated expense accounts.

The material formed the basis of an exposé that got widespread publicity when the agency Director was fired by the state Board of Education. The story scored a five or six on a ten-point scale of Louisiana scandals.

But it was enough for me to scratch out Director of Special Projects on business cards and stake my claim as an "investigative reporter."

CHAPTER EIGHT

MUCKRAKING NIRVANA

In August, 1972, I experienced a mucking thrill that has not been matched since. Crossing the I-10 Causeway in southeast Alabama on the way home from covering the Republican National Convention in Miami, I heard a news story on New Orleans radio station WWL that almost caused me to veer off the road into Mobile Bay.

Louisiana Attorney General William Guste—the official who approved my rubber check at Antoine's Restaurant eighteen months earlier—announced the indictments of three former bank executives and the Executive Director of a state government agency. His announcement included a statement that set my butt atwitter.

"I want to thank reporter John Camp of WJBO in Baton Rouge, who first called public attention to the subject matter resulting in today's indictments."

The criminal charges were a direct result of a scheme that I exposed eight weeks earlier. This was my first muckraking endorphin eruption. It caused a buzz that was comparable to the discovery of a potion that made me taller, handsomer, tougher and almost killed me. By the time I reached Baton Rouge three hours later, my initial excitement had begun to subside. It dawned on me that as an ostensible teller of truth and protector of the public till, I was responsible for the public floggings of four men who did me no harm. When I stopped drinking and started hanging around the Twelve Step fellowship, I underwent a conscience transplant. Damaging reputations of people that I knew only in the abstract contradicted my high-tone sober objectives.

The journalistic ecstasy I felt in smiting scoundrels seemed duplicitous for a guy who seemed destined to end up on the funny farm, in prison, dead, or all the above.

An ex-drunk named Dan Nealy put my concerns in perspective. He was my AA "sponsor"—the person who listened to me whine and offered advice based on his own experiences. I don't know why I identified with Dan so closely. We were very different. He was five years sober, a successful regional representative for General Motors, married to the same woman for twenty-five years, and a voracious reader of intellectual tomes like William James' *Varieties of Religious Experience*. For all I knew, the famed psychologist and religious philosopher was the brother of bandleader Harry James.

Dan's lack of reverence and wry sense of humor belied his deep spiritual nature. Perpetually flushed and showing a slight tremor from years of hard drinking, he seemed to fold inward when sitting—a posture shaped by thousands of cartons of cigarettes.

"You didn't cause those people's problems. They caused their own difficulties," Dan said after hearing of my sudden discomfort. He reminded me that I was only doing my job.

At the same time, he gave me the best advice I have ever received as an investigative reporter.

"Be damn certain your truth is the real truth."

The distinction is paramount to investigative reporting. Finding truth is its only purpose. And because truth is often imprecise, it can be altered, compromised or ignored completely. Interpretations depend on the honesty, prejudices and wisdom of the reporter. Dan had a tremendous influence in helping me establish a moral compass.

Listening to me proclaim in early sobriety that I didn't want anything to do with God, his only suggestion was to keep an open mind. When I finally recognized that my denial of a Higher Power put me at a disadvantage if I expected to stay sober, I took tentative steps toward spiritual growth by reciting the *Serenity Prayer*.

God, grant me the serenity to accept the things I cannot change, the courage to change the things I can, and the wisdom to know the difference."

The philosophy can be used effectively by believers and non-believers. Over time, I also latched onto AA's hackneyed slogans and aphorisms, like *One Day at a Time* and *Keep It Simple*. The phrases were maxims that guided me through tough times.

My gradual acceptance of a Higher Power was not nearly as difficult as I feared. Despite my fancy Tuscaloosa High School diploma, I was incapable of answering God questions that had forever perplexed mankind. So I came to believe that the capitalized three-letter word was a conceptual force that gave order and meaning to the human condition. The explanation has served me well.

Dan didn't deal in profundities in changing my contemptuous attitude toward AA's underlying principle of a Higher Power. His answer to the esoteric question of what is God's will for me was simple. "Do what makes you happy." I thought he was jacking me around. Pursuing what I thought made me happy got me to AA in the first place. But I confused happiness with instant gratification.

Until his death in 1978, I relied on Dan's advice to solve many dilemmas, as well as to protect me from a dangerous major benefit of sobriety. Success. Achievements have caused many sober drunks to forget where they came from. My bribery exposé was the first real test of keeping professional praise in perspective.

I started digging into the story when a lawyer friend mentioned a conversation with a *Newsweek* correspondent, who was investigating Small Business Administration guaranteed loans in Louisiana. Veteran reporter Hugh Aynesworth told the attorney that he was working under a deadline and regretted not having more time to develop the story. He had detected an odor of corruption in loans handled by a bank in Denham Springs, a small town 10 miles east of Baton Rouge.

A story of such complexity intimidated me. Nonetheless, I called Hugh. He had found no concrete evidence of wrongdoing, but suggested that I take a look at transactions involving the bank, whose Board of Directors were

close political allies of Russell Long. The Senator had appointed the Board Chairman to Louisiana's SBA Advisory
Commission. According to Hugh's sources, SBA-backed
loans were being funneled to firms secretly controlled by
bank officers.

The tip was my initiation into bona fide investigative
reporting. Although I was an apprentice muckraker, my
radio reporting background, three years as the host of a
public affairs talk show and limited experience uncovering mini-scandals gave me a practical knowledge of Louisiana's culture of wheeling and dealing.

Indeed, Louisiana scandals had entertained the nation
for decades. The antics of three former Governors were
depicted in Hollywood movies. The best known is *All the
King's Men*, an adaptation of Robert Penn Warren's Pulitzer Prize winning novel about a fictional populist Southern Governor. The 1949 film won three Academy Awards,
including Best Actor for Broderick Crawford's portrayal of
Governor Willie Stark.

Despite the novelist and poet's insistence that Willie
Stark was a fictional creation, his character was undoubt-
edly based on Louisiana demagogue, Huey P. Long. Penn
Warren spent eight years on the Louisiana State University
faculty—two of which overlapped the peak of the tyranni-
cal power of the man known as the "Kingfish."

But neither the book, the movie nor a re-make starring Sean Penn fully captured Huey Long's influence on
Louisiana and the nation. While reigning benevolently and

malevolently as a monarch, he radically changed the state's political, educational and social landscapes. He provided free school books for children, expanded higher education, and built new highways, bridges and hospitals. Like Penn Warren's character, Huey Long was willing "to sell his soul to get the power to do good."

Following his election to the U.S. Senate, he continued to serve as Governor. In Washington, the Kingfish was initially seen as a southern hick from a backward province. However, when he began promoting systemic changes in the United States, his populism struck fear in the hearts of Washington's political elite.

In the midst of the Great Depression, Long advocated limits on the personal wealth of individuals. He created the *Share Our Wealth Society*, which advocated the redistribution of America's resources. Under the banner, "Every Man a King," his ideas were a forerunner to many of President Franklin Roosevelt's New Deal policies.

In the Pulitzer Prize winning biography, *Huey Long*, historian T. Harry Williams hypothesized that several FDR initiatives to help the poor—Social Security, for example—were a direct response to Long's socialistic vision. His rhetoric on national radio broadcasts made him so popular that Democratic Party leaders feared he would become a Third Party Presidential candidate in 1936 and swing the election to Republicans. The Kingfish's spoiler role never came to pass.

On Sunday evening, September 8, 1935, Long was mortally wounded by an assassin's bullet in a corridor of Louisiana's Capitol building. He was forty-two years old. The exact motive of the shooting remains a mystery. The gunman, a twenty-seven-year- old physician named Carl Weiss, was killed on the spot by Long's bodyguards. Professor Williams, as well as other historians, have theorized that Weiss was mentally unbalanced and decided on the spur of the moment to kill a man he perceived as a tyrant.

Huey Long's movie script exploits were passed along to successors. His brother, Earl, got the Hollywood treatment. Paul Newman starred as "Uncle Earl" in the 1989 movie, *Blaze*. It was based on bizarre episodes that preceded Long's mental breakdown. Elected Governor in 1948 and again in 1956, Earl Long was committed to mental hospitals in the final days of his second term. Two brief confinements occurred in the wake of his publicized shenanigans with stripper girlfriend, Blaze Star.

The first trip to an asylum was actually a kidnapping. Without legal authority, his wife and nephew—Senator Russell Long—directed State Police troopers to shackle Earl and haul him to a Texas sanitarium. Because of the illegality of the abduction, he was quickly released and returned to Baton Rouge.

A local judge committed him to a Louisiana mental institution. But using gubernatorial powers, he fired the head of the hospital and appointed a new administrator, who immediately ordered his release. When Uncle Earl's term as Governor ended, the follies were topped off by his election to Congress. He didn't get the opportunity to take the sideshow to Washington. Only days before taking office, he died of a heart ailment.

Viewed in retrospect, Earl Long was probably bipolar or alcoholic, both perhaps. His wacky behavior was part of the debate that preceded the adoption of the Twenty Fifth Amendment to the U.S. Constitution. It establishes the line of succession, and outlines procedures when a President becomes incapacitated by sickness, injury, or goes nuts.

The third Louisiana Governor to have his name on movie marquees was Jimmie Davis. Prior to entering politics, Davis was an entertainer/actor/songwriter. He composed *You Are My Sunshine*, one of the world's most enduring songs. Davis starred as himself in the forgettable 1947 film, *Louisiana*. It traced his career from performer to politician. Campaigning with a guitar and country band, Davis was first elected in 1944. A dozen years later at the height of Louisiana's school desegregation crisis, he cast himself as a staunch segregationist and was re-elected. As a distraction to the state's futile efforts to resist integration, he rode his horse up the Capitol building's forty-eight steps at the entrance and dismounted outside the Governor's office.

Less entertaining, but more enduring in Louisiana's colorful political history was the career of the Kingfish's son, Russell. First elected in 1948, he served thirty-eight years in the U.S. Senate. As Chairman of the Senate Finance

Committee and head of the Joint Committee on Internal Revenue Taxation, Long rewrote the nation's tax laws. He was the antithesis of his daddy. Whereas Huey Long fought Standard Oil and other big corporations, his son created tax loopholes for oil and gas companies. Russell subscribed to trickle down economics in the belief that corporate tax breaks benefited his Louisiana constituency by creating jobs and expanding the state's economy.

When I moved to Louisiana in November, 1967, John McKeithen had just been re-elected to a second term as Governor. A half century after Huey Long's death, McKeithen was heir to the Kingfish's statewide political machine—a confederation of sheriffs, tax assessors and local politicians. As Governor, McKeithen took a relatively moderate stance on civil rights and other controversial social issues. He was Louisiana's first Chief Executive to bring African-Americans into the mainstream of government.

Before WJBO recruited me, I spent five years as a newsman at small California radio stations where I learned the fundamentals of broadcast reporting. My new employer was Baton Rouge's first commercial radio station, signing on in 1934. Though not in use, the second floor was testament to its history. A big auditorium with noise absorbing rubber-inlaid floors and acoustical ceilings was a vestige of radio's studio audience days.

I was hired as an interim replacement of Jules d'Hemecourt, a colorful newsman who was preparing to fulfill a six-month military obligation. Jules was an offbeat character with a staccato on-air delivery that emulated radio personality, Paul Harvey. A raconteur of Cajun dialect stories, he made several recordings and was much in demand as a speaker. WJBO planned to make us a reporting team following his reserve duty.

Meantime, I was a poor substitute for Jules' style of reporting, as well as his inimitable choice of clothing. He once arrived at a Governor's news conference in Bermuda shorts, brogans and a Budweiser promotional sport coat covered in a pattern of beer labels. Radio has always been the home of eccentric characters. He met the criteria.

WJBO's news programming centered on state government. Direct lines connected the newsroom to both the Louisiana House and Senate, allowing us to continuously record legislative proceedings. My duties included anchoring drive-time newscasts and producing a weekly syndicated Capitol report that aired statewide.

And news was breaking out all over when I got to Louisiana. The Legislature was in the process of appointing a joint committee to investigate labor racketeering. At the same time, government officials were issuing daily denials in response to *Life Magazine* allegations that linked them to organized crime. Added to those issues was the state's resistance to school desegregation. Louisiana's image was such that McKeithen purchased time on TV networks to tell the nation how much fellow citizens loved black folks.

They just didn't want to share restaurant food or attend school with people of color.

In the face of all the problems, Louisiana's economy was booming. Industrial expansion on banks of the Mississippi River made jobs plentiful in and around Baton Rouge—even though labor disputes caused near riots at some job sites. Charges were rampant about shakedowns and payroll padding, a practice known as featherbedding. At the center of most disputes was local Teamster's official, Edward Grady Partin.

Five years earlier, the U.S. Department of Justice under Attorney General Robert Kennedy relied on Partin as an undercover informant in a crusade to convict International Teamsters President James Hoffa. The Baton Rouge labor official testified as the star witness in a 1962 Chattanooga, Tennessee jury tampering trial that put Hoffa in prison.

Contractors and lawmen alike accused the Justice Department of ignoring Partin's racketeering—even protecting him—as a reward for his testimony. In an attempt to overturn the Chattanooga conviction, Hoffa's allies joined Louisiana critics in putting pressure on local authorities to prosecute Partin and discredit him as a believable witness.

Jules d'Hemecourt had been aggressive in reporting the intricacies of the Partin scandal. His stories disclosed evidence of illegal wiretaps, intimidation of witnesses and other wrongdoing. As a newcomer to Louisiana, the best I could do was keep a scorecard on the charges and countercharges.

Overlapping the labor racketeering tumult was a *Life* magazine exposé that linked New Orleans mob boss Carlos Marcello to several Louisiana officials, including an aide to Governor McKeithen. Investigative reporter David Chandler's stories also alleged widespread bribery, illegal gambling and unlawful tax breaks for Marcello-owned businesses by Louisiana's Revenue Department. A second legislative committee was empanelled to hold hearings on the magazine's allegations. Neither panel accomplished much more than providing great political theater. But for me, it was a crash course in Louisiana scandals and kept me busy in Jules' absence.

When he completed his reserve duty six months later, he came home with an idea for a program called *Topic*. The show gave us added time to report the ongoing circus. It was devoted to interviewing newsmakers and included listener participation. The Larry King approach was not original, but it was then cutting edge in Baton Rouge. For me, co-hosting *Topic* was the equivalent of advanced studies in public affairs, politics, crime and punishment, and a mixture of obscure topics that I really didn't give a shit about. However, the trivial knowledge came in handy when I took the title of muckraker.

Jules missed out on much of the erudition. He accepted a journalism fellowship at Columbia University and left me as the sole moderator. He later became a journalism professor at LSU. In 2008—not long after his retirement—he died of pneumonia.

Topic debuted in May, 1968, during unrelenting defiance in Louisiana and the South to social changes. Baton Rouge was about equally divided into white, gray and blue collars. A large segment of the work force depended on state government and LSU for livelihoods. Blue and gray collar workers were mostly employed in the oil, chemical and construction industries. The city demographics was moving toward majority black.

Though not completely disenfranchised, people of color struggled for a share of the benefits from Baton Rouge's economic boom, and the opportunity to provide their children with a good education. A dozen years after *Brown v. Topeka*, black children continued to attend segregated elementary and secondary schools even though their parents were among the first in the country to file a desegregation lawsuit. The 1956 litigation took forty-six years to settle, the longest standing deseg case in U.S. history.

Baton Rouge's Southern University was one of the nation's largest historically black colleges. For years, the school was relegated to second-class status in legislative budget allocations.

The city's daily newspapers still reflected many customs of the "Old South." News stories identified people as "Negroes" when race was irrelevant. The policy was a consistent gripe of mine on *Topic*. Although the newspaper publishing family owned WJBO, my bosses didn't complain. Or at least not to me. Regardless, the policy changed. And so did company hiring practices.

I hired the WJBO's first black reporter, albeit part-time. Bill Samuels was a 400-pound retired Army Sergeant. We met at a civil rights rally in which he was a participant. Bill was the regional representative of the Voter Education Project. When assigned to report on demonstrations, I didn't know if he would get a story or get thrown in jail.

Topic was a forum for local and national civil rights leaders like John Lewis, then head of the Atlanta-based Voter Education Project. Once a week on average, some aspect of Louisiana's racial divide was discussed. And as Louisiana became more racially inclusive, the show often sounded like a program of firsts. "Our guest today is (fill in the name), Louisiana's first elected black (fill in the position)." Not once in that volatile era did any of my guests predict we would see a black President in our lifetime.

Beyond civil rights and race, the show dealt with an endless stream of hot-button issues. Teamster leader Ed Partin was always eager to refute allegations that he lied during the Hoffa trial and deny that he had anything to do with the labor abuses that prompted legislative hearings on racketeering. New Orleans Crime Commission official Aaron Kohn—noted for seeing Mafia figures behind every bush—regularly came on the program to give the latest foliage reports. He expressed great confidence in the veracity of *Life* magazine's exposé of organized crime's influence on state government—as he should since he was one of reporter David Chandler's main sources.

Congressman John Rarick regularly pontificated on *Topic* about the civil rights hand-basket he believed was delivering the country to hell. The U.S. Representative eventually took his far-right views to the entire nation. In 1980, he received 41,000 votes as the Presidential candidate representing the American Independent Party.

I considered some of Rarick's politics goofy. But his views were liberal compared to a nineteen-year-old pimply-faced LSU freshman named David Duke. He won *Topic*'s title as the most uncontrollable guest to ever appear on the program. I'm ashamed to admit that I gave Duke his first exposure to an audience larger than a few people who heard him rant and rave on LSU's Free Speech Alley.

Claiming to be a spokesman for the National Socialist Movement, he contacted me to offer opposing views following a program that featured students representing an LSU anti-war group. Duke seemed relatively articulate, and I didn't check his background until the day of the show. That's when I realized he was a member of George Lincoln Rockwell's American Nazi Party. Though disconcerting, I figured to easily send Duke away with a swastika tucked up his ass. After all, I considered myself to be an accomplished interviewer accustomed to one-on-one confrontations with crazies.

He did me in, responding to rational questions with irrational speeches. But as a free speech advocate, I toughed it out. Using terms like "nigger" and "kike," the racial slurs and anti-Semitic comments were so inflammatory, I asked if he were under psychiatric care. More disturbing was the reaction of several call-in listeners who agreed with his views. These same listeners would picket the station a few weeks later after I refused to bring them on as guests.

When David Duke emerged years later as founder of the National Association for the Advancement of White People, a Ku Klux Klan Wizard, a successful political candidate and a symbol of racism in America, I was embarrassed to admit that I provided an early forum for his malevolence.

Despite being badly beaten by the teen-aged psycho, I was acquiring interviewing skills that became a hallmark of my career. The talk show honed a talent for bluffing and exaggerating my knowledge of issues. The technical term for my genius is bullshit artist—an essential muckraking ingredient. In contrast to my bluster, I learned to admit ignorance. "Are there questions I should ask you?" The answers were often surprising.

Uncovering the 1972 bribery scheme combined my bullshit skills with ten years of experience in rummaging through records at courthouses and in small government agencies. But I had to overcome a lack of confidence in dealing with big federal bureaucracies like the SBA—especially after an official was less than cooperative in our initial telephone conversation. To bolster my confidence, I took the unorthodox approach of arriving at the agency with a lawyer at my side. An attorney of sorts, I should say.

One of Baton Rouge's leading law firms represented WJBO, however, I was embarrassed to seek legal assistance for a routine inspection of records on what could very well be a wild goose chase. I solved the problem by hiring my own counsel, a one-legged attorney named Jack. He was a sporadic member of the anonymous fellowship. Before liquor took hold, Jack had been a prominent lawyer for a federal agency. Therefore, I assumed he knew about obtaining obscure public records. But dependability was not his strong suit. He quite frequently went on drunken binges, lost his prosthesis and summoned AA members to help him regain balance in life—a terrible metaphor.

Once the artificial limb was located, Jack attended a few meetings before going bar-hopping again. Literally and figuratively. A worse metaphor. Disc jockey witticisms aside, he happened to be sober when I prepared for a meeting at SBA's regional office in New Orleans. I offered Jack fifty bucks and a free lunch to accompany me.

Since he was coming out of an alcoholic daze from his most recent bender, I kept close tabs on him. Before our appointment, I bought him a less aromatic ensemble at a discount store. The new clothes didn't make the emaciated lawyer appear any less seedy.

His hands were palsied, his head jerked and he had a glazed look in his eyes. I doubt the federal official believed me when I introduced Jack as my legal consultant on government records and public access. The bureaucrat kept cutting wary side-glances, apparently fearing my lawyer would keel over at any moment. Jack said very little. He simply nodded at the appropriate moments, and the files were opened for my inspection.

To untrained eyes, the documents were mainly gibberish. Nevertheless, I gathered names of potential sources and found enough background material to begin asking reasonably intelligent questions. The most interesting tidbit was a memo disclosing an inquiry by the U.S. Comptroller of Currency into the bank's SBA transactions. Concurrent with the examination, the bank's President and its board Chairman resigned. The notation helped me piece together the framework of a series of reports.

Most investigative stories are a blend of tips, public records, interviews with people who have axes to grind, leaks from official sources, and serendipity. Exposés also evolve from trade-offs with prosecutors, lawmen and folks who have access to information beyond the reach of reporters. The more skilled a muckraker is at developing sources, finding documents and interpreting the material, the more successful he or she is at bartering deals with people with subpoena powers. An investigative reporting modus operandi is, "I'll show you mine, if you'll show me yours." My SBA homework provided material for a couple of deals.

Even though I did the leg work in gathering information about the bank, I lacked confidence in reporting what I uncovered. So I relied on trade-offs with the U.S. Attorney's office in Baton Rouge. I told a prosecutor what I found. He, in turn, promised to investigate my investigation. And I reported his investigation of my investigation.

"WJBO has learned that the Justice Department and the U.S. Comptroller of Currency have begun investigations of past transactions of the bank, etc......"

The contrivance was my early security blanket. Even so, most listeners probably didn't understand my convoluted story filled with twists and turns of SBA loans, changes in ownership of companies, and political ties of people involved in the transactions. I barely understood the stuff myself. Still, the revelations caught the attention of Senator Long. He denied any wrongdoing, though none had been alleged. In fact, I scarcely touched on his friendship with the bank Chairman.

I initially reported a series of five stories. None fell into the "holy shit" category, and my revelations were reaching a dead-end. The story gained new momentum when a mid-level executive at the bank called and asked to meet me at a local café. He repeatedly sought assurances that I would protect his identity.

We arranged a rendezvous the same night. He was so nervous I half expected him to say, "You will recognize me by the paper sack over my head."

At the designated location, he was easy to spot pacing back and forth outside the café. Rather than go in, he insisted we walk around the block and kept looking over his shoulder to ensure we weren't followed. Finally, he pulled a tattered newspaper clipping from his pocket. The article stated that Louisiana's Legislative Auditor had chastised a state insurance regulatory agency for depositing $2-million in non-interest bearing accounts at the bank.

"Find out what's behind this and you'll win a Pulitzer Prize," he promised. I didn't have the heart to tell him that radio reporters aren't eligible for Pulitzers.

Prior to racing away, he gave me one other lead—the name of a former bank executive who supposedly knew precise details of a scandal surrounding the bank deposits. The man lived with a girlfriend in Panama. The fidgety informant didn't know the woman's name.

As a nascent investigative reporter, the prospect of finding a woman in Central America whose name I didn't know seemed the equivalent of finding a black hole in outer space with binoculars. Undaunted, I found the mysterious witness in less than an hour. I called the bank and got a forwarding number. Such logic in investigative reporting is second only to looking in the telephone directory to locate somebody.

The guy didn't know much more than his former co-worker. However, he added another piece of information to the mosaic. He said the questionable deposits were arranged by a state official whose brother-in-law was a business partner of the bank Chairman. The official was identified as James Anderson, Executive Director of Louisiana's Insurance Casualty and Rating Commission, an agency that approves premium rates for policies covering homes, automobiles and other types of coverage.

I didn't understand that $2-million in non-interest bearing accounts substantially increased a bank's lending capacity. As a muckraking trainee, I was also vulnerable to rookie mistakes, including a bizarre development that taught me a valuable lesson about the dangers of playing "I'll show you mine, if you show me yours." Find out first if there is a "yours" before showing "mine."

Louisiana's newly elected Insurance Commissioner taught me the rule of caution. Sherman Bernard may be the least qualified man ever elected to a statewide regulatory position. Prior to overseeing the state's multi-billion dollar insurance industry, he was a house mover. I suspect he was alphabetically elected. His name appeared at the top of the 1971 ballot. He became one of three consecutive Commissioners to go to prison.

I met Bernard at a Baton Rouge Press Club newsmaker luncheon. Our conversation was so brief that I failed to grasp the depth of his ignorance. But assuming he had good sense, I asked if he knew anything about the questionable bank deposits.

"Yeah, I know a lot about it," he replied. "We need to compare notes."

Excited at finding a knowledgeable source, I agreed to meet Bernard for dinner. He arrived for our date with his nephew, Raymond Vinet, and a campaign advisor. Sherman told me that Raymond had investigated the bank deposits. But as we talked, I concluded that Vinet would have difficulty finding his pecker at a urinal, let alone digging into complex bank transactions. They were pumping me for information.

But what the hell? I was getting a steak dinner at one of Baton Rouge's finer restaurants. Playing along, I offered a fuzzy outline of the deposits, telling them that a former bank executive suspected payoffs. Without pinpointing Panama, I said the source lived with a girlfriend in Latin America. As the motley crew took copious notes, I smiled to myself while deciding to avoid them in the future. No such luck. Two days later, a statement was released suggesting they had collective IQ below triple digits.

"Insurance Commissioner Sherman Bernard announced today that he has uncovered a scheme in which a high official of the Casualty and Surety Division took kickbacks for depositing state funds in a non-interest bearing account," the release stated.

Fragments of our conversation were enhanced by tabloid-like misinformation. "A bank officer, who knew about the payoffs, was so afraid of an investigation that he fled to South America with his young blonde girlfriend."

I had said nothing about the guy fleeing. Nor did I describe the woman as a blonde. The couple lived in Central America, not South America. The stupidity of the release had no bounds. It got worse.

"Bernard developed the information with the help of WJBO Investigative Reporter John Camp," it stated. I was on the phone to Bernard's office even before I finished reading the release. A secretary referred me to brain-addled Raymond Vinet.

"Are you fucking guys crazy?" I screamed. "How could you attach my name to something like that?"

"Don't worry," he replied. "The *New York Times v. Sullivan* protects us."

The Sullivan case is a U.S. Supreme Court decision setting a high threshold for public figures to prove libel and defamation. In short, plaintiffs have the burden of proving reckless disregard for the truth and/or actual malice. Bernard was not protected unless imbecility was accepted as a defense.

A week later, Rating Commission Chairman, James Anderson filed a $3-million dollar lawsuit against Bernard. Anderson was not named in the news release, although he was obviously the person being accused. Fortunately for Sherman Bernard, I would produce evidence that saved his dumb ass.

The strangest part of the fiasco is that Bernard and his gang of morons helped me nail the story. The news release that cited me as a source led the bank President to conclude that I had the goods on him. Hence, he hired one of Louisiana's best criminal defense lawyers.

Ossie Brown was the first choice of guilty defendants. When he gave jury summations, his theatrics filled courtrooms with note-taking lawyers. Ossie paced in front of jury boxes—sweat on his brow and tears in his eyes. Long before Brother Jimmy gained fame as Baton Rouge's bawling orator, the criminal defense attorney was known for turning tears on and off like tropical rain showers. Tall and heavyset with a slight overbite, droopy jowls and hair slicked to a widow's peak, he had a revivalist's talent for influencing juries with his entreaties on behalf of clients.

Brown gained a measure of national prominence in 1970 by successfully defending Staff Sergeant David Mitchell, the first person to go on trial in connection with the 1968 My Lai massacre of 108 Vietnamese non-combatants. He was the only soldier acquitted. Ossie's most memorable moment in the Fort Hood, Texas court martial occurred when prosecutors presented surprise evidence. He grabbed his chest, keeled over and left the courtroom on a stretcher. Returning a week later in fine shape, Ossie denied the seizure was a stunt to delay the trial.

In 1972, he was busy running for District Attorney of East Baton Rouge Parish. Therefore, I was surprised to get a phone call from him inquiring about the Bernard news release. He explained in vague terms that a bank employee had retained him, but refused to identify the client. He promised to reveal the name as soon as he knew more about the case. I began calling him nearly every day. He told me to be patient. Patience wasn't my virtue. Indeed, impatience caused me to step across the line of ethical journalism.

After a couple of dozen calls, I told Ossie that if he helped me I might be able persuade my boss to endorse his candidacy. What a crock. I couldn't have influenced Doug Manship to endorse Mother Teresa. I don't know if Ossie believed me. But he finally identified his client as the bank's former President.

I had tried earlier to talk to the banker on the phone, and he hung up on me. But as a result of Bernard's news release, he and Brown both believed I was close to revealing the bribes. To soften the blow, Ossie devised a preemptive strategy to get immunity for the banker. The official would provide details of the pay-offs as an anonymous source. Presumably, law enforcement agencies would contact me for the name of my informant. My part of the bargain was to refer investigators to Ossie so he could negotiate a deal. The arrangement suited me. All I wanted was a story.

In a self-incriminating tape-recorded statement and an affidavit to satisfy WJBO's lawyers, the bank President identified all the guilty parties, listed dollar amounts, and outlined specific details of how the bank concealed the bribes. He offered a variety of excuses for his role in the scheme. "It wasn't my idea. I was only following orders, etc."

The confession notwithstanding, this was a high-risk story. I didn't have the U.S. Attorney or any official source to back up my exposé. And since a libel lawsuit had already been filed against Sherman Bernard, WJBO was almost certain to be sued. But after my story passed legal muster, Doug Manship gave me the go ahead to air the exposé. The story made a big splash in newspapers and on wire services. Ossie Brown got his wish. Investigators from the Attorney General's office contacted me to find out my source. I referred them to Ossie and he worked out a deal for the banker to testify against co-conspirators. Meantime, a $4.5 million libel lawsuit was filed against WJBO. Truth became a winning defense when criminal charges were filed. The lawsuit was dismissed.

Allowing me to rake muck in the face of certain litigation was a bold stance by WJBO. My background—personally, academically or professionally—did not inspire confidence that I was competent to sling mud. However, I now had the confidence of Doug Manship and our lawyers. And I took full advantage of the opportunity by producing a succession of investigative stories.

I revealed how Baton Rouge's Congressman borrowed thousands of dollars from a right-wing group trying to impeach Supreme Court Justice Abe Fortes, and then refused to repay the loan. I also disclosed questionable deals by newly-elected Governor Edwin Edwards. Other stories exposed fraudulent contracts awarded by the U.S. Department of Housing and Urban Development, and I uncovered a bid-rigging scheme between the Louisiana's Education Department and textbook companies.

Sober a little over two years, I started collecting national journalism prizes. The bank bribery story received the Radio Television News Directors International Award for Investigative Reporting, a DuPont Columbia citation, a National Headliners award and several regional and state journalism prizes. In awe of such recognition, I inundated major radio and television stations with a fifty-five-page *curriculum vitae* that was so voluminous it required a Table of Contents and a color-coding system.

The loose-leaf binder contained scripts of stories, copies of newspaper articles corroborating my claims of investigative reporting prowess and letters of commendation from fifteen personal and professional references, including the U.S. Attorney, Baton Rouge's Mayor and several other luminaries. The only thing omitted from the résumé was an award as the "Biggest Talker" in my seventh grade class at Blakely Island Elementary School in Mobile, Alabama—a prize that presaged the genius of a bullshit artist.

The encyclopedic tome resulted in a job offer that put me on a television merry-go-round from Baton Rouge to Miami to Boston to New York and home again prior to my tenure at CNN. In February 1973, I got a call from Gene Strul, the News Director of south Florida's NBC affiliate. He requested a film clip, causing me to wonder if he read my material. Radio newsmen don't have film clips. Nevertheless, I asked an advertising agency friend to point a camera at me while I read the "prize-winning" bribery exposé.

The resulting video barely resembled the person I saw each morning in the mirror. It showed a fat-faced character with droopy jowls, greasy cowlick and thick spectacles. His head jerked up and down like a bobble-head doll as he tried to maintain eye contact with the camera while at the same time reading the script. It was a dreadful impersonation of a television reporter. But conceding that the strange creature must be me, I sent the film to Miami. My expectations were low. Two weeks later, surprisingly, Gene called with a job offer. Did my film performance influence his decision?

"I could see you were not palsied," he said.

Those were the days my friend.

Better to crash a plane than to be shot to death.
Left to right: Barry Seal, Emil Camp

CIA photograph

Cocaine loaded in Nicaragua
From left to right: Pablo Escabar, Federico Vaughn (back to camera), Barry Seal

WBRZ TV

Barry Seal points to CIA installed camera.

Peabody Award for "Best Insurance Commissioner Money Can Buy"
Left to right: Richard Manship, John Spain, Me, Mike Haley

Left to right: Bob Courtney, me, Sailor Jackson

My introduction to Ted Turner.

First twenty-five members of Special Assignment Team.

Another day on the job.

Courtesy, Mike Haley

My last conversation with Jimmy.

CNN

CHAPTER NINE

KICKING SAND IN THE FACES OF BAD GUYS

My television debut in Miami, Florida in April, 1973 was memorable —not for reasons of journalistic enterprise, but because of the sartorial splendor I brought to South Florida's then NBC affiliate, WCKT. For my first on-camera appearance, I wore a dazzling ensemble consisting of a double-knit white-on-white polyester suit, a glistening black silk shirt and a seventies-style wide-body white necktie.

In Baton Rouge, the attire embodied the height of fashion among politicians, barroom bookies and ambulance-chasing lawyers with whom I had associated. But peering into the camera lens through tinted spectacles that turned opaque under bright studio lights, I sensed a lack of appreciation for my debonair bayou garb. The suspicion was confirmed the next day.

"I thought we hired this guy to investigate the Mafia, not join it," the station owner complained to News Director Gene Strul, who was oblivious to on-air cosmetics.

He had his own concept of TV news. Short in stature and patience, Gene was an arbitrary and dictatorial editor. He wielded a heavy pencil to scripts that failed to meet his standards, which were often ambiguous. As stories were prepared for the six o'clock news, anxious reporters paced outside his glass-enclosed office. Scripts were returned with scribbled notes. Arguing was futile. "Change it," he replied.

Gene's undiplomatic demeanor extended beyond WCKT's staff. He rebelled against the arrogance of network news people who treated affiliates like video stores. High-profile NBC correspondents and producers swaggered into local newsrooms making multiple demands for assistance. If major stories were breaking, networks wanted first dibs on the video of local stations. Gene put WCKT's needs ahead of the network. He was an unpopular guy at NBC's headquarters in New York's Rockefeller Center.

For a little guy, Gene had big balls. His willingness to take up causes was evident by the many awards and plaques lining the station's lobby walls. In four years as the station's chief muckraker, my investigative reports would be cited for two Peabody awards and numerous other prizes. Gene imbued me with a crusading style of journalism. He refused to let go of stories if there were still angles to chase.

WCKT was a pioneer of ambush "gotcha" reporting that featured undercover video. We sometimes peeked at folks for no purpose other than they were there. Driving along Collins Avenue in Miami Beach one day, I noticed Meyer Lansky walking his dog. At my suggestion, the photographer started shooting grainy and unstable film as the van crept along beside the so-called "wizard of organized crime." Lansky saw me, but not my partner behind darkened windows in the rear compartment. Concerned he was being followed by God knows who, he picked up the small poodle and scurried away.

We were onto a big story that raised important questions. Did Lansky curb the animal when it shit? Was he armed with a pooper-scooper? And why were we filming an old man walking his dog? I guess because Lansky was notorious. Anyway, WCKT found a rationale to use the video—an anniversary of some criminal trial as I recall.

Regardless of how innocuous the activities, people on grainy black and white undercover film looked guilty. Consequently, the snoop van—painted in the same color scheme as a telephone company repair truck—was as essential to us as a camera.

Aside from the Lansky video, most of our undercover film had a purpose. Gene and Assistant News Director Dave Choate believed in kick-ass reporting.

Dave was my strongest advocate in the station, and closest friend outside of work. He soothed the damaged psyches of newsmen who incurred Gene's wrath. His easygoing personality made him and Gene an archetypal good guy/bad guy tandem. But Dave was no pushover. Underperforming reporters and photographers found themselves assigned to cover flower shows, week-end festivals and bottom-of-the-newscast stories.

My television premier was apropos of the WCKT's penchant for tabloid reporting. I disclosed "intimate" details of a sting operation targeting a lecherous local judge who spent large sums of money on party girls—one of whom happened to be a longtime IRS snitch. A lover's quarrel inspired her to exact revenge by providing revenue agents details of the jurist's lavish lifestyle. An investigation disclosed that his fun and games were supported by a few lawyers who regularly appeared in his courtroom. The IRS probe put the playboy's job, reputation and freedom in jeopardy. Not to mention his marriage.

When the judge failed to return telephone calls, I showed up at his home. I discovered he was no longer welcome there. So I convinced his indignant spouse to share feelings about her wayward husband's peccadilloes. In a Jerry Springer-like "exclusive," the woman said something to the effect that he was a no-account son-of-a-bitch, and she would take great pleasure in performing surgery on his genitals.

The tale, as tawdry as it was, allowed me to begin listing my occupation as television investigative reporter. With the Watergate investigation rapidly gaining momentum, muckraking was coming into style. Miami's two other network affiliates had fulltime investigative reporters. Like me, the competitors were television neophytes. We regularly stumbled over one another while prowling South Florida for scandals.

From the rear compartment of WCKT's snoop van, photographers and I tracked organized crime figures, corrupt politicians, and other villains. When caught, I leapt from the van with a microphone in hand and the camera grinding away as I fired discomfiting questions at our prey. It was good television, bad journalism. But that was the way of investigative reporting in the early and mid-seventies.

Establishing investigative reporting bona fides in a strange city begins with finding sources. Not long after arriving in Miami, I fell into a trap that befalls naïve investigative reporters. I fell in love with my sources. They were so easy to seduce that I judged them as sluts. The opposite was true. They were using me. I got cozy with cops and prosecutors, who were willing to exploit gullible reporters.

In Louisiana, I did much of my own digging. But to use an Alcoholics Anonymous phrase, I found an "easier softer way" in Florida. Friendly lawmen fed me stories. The shortcut got my face on the TV screen and eventually helped me collect journalism prizes. Using the drinking analogy again, I would suffer story-after hangovers.

My earliest sources enforced the least of Miami's problems. Assisted by Miami Beach vice squad investigators, I invaded the province of little old ladies by revealing that several charities sponsoring high-stakes bingo games were fronts for unscrupulous operators who skimmed the proceeds. When cops shut down a couple of bingo parlors identified in my series, I risked being attacked by an umbrella swinging gray-haired brigade. So I focused on another vice.

Miami Beach morals protectors provided me material for the tawdriest story of my career. I launched a fearless probe of massage parlors. Salons with exotic names like Salome, Grecian Girls, and China House were actually "jerk-off" joints. Undercover detectives made the discovery while assigned to the dangerous task of getting massages.

"When she began to manipulate my penis," one arrest report stated, "I identified myself as a police officer and placed her under arrest. Did not ejaculate." What a guy.

I proposed a single story to Gene based on the police reports. He wanted a series—plus corroboration. He sent me on a company-paid tour of every south Florida massage parlor that advertised in local newspapers. Traveling the grease circuit, I determined beyond a shadow of doubt what services were offered.

"Ironically, the movie *Deep Throat* has been banned from Miami Beach," I intoned in my first report. "Yet, it's possible in Miami Beach to purchase the real-life version of the sexual activity that is the movie's theme. Oral sex."

How I developed conclusive evidence remains confidential. To paraphrase a Las Vegas motto, what happens in massage parlors, stays in massage parlors. Suffice to say that I disclosed the services of thirteen places. An on-screen graphic designated "M" for masturbation, "OC" for oral copulation, and "I" for intercourse.

Below each was a price list. A massage parlor at the rear of an auto body shop in an industrial area charged five-dollars for a hand-job. The bargain probably caused a traffic jam in the neighborhood. The horny man lobby had more influence than I realized. There was no outcry to shut down the places. So I retired from the vice beat to tackle legitimate issues.

My first substantive series revealed patterns of favoritism by judges in assigning lawyers to represent indigents in criminal proceedings. Meeting clients for fifteen minutes or less in courthouse corridors, favored attorneys collected fees for convincing defendants to cop pleas to reduced charges. Innocence was irrelevant. Plead guilty to a lesser crime and walk. Otherwise, take your chances.

I have nothing against lawyers. They are among an investigative reporter's best friends. But a disproportionate number are vulnerable to exposés. After reporting the plea bargain scam, I disclosed an ambulance-chasing scheme in which attorneys and doctors conspired to inflate insurance claims arising from minor traffic accidents. One doctor/lawyer team I identified handled more than 300 separate lawsuits in tandem. All involved soft-tissue injuries such as whiplash. None went to trial.

Rather than risk jury verdicts, companies settled claims in the range of $20,000—half of which went to the lawyers and doctors. One cocky Miami barrister was so successful in bleeding insurance companies that he named his yacht, *The Whiplash*.

My early Miami exposés were more "gosh darn" than "holy shit." But I was building a list of sources. The big south Florida news then was an ongoing trial called the "market scandal." Two judges and several cronies were linked to allegations of political patronage, payoffs, and judicial corruption. The investigation got its name from a food market and café where the deals were allegedly made. WCKT reporter Brian Ross—on his way to becoming one of network television's best-known muckrakers—was assigned to cover the trial. Gene told me to find scandals of equal magnitude.

Historically, the most powerful Miami politician was Dade County's State's Attorney. For twenty years, the late Richard Gerstein held the office. He was a source for scores of reporters, including *Washington Post* journalists Bob Woodward and Carl Bernstein. Gerstein investigators uncovered a money-laundering operation that financed the Watergate break-in—pivotal evidence in the *Post's* pursuit of the President.

Tall and bald, Gerstein's most distinctive feature was a glass eye. The World War Two souvenir prompted lawmen to nickname him "Cyclops." He was the target of federal and state investigations throughout the 1970's. Despite allegations of corruption, he was enormously popular with voters and a staff of young lawyers. Ambitious assistant prosecutors were elected and/or appointed to judgeships and other important government positions. Among Gerstein's protégés was former United States Attorney General Janet Reno, who succeeded him as Dade County's top prosecutor.

The judges accused of conspiring to fix cases in the "market scandal" had close ties to Gerstein. And although a jury found them innocent, the corruption investigation was expanded to encompass their mentor. A joint probe by IRS agents, the Florida Department of Law Enforcement and Dade County's Organized Crime Bureau was coordinated by the U.S. Justice Department's Miami Organized Crime Strike Force.

A detective in OCB, as the Dade Organized Crime Bureau was known, told me of a mysterious Saturday morning rendezvous involving Gerstein, a prominent judge, a convicted bookmaker and a Las Vegas gambling junket operator with links to mobster Meyer Lansky. The meetings purportedly took place like clockwork at Lincoln Road pedestrian mall, a popular Miami Beach shopping center. As a follow-up to the tip, I staked out the mall in the snoop van.

I felt like Judas. Prosecutors in Gerstein's office were helping me on other stories. But a muckraker's stock in trade is betrayal—a contradiction of "rigorous honesty," which is an underlying principle of AA's Twelve Steps. Throughout my career, I came up with rationalizations for my perfidy. Only one made much sense. I was doing my job.

True to the cop's lead, Gerstein and Judge David Goodhart arrived in separate cars every week on a predictable schedule. Goodhart was Gerstein's former top assistant. From a parking lot, we filmed the meetings. They always followed the same routine. The two men first went to a barbershop—unusual because Gerstein was bald and Goodhart lived twenty miles away. Bookmaker Marty Ash was waiting for them to arrive.

Following a brief chat, the judge and prosecutor went next door to a clothing store, where they met with Las Vegas gambling junket operator Hyman Lazar. He was purportedly one of the nation's biggest layoff bookmakers—a vocation that entails taking bets from other bookies to protect them from catastrophic losses. Hymie's Miami gambling connections enhanced his legal occupation as a casino junket operator. He knew Miami's high rollers, their betting habits and credit worthiness.

Until Gerstein underwent heart surgery, the mall routine seldom varied. Even as he recuperated, Goodhart continued the trysts. My photographer and I were not alone in spying. Reporters from competing stations also filmed the meetings. The place was also crawling with undercover agents.

"After a while that stakeout got to look like a used-truck lot," *TV Guide* reported in an article about Miami investigative reporting.

The funny thing is nobody knew the purpose of the meetings. Gerstein and pals could be holding Bible study meetings. Regardless, our candid camera video made the confabs look sinister—especially after I learned that Lazar and Meyer Lansky had breakfast together most weekdays at Wolfie's restaurant, a popular Miami Beach hang-out for politicians, gamblers and sportsmen. The "wizard" was then a drool or two short of a nursing home. But lawmen saw him lurking behind every palm tree.

Five months before I moved to Miami, Lansky unwillingly returned to the United States from Israel to face tax evasion and contempt of court charges stemming from an alleged conspiracy to skim money from a Las Vegas casino. Denied citizenship in Israel, Lansky took an excursion through Latin America to find a safe haven. No country would take him. Out of options, he arrived in Miami to be greeted by federal agents and the media. A WCKT reporter provided the highlight, addressing his wife as "Godmother."

The mobster's legend is arguably part myth. He had long associations with Mafia boss Charles (Lucky) Luciano and childhood friend, Benjamin (Bugsy) Siegel. Both men were long dead when Lansky returned to Miami. Cancer killed Luciano. Mob bullets did in Siegel, a trailblazer in the Las Vegas casino industry. Lansky did not feel so good himself. Or so he claimed. An alleged heart condition put him in the hospital several times, often coincidental to grand jury subpoenas and trials. He claimed his notoriety was a fantasy kept alive by lazy journalists, who failed to question police propaganda. I was among the guilty, reporting many stories that propagated the mystique.

The indictment leading to the airport spectacle stemmed from the ramblings of a self-described "Mafia Lieutenant" named Vincent (Fat Vinnie) Teresa. The longtime

FBI informant was the main witness at Lansky's trial. His testimony was so incredible the jury laughed at him, and quickly returned an innocent verdict. Afterwards, Teresa disappeared into the federal witness protection program from whence he periodically emerged to relate implausible tales that were memorialized in a book titled, *My Life in the Mafia*.

Cops in Teresa's hometown of Boston described him as a small time street criminal and a big time kook. I dealt with Vinnie a couple of years after the Lansky trial. He once promised me an exclusive interview about a South Florida gambling operation headed by Hymie Lazar. To do the interview, he asked me to send him First Class airfare to travel to Miami from an undisclosed location. I passed on the "exclusive" after determining his information had been lifted— incredibly—from my previous exposés.

I learned of the Lansky/Lazar breakfast meetings in the latter stages of my Lincoln Road spying expedition. So we parked our van across the street from Wolfie's and filmed the two men entering and leaving. Getting pictures inside was a problem. Since my face appeared on Channel Seven, we had to recruit a new member to the spy team. The young producer will mercifully remain nameless.

He was terrified of being caught, tortured and killed. But after assuaging his fears, he reluctantly dressed as a telephone repairman and undertook a mission to get snapshots with a miniature camera concealed in a cigarette pack. Technology had not yet come up with tiny video cameras that can be hidden in lapels.

On the appointed day, the nervous producer got out of the van without being pushed. Although a non-smoker, he paused to light up outside Wolfie's. In a greatly exaggerated motion, he inhaled deeply and began coughing to near collapse. We laughed so hard, I feared the movement of the van would attract the attention of passers-by.

Catching his breath, he staggered inside and found a table as far away from other diners as possible. Lansky, Lazar and friends also wanted to sit away from the crowd. They chose a table adjacent to the producer. It's a wonder he didn't have a coronary. But he sucked it up and snapped off a roll of black and white film. The photographs were an important visual element linking Gerstein, Goodhart, the junket operator, a bookmaker, and the "wizard." After weeks of surveillance, all we needed was a plot.

Plot or not, Miami's three major stations led nightly newscasts on May 28, 1974, with stories disclosing that the federal Organized Crime Strike Force had subpoenaed witnesses to testify before a grand jury. The CBS and ABC affiliates carried tightly edited five-minute stories. My report was a rambling twenty-minute epic, a virtual "Who's Who" in South Florida gambling. In addition to undercover video, I gave detailed biographies of all the bookmakers and political deal-makers involved in the wide-ranging investigation. Included in my report were arrest records, nicknames and every trivial piece of information I had gathered. Gene delighted in minutiae.

What was Lansky's breakfast fare? Based on our undercover producer's answer, I reported it was a "high cholesterol breakfast of bacon and eggs." Given his terror of being executed on the spot, I was skeptical that he noticed. But Gene insisted I put it in my script. The tidbit was subsequently included in stories by other news organizations, obviously plagiarized from us since we were alone in reporting Lansky's meal.

Richard Gerstein displayed more fury than concern about the investigation. His anger was easy to detect. He got spitting mad. Literally. Interviewing him on the day the story broke, I received a veritable shower. He offered no explanation for the meetings, other than to say his encounters with bookies were accidental.

A grand jury soon began hearing testimony of gamblers and organized crime "associates"—a term describing anyone within shouting distance of targets of a mob investigation. Most witnesses took the Fifth. They were then hustled before a judge, given immunity from self-incrimination, and ordered to testify. Goodhart made a brief appearance before the panel. Gerstein was not subpoenaed.

As the weeks rolled by, Strike Force investigators became increasingly frustrated. And so did the media. I began having serious misgivings about the investigation. Given the scope of the inquiry and the number of people involved, the lack of progress was puzzling. Regardless, I staked out the courthouse and tried to interview witnesses who came and went. Our undercover film was replayed over and over in my reports.

A conversation with an AA friend set me to wondering about the inquiry. He had business ties to a key character in the probe. According to him, the feds were asking the wrong questions. He characterized the Lansky/Lazar daily breakfasts as aging gamblers talking about the good old days. The mall conferences, he said, were a different matter. Those discussions supposedly dealt with a political slush fund established by racetracks. I gave credence to the information since my friend had no reason to mislead me.

Florida law banned pari-mutuel companies from making political contributions. To evade the law, my pal said tariffs were imposed on a business that was new to me—on-track bookmaking. The services were valuable to high-rollers. On-track bookies granted credit. Bettors didn't have to bring wads of cash to the track. Secondly, their wagers by-passed pari-mutuel windows, making it difficult for the IRS to trace winnings. Some tracks allegedly turned a blind eye to the illegal activity. But for a price. On-track bookies were required to contribute to a political fund overseen by Gerstein.

The explanation of the Lincoln Mall meetings seemed implausible. Still, I attempted to corroborate the tale in an undercover filming foray at Hialeah Racetrack. I use the term "undercover" loosely. In the Florida heat, my photographer looked ridiculous trying to conceal a camera beneath a heavy coat as we strolled through the track. What's more, nearly everybody looked like a bookie.

Unable to independently confirm the yarn, I passed the information to my cop sources in hopes that they would follow-up and leak the results of their investigation to me. But they were convinced the meetings had more sinister purposes. And nothing of substance ever emerged from the Lincoln Road "scandal."

Remarkably, I collected my first George Foster Peabody medallion for secretly filming meetings that forever remain a mystery. The Peabody announcement coincided with my three-year sobriety anniversary. I still attended several AA meetings every week, which helped me keep my "award-winning reporting" in perspective.

Meetings in Miami were considerably different than in Baton Rouge where the fellowship was still relatively small. In my new home, I shared my "experience, strength and hope" with an eclectic array of ex-drunks that included the Miami-Dade Mayor, a rock and roll star, friends of Meyer Lansky and gold-chained characters whose colorful histories had to remain secret until the statute of limitations expired. But wherever I went to meetings, the principles that kept me sober were the same.

Staying close to AA was a remedy for handling the dangers associated with my sudden and improbable success as an investigative reporter. I heard things I needed to hear. Shortly after receiving the Peabody citation, I was in Baton Rouge on vacation when an unlikely character gave me lesson in humility.

In an anonymous fellowship, people were often referred to by nicknames like "Sick Ed," "Crippled Arthur," "Blind Nick" and "Peg-Leg Jack." Sensitivity was not our strong suit. One obnoxious character was called "Crazy Leonard," mainly because he was nuts. His personality problems had caused him to fail at nearly everything he tried, except staying sober. Leonard found a level of acceptance in AA.

"I read about your big award in the newspaper," he said at a meeting during my Baton Rouge visit. We were never particularly friendly, so I braced for a punch line. Instead, he made a comment I have always remembered. "I figure a little piece of the award belongs to me."

Tears welled in his eyes. Mine, too. A man of so few accomplishments outside AA was vicariously sharing in my sober success. And rightfully so. I was a surrogate for many less successful AA members.

By 1975, I had become a fulltime whore for Miami law enforcement and in the process, added a second Peabody medallion to my collection for a series of stories on so-called "Mafia" figures, who moved to the land of sunny skies and sandy beaches to escape a blizzard of subpoenas in the Northeast. My "Peabody award-winning" exposé featured undercover video of alleged hoodlums engaging in suspicious activities such as taking out the garbage or going to the post office.

As I later discovered, the characters we filmed in the wild were mostly small-time crooks with names that ended in vowels. They didn't belong to intricate crime organizations, but would have relished a chance to join. My arrival on the Mafia scene was tardy by a few years. Survivors of early crime syndicates were kept busy attending funerals. Or getting buried themselves. Blood-oath Sicilian traditions died with them.

As a latter day "Mafia" hunter, I skulked around south Florida with the aid of law enforcement intelligence reports that were replete with distortions, contradictions and misrepresentations. The Mafioso I stalked were a far cry from the *Godfather's* suave Michael Corleone. These guys were barely literate gamblers, loan sharks and extortionists who engaged in opportunistic and primitive crimes. Most were Italians.

But the menacing loan shark warning, "I'll kill your children, rape your wife and cutoff your nuts if you don't pay what you owe me," was not the exclusive copyright of any ethnic group. The age-old threat was used by Hispanic, Irish, Russian and African-American crooks, as well as descendants of Mayflower immigrants. Indeed, "organized crime" in south Florida was a disorganized potpourri of every ethnic culture.

Cop sources got me started on the Mafia series by giving me material that disclosed links between a New Jersey crime figure and a Miami Beach real estate investor named Howard Garfinkle. He had acquired $60-million worth of

Florida property in a matter of a few months. The rotund thirty-nine-year-old ex-convict's holdings included Miami Beach's famed Eden Roc Hotel and the nearby beachfront Imperial House condominium complex where he maintained penthouse offices. His home was a luxurious Miami Beach gated estate.

Garfinkle represented himself as a patron of the arts, pledging $3-million to the University of Miami for expansion of the Love Art Museum—a contribution that was never delivered. He was a world class deadbeat, a defendant in millions of dollars of lawsuits and an ex-con who had served prison time in New Jersey for bad checks, obtaining money under false pretenses and transporting counterfeit securities.

He also had a secret partner, former fellow inmate Joseph Paterno—no relation to the football coach. Non-coaching Paterno was identified in law enforcement intelligence documents as a "top ranking member of the New York Mafia family of mob boss Carlo Gambino." He was under subpoena by the New Jersey Crime Commission before taking up residence in a waterfront home a few blocks from Garfinkle's estate. Paterno's automobile was registered to the entrepreneur's real estate company. And telephone records revealed the two men were in daily contact. Dade County's Organized Crime Bureau was keeping close tabs on Paterno and two dozen transplanted hoodlums from the Northeast. An intelligence analyst slipped me a twenty-two page confidential analysis giving backgrounds and criminal histories of the racketeers.

Based on the document, I reported a "know your Mafia neighbor" series. A great deal of my "reporting" consisted of sneaking around and filming faces to match the names in the document. When the series aired, an on-screen graphic identified our video as "WCKT Undercover Film." Images of mobsters embracing one another appeared ominous, even though they were doing nothing more than exchanging greetings.

Instead of a Peabody citation, my undercover efforts deserved an Emmy for "Best Slapstick Comedy in Pursuit of Gangsters." The project was a laughable adventure. After the aforementioned *TV Guide* article revealed that our spy van was disguised as a telephone company truck, it displayed the name of a fictitious plumbing company called GMS—the initials of News Director Gene M. Strul.

South Florida must have been beset with plumbing problems. Our undercover filming was occasionally interrupted by folks banging on the door to get us to unstop toilets. Had we brought along a plunger, we could have started a successful business.

WCKT photographers were not eager participants in the project, especially when I told them the first target of our mission was "hit man," Joe Paterno. And it's a wonder we weren't killed. Not by him, but rather by my incompetence as a race driver.

Because Joe's home was hidden behind a high fence, we decided to play like cops and tail our man. The first time out, his driver immediately spotted the van and tried to outrace us. I knew how to cut him off at the pass. We arrived at the shortcut intersection at the same time as Joe's car. I slammed on the brakes, sending the photographer tumbling through a curtain that concealed the rear compartment. He was hanging over my shoulder in the front seat. We wrestled to disentangle ourselves in full view of the quarry.

Still, we continued the pursuit and caught up when Paterno's driver had to stop for gas. As the photographer tried to get video, I circled the gas pump like a wolf after prey. Joe kept adjusting the windshield visor to conceal his face. Finally, I heard the camera purring and stopped the van—directly in front of a car wash exit. Automobiles were on an assembly chain inside. An attendant shouted at me to move. My photographer kept saying, "Just a few more seconds." Seeing Joe's piercing glare convinced me that he was, indeed, chief of an assassination squad. I had a sinking feeling his squad might come looking for us if we didn't get the hell out of there.

The most overrated character in the undercover follies was Anthony (Tumac) Accetturo. His nickname was taken from *One Million Years BC*—a low budget movie featuring a club-wielding caveman of the same name. The moniker was appropriate, given Accetturo's Neanderthal-like appearance, and his alleged penchant for wielding baseball bats to collect loan shark debts. The OCB intelligence document described him as having "more power than any other organized crime figure residing in south Florida."

Like Joe Paterno, Tumac's reputation caused us a bit of trepidation. According to a New Jersey report, cops once annoyed him by spying on his activities from an undercover van. To express displeasure, he set fire to the vehicle with the cops still inside. They escaped unharmed. Still, the incident was unsettling, especially during our first stakeout of Accetturo's home in an upscale Broward County neighborhood. We parked the snoop van a couple of hundred feet from Tumac's and climbed into the rear compartment. Somebody apparently saw us and called the police. Minutes later, a patrol car arrived. I crawled into the driver's seat and displayed news credentials.

"We're filming the Mafia," I whispered.

The cops were laughing as they drove away. Seconds later, Tumac and three henchmen walked outside his residence and stood in the driveway. Either intentionally or unwittingly, they were posing for the camera. In a very animated conversation, the three men kept pointing to our vehicle. I thought I detected a distinct odor of smoke.

When my rotating team of three photographers was on other assignments, I sometimes grabbed a 16mm silent camera and chased mobsters around in my Chevy Vega. I learned six years later how "uncool" my surveillance efforts were. While working on an ABC *Close Up* documentary, I interviewed one of Tumac's former lawyers—an ex-IRS agent named Peter Aiken. For my entertainment, he retrieved pictures buried in his files. The photos showed me hanging out the window of the car with a camera as I attempted to film Tumac in the incriminating act of crossing the street to Aiken's offices.

In four months of filming so-called "wise guys," we only missed a few of our twenty-plus intended targets. Turns out that I should have asked the ones we couldn't find to pose for our cameras. When the series aired, the biggest complaint came from Emilio (The Count) Delio, a former Newark, New Jersey bookmaker and loan shark. We could never locate "The Count," and I had to use a mug shot in the series. Meeting face-to-face at the federal courthouse in Miami, he was terribly upset.

"Why did you use that picture? It made me look like a common criminal."

Emilio Delio and most of the featured characters in my series were eventually subpoenaed before grand juries and we got better video. But not without more hilarity. When Joe Paterno arrived for his appearance, my photographer backpedaled in front of him as I fired questions. He walked silently, his gaze cutting through me like a laser.

Suddenly, my cameraman ran into a telephone pole and went topsy-turvy to the ground. I stumbled on top of him. We acted as if nothing happened. I continued asking questions as the cameraman positioned himself on his knees. For a second, Joe's menacing demeanor seemed to soften. I detected a hint of a smile. Maybe we wouldn't be targets of his assassination squad after all. Even mobsters need comic relief.

Anthony Accetturo's appearance before a grand jury was less comical, and created a very awkward situation for me. I helped keep him out of jail. As Tumac was leaving the Broward County Courthouse, a photographer and I followed him into the elevator and onto the street. Later in the day, I was contacted by attorney Peter Aiken.

"Did you see Tony assault anybody?" he asked. "He has been arrested on charges of battery on a police officer in the elevator." Obviously, I was going blind. I saw nothing of the sort. I viewed the film twice before finding the premise for the allegation.

When Accetturo reached to press the elevator button, his arm brushed against a police photographer. The contact was negligible. Yet, the cop later testified he felt intimidated. Tumac was on parole for a previous assault, and it only took a misdemeanor conviction to send him back to prison. Subpoenaed as a defense witness, my testimony and the film resulted in an innocent verdict. Defending hoodlums was not fun.

Following Accetturo's return to New Jersey, he was characterized as the leader of a "Mafia crime family." As such, he and nineteen members of his "family" were indicted in 1988 for racketeering. The trial was notable because it lasted nearly two years, the longest criminal trial in U.S. history. Astonishingly, the jury took only two days to declare all of the defendant's innocent—a misnomer, for sure.

Tumac revealed the reason for the quick acquittal five years later. One or more of the jurors had been bribed. He made the disclosure during plea bargain negotiations in an unrelated New Jersey case. The jury tampering case was never pursued. By then, he was a snitch. Charged with multiple murders and an array of other crimes, he turned on former associates, claiming they had squealed on him. He said there was no longer honor among his band of thieves.

The Accetturo trial is the subject of *The Boys from New Jersey*, a book by Newark *Star Ledger* reporter Robert Rudolph. The proceedings were also the basis of *Find Me Guilty*, Sidney Lumet directed film. Relying on trial transcripts, the comedy depicted the antics of the Accetturo co-defendant, Jackie "Fat Jack" DiNorciscio. He served as his own lawyer and gave a twenty-one-month stand-up routine that was believed to have influenced the jury. However, Tumac's confession of jury tampering suggests that DiNorciscio's impact on the outcome may have been exaggerated.

Anthony Accetturo's reputation as a mob boss may also have been greatly exaggerated. According to his former lawyer, I facilitated his climb up the organized crime charts. Peter Aiken characterized Tumac as a minor hoodlum prior to my portrayal of him "as having more power than any other organized crime figure residing in south Florida." The publicity caused his loan shark and extortion victims to tremble in fear when he came to collect.

Shortcut journalism had made me a PR man for criminals, as well as cops.

CHAPTER TEN

A LOSS OF FAITH

The "know your Mafia neighbor" and Lincoln Mall "exposés" were examples of media manipulation. Me being the media manipulated. I failed to recognize my susceptibility to law enforcement propaganda until Florida Governor Rueben Askew ordered a statewide investigation of illegal gambling and racketeering—a decision that was influenced, in part, by my "know your Mafia neighbor" and Lincoln Mall "exposés."

The Governor's appointment of a Special Prosecutor gave me a chance to meet the underworld figures named in the Dade County Organized Crime Bureau's "intelligence" analysis. A special grand jury was empanelled to hear witness testimony in venues throughout the state. Gene Strul wanted me to be a witness to the proceedings.

The investigation was akin to a traveling circus. And like the old joke of the guy who refused to quit his circus job shoveling shit behind elephants in order to stay in show business, I followed behind the grand jury shoveling muck to keep my face on television.

I wasn't quite ready to cast cop friends aside, but my faith in them was beginning to wane. Characters like Anthony Accetturo failed to live up to their billing. He was a bad-ass criminal. However, by standards of blood oath Sicilian traditions he was faux Mafia. Tumac ruled a gang of simple-minded criminals by brute force. He was an early version of Tony Soprano—the fictional thug featured in the *HBO* series. The TV show accurately portrayed the kind of "Mafioso" that I encountered in Miami.

Meyer Lansky was different. The diminutive "wizard of organized crime" was never known as a strong-arm guy. He could read and write, which made him a mob intellectual. When the statewide grand jury first convened, Lansky was the star attraction. As he walked down the corridor of the Broward County Courthouse in Fort Lauderdale for his first appearance, he was besieged by photographers and reporters.

"Do you plan to testify?" they shouted. "Will you take the Fifth?" "Are you involved in organized crime?" The "wizard" said nothing. Observing the ludicrous scene, I couldn't resist asking a question that finally elicited a response.

"What is your assessment of Lee Strasberg's portrayal of you in *Godfather Two*?" Everybody roared with laughter. Lansky stopped for a moment, smiled and patted me on the shoulder. "After following me around, John, you should've played the role."

As expected, he refused to testify. Eventually, he was given limited immunity that required him to answer questions within the scope of the grand jury investigation. Because of an alleged heart condition, his testimony was limited to one hour in the morning and an hour in the afternoon.

Like me, Lansky followed the panel on its journey across the state. Despite immunity, he remained unresponsive beyond an admission that he was once a professional gambler and acquainted with other gamblers. He kept a card with him that stated in effect, "I respectfully decline to answer the question because it does not fall within the scope of issues this grand jury was empanelled to investigate."

Oddly, a few cops assigned to the grand jury were in awe of the "wizard." One even asked him to autograph a Lucky Luciano biography. "All that is written is not truth," Lansky inscribed. It will probably never be known how much that has been written about him is truth. Law enforcement files are filled with allegations of guilt by his associations. He was arrested a few times in the 1920's and quickly released. In the 1950's, he served a short prison sentence for illegal gambling.

When I spent time alone with Lansky and his lawyer outside grand jury rooms, he smiled about his reputation as the "financial wizard of organized crime," reiterating that he was merely a professional gambler. The most noteworthy insight given me was provided by his longtime attorney, E. David Rosen.

The lawyer told a strange story of receiving a call from a Life magazine reporter for comment on an upcoming article that accused Lansky of ordering the murder of a Michigan racketeer. Rosen relayed the question to Lansky, who laughed and said it could not be true. The purported victim was alive. Rosen said he told the magazine that the man was among the living and provided an address. Yet, he remained dead in the *Life* article. Thereafter, the "wizard" concluded it was a waste of time responding to journalists. Lansky looked on silently as Rosen related the anecdote.

In contrast to his reputation as a financial genius, Lansky left only a modest estate when he died of natural causes in January, 1983. His widow had to rely on a son and the generosity of friends for her well-being. Beyond the Lansky legend, I also found the truth to be elusive in much that was written in the Organized Crime Bureau intelligence documents—my primary source of Miami mob lore.

The nephew of Emilio (The Count) Delio was identified as a "Lieutenant" in a major organized crime family. In truth, he was a chicken-plucker at a wholesale meat market. Delio's portrayal as a "Mafia kingpin" also seemed vastly overstated. He was described as "the official greeter for visiting New Jersey organized crime figures."

I couldn't picture the pear-shaped gambler on an airport concourse holding a placard, "Welcome to Miami, Mafia brothers." Like my encounters with Lansky, "The Count" and I chatted as we sat in courthouse corridors prior to his grand jury appearances. The seventy-year-old "mobster" was long past his prime as a leg-breaking loan shark, a specialty attributed to him in the OCB document.

"I'm a goddamned corner bookmaker," he told me in a gravelly voice.

Despite the purported secrecy of the Mafia brotherhood, several of my Mafiosi members seemed to enjoy their celebrity status. A loan shark named Frank Boni showed up staggering drunk for his grand jury appearance. Lurching down the hallway, he shouted, "I want to meet John Camp. Where is he?" I introduced myself.

"I just wanted to shake the hand of the man who made me famous." He was sent home by prosecutors and ordered to return sober the next day to testify.

The physical perils of investigative reporting are mainly fables perpetuated by journalists to add mystique to the craft. I rarely felt threatened in reporting on organized crime figures, alleged hit men, drug smugglers, Ku Klux Klansmen and scores of other nasty characters. An exception was a union goon who promised me information about an insurance scam involving his boss. I recognized the name when he called. He had been indicted a few weeks earlier for busting heads at a non-union job site.

We agreed to meet at a Howard Johnson's restaurant on the outskirts of Fort Lauderdale. As I arrived in the parking lot, his car pulled alongside, and he told me to get in. I complied instinctively and off we went into the Everglades along a highway known as "Alligator Alley." Only then did it occur to me that I was seated next to a giant, a head taller, weighing three hundred pounds, and under indictment for attempted murder.

Speeding past the last vestiges of civilization, I worried that this was a set-up. I had recently exposed an insurance scam involving the business manager of his union. As I contemplated my fate, he rattled off a list of criminal activities in the local. But I was so busy considering ways to get out of the car that I barely heard him. It would be a better story if he planned to kill me, and I fought my way to safety. But he was a true informant. The incident made me more cautious in meeting sources at out-of-the-way places.

In Mexico, Colombia and other countries, killing reporters is commonplace. Shooting the messenger is rare in the United States. However, as recently as 2007, a gang was arrested for killing Oakland, California *Post* editor Chauncy Bailey in reprisal of his reports alleging that a Muslim bakery was a front for criminal enterprises.

In June, 1976, *Arizona Republic* reporter Don Bolles was killed by a bomb planted in his automobile. The Bolles' murder was the impetus for the growth of Investigative Reporters and Editors, (IRE). To send a message that killing journalists doesn't kill investigations, IRE formed a team of journalists to finish the Bolles story. A comprehensive series of investigative stories appeared in several newspapers. A crooked land developer featured in the exposé was later convicted of the murder. The IRE posse approach to muckraking was so controversial that it has not been repeated.

A posse wasn't necessary to protect me from the sad sacks who came and went in the course of Florida's state-wide grand jury proceedings. My close-up view of these desperados reinforced a sinking feeling that I had failed to abide by Meyer Lansky's admonition, "All that is written is not truth."

As a rule, cops don't maliciously mislead reporters. But regardless of the profession, people want to see tangible evidence of their hard work. Because of the complexity of organized crime investigations, most never reach the indictment stage. So when underworld characters are ar-rested, lawmen loudly trumpet their successes. Such was the case in August, 1975, when I witnessed a spectacle in-stigated by detectives from the Organized Crime Bureaus of both Dade and Broward counties. The two agencies conducted a joint raid on an Italian social club purported to be a Mafia hangout.

Prior to the bust, television and newspaper report-ers were alerted that something big was going down. We were summoned to a midnight rendezvous and briefed on "one of the most significant raids on organized crime in the last decade."

Afterwards, we moved in a convoy to Hallandale and positioned a block away from an unimposing one-story building said to be the site of a mob-connected gambling operation. A wrecker moved into position and attached a hook to a steel-reinforced backdoor. "Police, open up!" someone shouted. Without waiting for a response, the door was jerked from its hinges. Weapons drawn, cops stormed inside.

A half-hour later, reporters were treated to the sight of a bunch of elderly Italian men sitting like mannequins at card tables with chips still in front of them. The suspects were ordered not to move until television and newspaper photographers got video. Following the photo session, twenty people were marched to police vans. Detectives recited the criminal histories of each suspect parading before cameras.

I recognized Emilio Delio, who seemed to pop up everywhere. "The Count" alternately laughed at cops and glared at newsmen. Asked to comment, he shrugged, "I'm no angel, if that's what you mean."

As far as I know, neither Delio nor any of the characters in my "Peabody-award winning" series were angels. Few, though, were the kind of gangsters depicted in law enforcement documents. Or my television exposé.

A pivotal turning point in my loss of confidence in police intelligence was an incident that followed a casual conversation with an OCB detective. I mentioned to him that a chatterbox criminal defense lawyer made a doubtful claim to me that Meyer Lansky owned a stake in a chain of pornographic movies that were used for a money-laundering operation. The cop said he had never heard the story. A few weeks later, I ran across Lanksy's porno connection in OCB files. The information was attributed to a source "believed to be reliable." The date of the entry indicated the source was me.

My delusion of maintaining an arms-length relationship with Florida lawmen was finally expunged once and for all in the latter stages of the statewide grand jury probe. I was asked by a prosecutor to meet with the panel. He assured me there was nothing to be concerned about. The jurors simply wanted my advice on an issue. So I stepped inside.

"Our final report is being prepared," the jury foreman said. "We need your advice on how to ensure maximum news coverage."

I stammered some kind of answer, knowing with certainty that jurors saw me for what I was—a cop whore. Reformed prostitutes are often self-righteous to a fault. That may explain my longstanding distrust of lawmen.

The nation's future Attorney General was among the first to confront me about my public relations sideline. Janet Reno was then a thirty-seven year-old Assistant State's Attorney in Richard Gerstein's office. Even though I ravaged her boss in the Lincoln Mall series, we maintained a cordial relationship. I even acted as her chauffeur.

The offices of the State's Attorney were in a complex two miles from the Dade County Courthouse. A shuttle ran back and forth. If I happened to be heading to the courthouse and saw acquaintances at the bus stop, I usually offered them a ride. A couple of times, the lanky prosecutor crammed into my Vega, her knees touching the dashboard.

My casual friendship with Ms. Reno was severely strained in September, 1975. I accused her of foot-dragging in the prosecution of an insurance fraud case. The inquiry had begun after an ambulance-chasing attorney solicited a Dade County detective as a client. The lawman was investigating a burglary at the lawyer's waterfront home and mentioned that he had a minor fender-bender accident en route to the shyster's residence.

"You're sitting on a gold mine," the attorney advised him. To dig gold, the detective was referred to a specific doctor and told to complain of a sore neck. The lawyer promised to take care of everything else. The investigator immediately reported the solicitation to his superiors, who instructed him to go along with the ruse.

At every step, conversations with the lawyer and doctor were secretly recorded. The tapes were then turned over to Reno. Fourteen months passed and no charges had been filed. Frustrated by the delay, transcripts of the tapes were leaked to me. In a "gotcha" interview, I questioned Reno about her timid approach. She was rip-shit. Her eyes welled and her lips quivered in anger.

"I know yellow journalism. My dad was an investigative reporter for thirty years," she ranted. "You're nothing more than a yellow journalist and an OCB mouthpiece."

My defense was that the suspects had conspired on scores of claims while she dawdled. Reno didn't consider that relevant. In newspaper comments, she blasted OCB and me. "The release of this evidence will seriously hamper and in all probability prevent a successful prosecution of a major insurance fraud."

Despite her protestations, the scammers were ultimately convicted. Reno's deliberate nature as a young prosecutor was a precursor. Two decades later as U.S. Attorney General, she was repeatedly criticized for not being aggressive enough in the investigation of the Clinton White House. Antithetically, her prudence was an admirable quality. After succeeding Richard Gerstein as Dade County State's Attorney in 1978, she advised her staff to always remain alert for "signposts of innocence" in prosecuting cases. It is an important admonition. Too often, prosecutors ignore—even conceal—exculpatory evidence. For them, winning is more important than truth.

Over the course of my career, I regularly reassessed my perceptions of truth and my tactics in pursuit thereof—sometimes retrospectively. Investigative reporting is fraught with pitfalls and I frequently stumbled.

There was always the temptation to rely on ambush interviews and undercover video as a substitute for good journalism. My mugging of the widow of a murder victim caused me to re-think the propriety of sneak attacks.

Prominent Miami Beach criminal defense lawyer Harvey St. Jean—peripheral character in the Lincoln Mall investigation—was murdered in 1975 in a parking lot near his office. An imprisoned Colombian drug smuggler was suspected of hiring a hit-man to murder the attorney. St. Jean had collected $120,000 from the Colombian, ostensibly to bribe a federal judge. It was an old trick. Lawyer promises to fix a case he believes is winnable. Lawyer loses. Lawyer tells his client the judge reneged. When St. Jean lost, the client demanded a refund. The attorney made the fatal mistake of ignoring him.

The murder didn't end the disgruntled client's demands. St.Jean's law partner received a letter stating in effect, "It's up to you to settle the account." He was scared out of his wits and went into hiding. Showing extraordinary persistence for a man suspected of ordering the murder, the Colombian filed a handwritten claim in Probate Court seeking restitution from the lawyer's estate.

The petition alluded to a bribery scheme and identified St. Jean as a conduit for a payment to an unnamed "third party," presumably the Judge. The widow took the claim seriously. She agreed to meet the suspect at the Dade County jail where he was awaiting transfer to a federal penitentiary. In a trade-off of information, I told a homicide cop about the crudely written probate claim. In turn, he tipped me to the date and time of the jail house meeting. When Mrs. St. Jean arrived in the parking lot accompanied by her attorney, the cameraman and I leaped from the van.

"Why are you meeting the man who arranged your husband's murder?" I yelled. The lawyer tried to shield her. But I continued my wretched questioning.

"Are you planning to return the money your husband stole?"

I was embarrassed watching the film. It softened my approach to ambushing unsuspecting targets. I already had qualms about the tactic, which began a few weeks before when I stormed the office of an unsuspecting target, lights ablaze and shouting questions as he cowered behind his desk. Viewing the film, I wondered about my reaction under similar circumstances.

This is not to suggest that I became a diffident, goody-two-shoes reporter. But private citizens have a right to refuse interviews. Public officials are different. I had no misgivings about waylaying stonewalling politicians and bureaucrats with a camera. Nor did I exempt miscreant private citizens at the vortex of important public policy issues. Since I defined what public issues were important, it was easy to abide by the new code.

—

Improving my journalistic principles ran parallel to values I learned in AA. Five years sober in 1976, I was very much involved in the fellowship. Despite warnings about our too-early-in-sobriety marriage, Patricia and I had built a stable relationship. So stable, in fact, that she knocked me for a loop by announcing she wanted to be a momma.

The idea of starting anew as a daddy scared the hell out of me. I was only then reconciling with my three daughters and, to a lesser extent, with my son. His drug addiction led to repeated arrests and an Arkansas prison sentence for writing bad checks.

Although I had doubts about a fatherhood rerun, I agreed to file an application with the appropriate state agency. I figured nobody in their right mind would consider me as an adoptive father. But a few weeks later, we were contacted for an interview. I was resolved to being completely honest about my alcoholism, my failures as a father, and the concerns I had about starting a new family. When the caseworker arrived, I recited my alcoholic résumé.

"I understand the miracle of recovery," she said. "My brother has been in AA for eight years, and his life has completely turned around."

It was one of the benevolent coincidences that seemed to occur regularly in my sober life. We were soon declared suitable to adopt and placed on a waiting list for our new baby. Several weeks later, the caseworker called with news that she had found the perfect match for us.

"I've located brothers seven and three years old."

"We must have a bad phone connection. I thought you said brothers, seven and three years old." I understood her correctly. No infants. Growing boys.

After coming this far, the least we could do was meet them. The introduction took place in the friendly surroundings of a municipal park. Such encounters are both awkward and poignant. Parents and kids are auditioning for each other. The boys had lived in foster homes for more than a year and knew the score. They were neatly dressed in hand-me-down outfits, had fresh mop-top haircuts and displayed their best conduct.

Robert and Edward were taken from their birth mother because of her drug use and inability to properly care for them. Getting acquainted with us was low-key. While the social worker observed, we ate donuts, walked in the park and tossed a Frisbee. Rob and I watched a softball game. He said he liked playing ball but didn't own a glove or bat. I promised to get him equipment if he visited Patricia and me. Any doubts that I had about the adoption quickly diminished. We were all very comfortable together.

A week later, the caseworker brought the boys to visit us at our condo in North Miami. We headed straight for *K-Mart* to load up on gifts, including a glove, ball and bat for Rob. No gift was ever more appreciated.

"You said you would get me a glove and bat and you did," he kept repeating. He had lived a life of broken promises.

By the end of the day, Patricia and I were committed to making them a part of our lives. The adoption papers were signed in April 1976. It was my opportunity to correct my past failures as a parent. I dedicated myself to putting the needs of Rob and Ed ahead of my self-absorption—a goal easy to imagine but difficult to accomplish.

Prior to the adoption, I didn't realize the level of emotional energy that Patricia and I devoted to the marriage. Until now, our marital bond revolved around Alcoholics

Anonymous. The program met our spiritual and social needs. The adoption took our focus off of each other and gradually changed the relationship.

—

Even as my collection of awards grew, I could not rid myself of deep-rooted professional insecurities. As a defense mechanism, I embellished the importance of every bit of recognition that I received. A mid-seventies proliferation of post-Watergate books, news stories, and movies made muckraking an honorable craft and gave me bragging rights of being one. I got an ego boost from seeing my name in a *TV Guide* article and an obscure book titled *The Investigative Journalist: Folk Heroes of a New Era*. The only local television "folk heroes" in the book were a crosstown rival and me. I edged him out by a full paragraph in the book—a cause for celebration.

I had mostly weaned myself off the law enforcement teat and began doing my own digging. Very well, too. One of my exposés caught the attention of federal prosecutors, even though it was ignored by the media. My curiosity was peaked by a short article in a Miami business journal that reported the financing of a Broward County condominium development called the Executive House of Inverrary.

Ignoring a history of failed construction projects, the Teamster Pension Fund of New Jersey's Bergen and Passaic counties loaned brothers, Frank and Thomas Romano $4.7 million. It was the biggest ever real-estate loan by the

fund. For years, it had been a piggybank of the union's former boss, Anthony (Tony Pro) Provenzano.

Checking public records, I learned that a restaurateur
cousin of the Romano brothers held a forty-percent interest in the project. Less than a month before the loan, he
was photographed playing golf with Tony Pro at an exclusive golf club in California.

Real-estate records also revealed a convoluted deal in
which Provenzano acquired Thomas Romano's waterfront
home in Hallandale for $50,000 below market value. At the
same time, Tony Pro received an additional $50,000 in cash
in the transaction.

After documenting the dealings, I barged into the
Romano brothers' offices asking questions on camera.
They gave answers so straightforward that the film was
later subpoenaed by a federal grand jury in New Jersey.
The Romanos admitted that their cousin received his forty-
percent cut for arranging the Teamster loan through Tony
Pro. They also conceded that Provenzano got a sweetheart
deal on the waterfront home.

The timing of my story, July 30, 1975, was serendipi-
tous. As I was finishing research, Jimmy Hoffa mysteriously vanished. He was supposedly heading to a meeting
with Provenzano. As reporters scrambled to find Tony Pro,
a photographer and I tapped on the door of his recently
acquired Hallandale abode. Looking like someone out of
central casting for *The Godfather*, he came to the door in
Bermuda shorts, an expensive brocaded shirt and holding

a huge cigar. Forcing a smile, he denied any knowledge of Hoffa's whereabouts. The smile vanished when I tried to question him about his dealings with the Romano brothers. He offered a terse "no comment" and slammed the door shut.

The Romanos were subsequently indicted and convicted of diverting funds from the condominium loan. Provenzano was never charged in the investigation. However, he was convicted in 1988 in another racketeering case and died in a federal penitentiary. Jimmy Hoffa still hasn't called home.

I'm regularly asked the origin of investigative stories. My answer is that exposés beget exposés. The highest compliment is a tip from former adversaries. In early 1976, an attorney who previously represented a target of my muckraking tipped me to a story of widespread corruption in Miami's Building Inspection Department.

Two years earlier, seven people were killed when the south Florida headquarters building of DEA collapsed under the weight of fifty-seven automobiles parked on the roof. Inspectors had approved the parking deck, despite warnings by structural engineers that the building was not sturdy enough to support the weight of a thick concrete slab, let alone the cars. My lawyer source represented the family of one the victims. He provided me depositions and other evidence disclosing that the foreman supervising the deck construction had a history of making payoffs to city inspectors. The information became the basis of two investigative stories that in turn led to comprehensive series.

A newly retired police detective, who watched my first two stories, had conducted an undercover operation that documented a pervasive pattern of bribes on numerous building projects. He gave me transcripts of secretly recorded conversations in which city building inspectors were heard accepting bribes as small as fifty dollars to overlook serious construction defects. One inspector was caught on tape signing off on a structure without even entering the building because it was raining.

"There's no way I'm going up there and check that. It's too fucking wet. Let me sign it," he told the builder.

The ex-cop collected overwhelming evidence of rampant corruption. However, the Dade County prosecutors failed to indict anyone. Instead, inspectors were allowed to quietly retire with full pensions. When questioned, city officials and prosecutors blamed each other for the manner in which the investigation was handled.

Following my disclosures, the probe was reopened. But by then, potential witnesses were long gone. The extent of the shoddy inspections hit home in 1992 when Hurricane Andrew struck south Florida and flattened thousands of structures.

The building inspection series was my final story of any significance in Miami. Patricia and I were looking to move from our cramped two bedroom condo to a neighborhood with better schools when I ran across an ad in *Broadcasting* magazine that seemed tailor made for me.

"Seeking Director of Investigative Reporting. The ideal candidate is a tenacious, creative, accurate and hard-working journalist dedicated to his or her craft and to exposing abuse of power wherever it may exist."

Even though my Miami Peabody awards were tainted by my over-dependence on cop-sources, that didn't stop me from beginning all job application letters with, "Dear Sir or Madam, I am a Peabody award winning, etc."

The phrase was a door opener. How else does an un-dereducated ex-drunk from Tuscaloosa High School find himself seated in a plush leather chair in the Harvard Club on Boston's Commonwealth Avenue being interviewed for an important journalism job by Professor Oscar Handlin, a Pulitzer Prize winning historian who spoke so softly through clenched teeth—an affectation of many high brow intellectuals—that I scarcely heard a word he said? I must have nodded and smiled at the right times.

The meeting was the final of five interviews before I was hired as Director of Investigative Reporting for WCVB—a Boston ABC affiliate then described by the *New York Times* as "the best local TV station in America." The multi-member investigative unit was WCVB's latest innovation. I seemed an unlikely candidate to head a department in such a high-falutin' environment. However, station executives were unfazed by my modest academic background and trailer trash history.

The search committee was led by Bill Poorvu, the station's Vice President and Treasurer. A Harvard graduate and faculty member, he was a quintessential preppie. I expected him to break into a few choruses of "Boolah, Boolah" at any moment.

News Director and committee member Jim Thistle was a fidgety, chain-smoking pragmatist. He climbed through the television ranks as a photographer, field producer and news executive. Jim was the least enthusiastic over the new endeavor. An investigative unit would consume his production and technical resources. Jim's vacillation later manifested itself in the attitudes of other newsroom personnel.

WCVB Editorial Director Phil Balboni was the only committee member to address my academic deficiencies. I was equipped with sufficient polysyllabic bullshit to bluff my way through his interrogation. He envisioned doing commentaries in conjunction with investigative unit exposés.

My most spirited supporter was Public Affairs Director Larry Pickard. He foresaw a unit that developed segments for a planned magazine show. In the last days of a long TV career, he was nearing retirement—the lone committee member without a college degree. He would soon obtain that degree from Boston University.

With committee approval, Bill Poorvu offered me a job that paid $10,000 a year more than WCKT. A three-year contract included annual raises and moving expenses.

At Bill's suggestion, Patricia had accompanied me to Boston. To get a feel of the city before making a decision, we took a ride on the MBTA. Fortuitously, we chose the Green Line that took us to Brookline, Newton and suburbs with the kind of New England ambience found on postcards. Choosing another subway line may have discouraged us from moving to the country's fifth largest TV market.

Gene Strul was moderately distressed by my departure. But he was accustomed to seeing reporters come and go. WCKT had been a jumping off point for the careers of many newsmen. Nonetheless, we had worked well together. As matter of formality, he offered me a small salary boost. However, I couldn't pass up the opportunity.

With the benefit of hindsight, I now recognize that my experiences in Miami and Baton Rouge had more in common than I realized. Bigger does not necessarily translate into a better environment for investigative reporters. It is the ownership of television stations that makes a difference. WCKT and Baton Rouge's WBRZ were both family owned. The bottom line of the balance sheet was certainly important. But there were no stockholders to please. Nor did they bow to pressure from advertisers and politicians.

Edmund Ansin and his father, Sydney, had acquired WCKT in 1963. The Federal Communications Commission stripped the previous owners of the license for ethics violations. Ed ran the station. And like my Louisiana journalism hero, Douglas Manship, he displayed courage in a business known for spinelessness.

I first became of aware of his oversized testicles in the midst of the Lincoln Road investigation when he asked if I were doing a story on a particular racetrack owner—an advertiser with a lot of pull in Miami. I confirmed that the guy was part of an exposé. Ansin was unfazed.

"That's fine. He's been calling me, and I don't want to return the call if you're doing a story."

Ed showed the same toughness a dozen years after I left Miami. NBC threatened to strip WCKT of its network affiliation because of the station's refusal to carry mandated programs. The threat became a reality when NBC bought the CBS affiliate. In turn, CBS tried to buy WCKT. When Ed rejected a lucrative offer, people thought he was crazy.

As the bell tolled midnight December 31, 1989—the final day of the WCKT's NBC ties—he shrugged off reports that his stubbornness might cost him $100-million.

"It doesn't bother me," he told a mutual friend. "I still own my TV station."

Ed enjoyed the last laugh. He changed the call letters to WSVN, and the station operated as an independent. Very successfully. At a time when news departments were shrinking, WSVN expanded, though not without criticism. The station was disparaged for pioneering "if it bleeds, it leads" sensationalism.

The new format made Gene Strul's tabloid approach seem like the BBC's reverent account of a death in the

Royal family. But investigative reporting survived. Carmel Cafiero, recruited by Gene from Baton Rouge in 1973 at my suggestion, eventually took over the role as muckraker. Thirty-plus years after I left, she continues to dig dirt.

By placing an emphasis on news and public affairs, WSVN prospered as an independent and emerged as south Florida's most profitable station—thanks in part to the introduction to viewers of reporters like Rick Sanchez. He personifies a breed of reporter who believe viewers tune in to see them, rather than learn what is going on in the world. Maybe they are right. He is a CNN anchor as this is written.

Anyway, WSVN was among the first stations in 1996 to sign on as an affiliate of "Fair and Balanced" Fox News. By then, Ed Ansin's Sunbeam Broadcasting had bought the CBS affiliate in Boston. The sale caused many staid TV pundits to wring their hands in anxiety that a Sanchez clone would be sicced on New England. But like it or not, there is no fighting television's emphasis on personality over content, and murder and mayhem over substance. Viewers are given what they apparently want.

And get what they deserve for watching.

CHAPTER ELEVEN

A REDNECK IN BLUEBLOOD LAND

I learned in Boston that bigger is not better—especially for a misfit. Before my arrival in New England, a *Boston Globe* article hyped me in glowing terms as "A nationally-known television investigative reporter, whose exposés of corruption and racketeering won him prestigious Peabody Awards in successive years, plus numerous other journalistic honors, joins Ch. 5 next month." It was nice to read, but the newspaper missed a more interesting story. I possessed a résumé unlike any investigative journalist in Boston. Or in most major cities for that matter.

Anyway, Bill Poorvu told the *Globe* the unit was "unique because of its absolute independence. The investigative team would devote its undivided attention "to rooting out the abuses of power, wherever they may exist." Unfortunately, I was not up to the challenge. My crimson nape was evident from the day I first parked an electric blue AMC Matador with racing stripes in a spot reserved for WCVB department heads.

Although my wardrobe of polyester suits and plaid jackets was less tacky than the white-on-white costume I wore for my 1973 television debut, I only had to glance at the people around me to realize I needed to make an emergency trip to Filene's Bargain Basement. But fashion was the least of my shortcomings in a city famous for its

Beacon Hill elite. I was sorely lacking academically, personally, professionally and culturally.

There is an AA twist on the old story of a New England farmer telling a lost city slicker, "You can't get there from here." The AA version for members who rise from the gutter to improbable positions is "You can't get here from there."

That's the story of my life.

—

I was sixteen-years-old when I graduated from Tuscaloosa High School and barely seventeen when I was expelled from the University of Alabama. During my single semester in an institution of higher learning, I failed every class. It was a blow to momma and daddy. Despite high school mediocre grades, they believed their only child was an under-achieving genius and enrolled me in college.

Daddy, a civilian inspector for the Army Quartermaster Corp, was transferred from Tuscaloosa to Columbus, Georgia a month after my high school graduation. So my "higher education" began two hundred miles from parental supervision.

Momma and daddy were convinced that a college degree would make me "somebody." Being "somebody" was a household mantra. Neither of my parents made it past tenth grade and struggled financially most of their lives. Helping me unpack in a university dormitory was a new and exciting experience for them. Sadly, the excitement soon turned into shattering disappointment.

In February, 1953, a self-appointed protector of my welfare informed daddy of my expulsion. That was only the beginning of the bad news. More stunning was news that my high school sweetheart was pregnant, and we planned to elope. Actually, Glenda Adams and I were already on the road to Mississippi to recite our vows. There was also another tidbit to disclose. Daddy's little boy had developed a serious drinking problem.

During my five month college stay, I drank at every opportunity and usually got falling down drunk. I had discovered in my high school senior year that booze helped me overcome the inadequacies I felt among older classmates. My insecurities hibernated while I was under the influence.

Therefore, I obliterated a sense of impending doom with a bottle of gin the night before my parents got the news of my failure. But the day of reckoning was now upon me. The notice of my expulsion was in the mail, Glenda was pregnant, and I was certain that her daddy was going to kill me. The only solution was to drink until I passed out.

Waking the next day, I took frantic steps to handle my predicament. At about the same time daddy received the telephone call, I persuaded a pal to chauffeur Glenda and me sixty miles to a marriage mill in Lowndes County, Mississippi.

For couples in a hurry, there were no blood tests or waiting period. Sign a marriage certificate, stand in front of a Justice of the Peace and become legal. In this instance, he made a feeble attempt to dissuade us from taking the big step. He noted that we didn't look old enough to get married. But he didn't care as long as I paid his fee.

Moments before the ceremony, a sheriff's deputy entered the office with a prisoner in tow. He echoed similar concerns about our ages, and even made a half-hearted attempt to scare us by claiming our parents called him to stop the wedding. The lie wasn't nearly as convincing as the certainty of what was going to happen when Glenda's daddy found out I got his oldest daughter pregnant. He was a former boxer with a bad temper.

After the deputy had his say, he handcuffed the prisoner to a telephone pole outside and stood as a witness while the Justice declared us pregnant child bride and hung-over child groom. We were back in Tuscaloosa before dark. By then, my parents were in town. Fearful of the family reunion, I had my friend take Glenda to her home while I went into hiding to try my hand at forgery. Using whiteout, I predated the wedding certificate to September. Perhaps this would spare me an ass-whipping.

Around eight o'clock, my bride tracked me down to report that our parents were gathered at her home awaiting my appearance. She had already confessed to both families that we were married, and she was pregnant—in that chronological order. Recognizing the moment of truth had arrived, I conjured lies for my speech in presenting the crudely forged marriage certificate at the impromptu wedding reception.

A grim group of prospective grandparents greeted me. The somber delegation listened as I attempted to convince them that we were an old married couple. I produced the marriage document as proof. Daddy noted that the ink was still wet. I immediately confessed to being a forger. Everybody was in a state of shock. Luckily, Glenda's heartbroken father was so numbed by the news he didn't have the energy to beat me up.

Options were discussed. Annulment was rejected as impractical because of the pregnancy. Abortion was never considered. The only solution was acceptance. To avoid the disgrace of a premature baby, our parents jointly decided to get us out of Tuscaloosa. Glenda's belongings were packed into my parents' car, and we headed to Georgia. Our wedding night was celebrated where it began. In the backseat of daddy's car.

As under-educated seventeen-year-old newlyweds with a child on the way, we seemed destined for one of those pockets of ugliness called "trailer parks." Trailer parks have no resemblance to neat, tree-lined mobile home communities where silver-haired AARP members exchange memories and discount coupons. Nor do they look like Mother Nature's tornado targeted, "it sounded like a freight train" working class neighborhoods like the one where daddy died in the only home he ever claimed pride of ownership.

In my mind's eye, "trailer parks" are sinister-looking roadside ghettos with dilapidated mobile homes

pockmarked by peeling aluminum siding, air condition-
ers tilting precariously from window sills, and battered
old cars and trucks mounted on concrete blocks as monu-
ments to the procrastination of no-accounts who drink
whiskey, smoke dope, and force their families to live in
such odious conditions. That seemed our destination. And
if life were truly fair and we got our just desserts, we would
have ended up there—borrowing jumper cables from our
next door neighbor, Jimmy Swaggart.

I was as ill-equipped to be a husband and daddy as
anybody could be. My work experience consisted of bag-
ging groceries at a supermarket, and a few days trying to
sell Bibles door-to-door one summer. Now, as a married
man in Columbus, I embarked on new careers. The first job
was folding clothes in a coin operated laundry. That lasted
eight hours—two hours longer than my second career of
selling food and oil change discount coupons. Neither career panned out, so I pursued the best option for a seven-
teen- year-old future daddy lacking any discernible skills.
I enlisted in the U.S. Air Force.

Six hours elapsed between the time I walked into a
recruiter's office and my departure from Columbus on the
way to Basic Training at Lackland Air Force Base in San Antonio, Texas. Three months in Texas was followed by eight
months in Communications School at Keesler Air Force
Base in Biloxi, Mississippi. Glenda and I rented a one-room
studio apartment in an old mansion facing the Gulf of Mexico. And like kids playing house, we tried to act grown up.

Michael was born at Keesler's hospital in September, 1953. He came home to immature parents, one of whom was a nascent alcoholic. His future would be marked by years of tragedy.

The Air Force offered better opportunities than folding clothes at a Laundromat or selling coupon booklets door-to-door. Liquor, however, interrupted my quest to become "somebody." At every assignment during my four years in the military—Texas, Mississippi, Okinawa, and Northern California—alcohol-related incidents got me in trouble. Before and after reaching the legal age to buy booze, I had car crashes, barroom brawls and run-ins with cops. My crazy behavior finally resulted in a referral to a military shrink. The session lasted half an hour. He asked why a young kid like me drank so much. I said "I don't know." He said, "Don't drink so much." I said, "Okay."

The advice worked for a few months. I held on to my buck sergeant rank and finished my Air Force career at a radar installation across the bay from San Francisco. Given my antics, an Honorable Discharge in 1957 bordered on miraculous. By then, our family had expanded. Patti and twin daughters, Sherri and Terri, were born a year apart.

For four years, the Air Force served as surrogate parents—putting food on the table, keeping a roof over our heads, providing health care, and occasionally spanking me for misbehavior. I had to fend for myself in civilian life. Momma and daddy had moved to southern California two years earlier, and we settled nearby.

The military taught me Morse code and teletype operation. Neither craft was in demand in civilian life. Setting out to find my calling, I changed jobs and addresses five times over the next two years.

I was first a butcher-trainee in a supermarket. A month later, I was fired in possession of all my fingers—"a miracle," said the meat-cutting supervisor. The thrill of whirling knives was followed by a lazy man's job as a timekeeper in a Fruehauf Trailer Company factory. Every hour or so, I walked along an assembly line to determine if all the workers were still there. Glenda, the four children and I were cramped into a converted garage in an industrial neighborhood near Fruehauf.

After surviving a year of monotony, I decided to seek my fortune as a door-to-door salesman. Attempts to sell the *Great Books of the Western World* took us to the brink of starvation. But it was great experience for a future muckraker. Persuading a plumber that plunging toilets is made easier by reading Aristotle is far trickier than convincing bureaucrats to turn loose of sensitive documents.

Following my *Great Books* failure, I became a Fuller Brush man. Selling brushes and household products put food on the table. But not enough. When a Cocker Spaniel nearly made me a soprano, I turned in my brush case to join an itinerant band of hucksters selling massage chairs at West Coast fairs and carnivals. The vibrating chair tour was a drunken road trip. I returned home hung-over, broke and in despair. We were now on the verge of eviction from our North Hollywood apartment because of rent delinquencies.

Although long-term sobriety was a dozen years away, I was beginning to see a connection between my drinking, job-hopping and irresponsibility. Periodically, I went "on the wagon." And short-term abstinence paid dividends. I was hired as a truck-driving potato chip salesman. For the first time in civilian life, I brought home regular paychecks.

Just as importantly, I learned a work ethic, showing up on time and staying until the work was finished. Steady wages allowed us to buy a home, a late model car, and give a passable imitation of "middle class." I managed Michael's peewee baseball team, participated in non-drinking social activities and we attended church.

Regrettably, "on the wagon" is an easily broken vow. And my sporadic drinking episodes were usually disastrous. After celebrating with potato chip co-workers at the Los Angeles Coliseum where the Dodgers first played when moving West, I got so drunk I could barely stand up. Following the game, we were in a minor traffic accident. The driver of the other car turned out to be pitching star, Don Drysdale, and a crowd gathered as police wrote a report. I was a passenger in the backseat and told to stay there.

But certain that Drysdale would love to meet me, I emerged to introduce myself. The cops investigating the accident ordered me back in the car. Offended, I took a swing at one of L.A.'s finest. I was charged with disturbing the peace and hauled to jail. It was not my first trip to the slammer, nor the last.

While under the influence, I had a fondness for losing battles with gendarmes. Overseas, I kicked a Japanese policeman who was ejecting me from a nightclub. Rather than beat my brains out, he released me to the military. My commander gave a stern go-and-sin-no-more lecture.

The night I returned from Japan, Seattle cops put a sizeable knot on my head after I flailed at them. They were summoned because I mistook a public sidewalk for a urinal. After a night in jail, my fate was again left to the military. I received another lecture.

In Northern California, I was taken to jail after a DUI arrest. This time, I managed to keep the misadventure a secret from the military and avoided a lecture. Instead, a judge lectured while imposing a fine of a couple hundred dollars.

The arrest in Los Angeles was acutely embarrassing. Co-workers had witnessed my alcoholic insanity. The charge was dropped on the condition that I attend Alcoholics Anonymous meetings. It seemed rather harsh to make me associate with a bunch of drunks, winos and skid row bums. But I attended a couple of meetings and was surprised to see people all spruced-up. They appeared almost normal. I was happy for them.

In spite of tumbles from "the wagon," I kept my potato chip job. My gentle touch stacking and rotating bags of potato chips had the makings of a long career. But ever since I first learned to turn a radio dial, I had a fantasy of becoming a play-by-play sportscaster. My goal was later amended to be a rock and roll disc jockey. Using the GI Bill, I enrolled at Columbia School of Broadcasting in Los Angeles.

I dropped out after four semesters. Too often, I was sidetracked on the way to classes by visits to taverns. That didn't deter me from applying for an announcing job at one of the biggest stations in Los Angeles. Invited to audition, I suffered a humiliation that nearly ended my plans for a radio career.

After an engineer sat me down to read news copy, my southern drawl generated smiles, giggles and guffaws in the control room. Seeing the reaction, my audition went from bad to god-awful. The engineer must have felt sorry for me. Before leaving, he gave me some advice. "The President's name is pronounced I'zan hou'er, not Aaahs'an-haar."

Realizing nobody would hire a broadcasting school drop-out who couldn't pronounce the President's name, I gave up. Rather than relive mortifying rejection, it was better to spend the rest of my life delivering potato chips. Fortunately, JFK was elected three years later. I was able to pronounce Kennedy. And a new opportunity came along,

During the 1961 Christmas holidays, I cried on my uncle's shoulder about my unfulfilled disc jockey and sports announcing dreams. Uncle Harry was dad's younger brother. A sales executive at NBC's Los Angeles affiliate, he had suggested four years earlier that I enroll in broadcasting school.

A few days after our conversation, a co-worker of my uncle mentioned that a former NBC engineer was looking for an announcer-salesman at a small Northern California station he owned. Calling itself the *Voice of the Mother Lode*, KVML was located in the historic gold rush town of Sonora in the foothills of the Sierra Nevada Mountains, three hundred miles northeast of Los Angeles. Before contacting the owner, I divined a phony résumé which listed experience as an announcer for the Armed Forces Radio Network and an Alabama station with call letters that I fabricated.

References were unnecessary. I was the only applicant for the low-paying job.

Glenda, my parents and friends were all understandably skeptical about my giving up the security of potato chips for an unknown future in radio. But Glenda agreed to go with me to Sonora. Seeing the town was all it took to get her support. Creeks and rivers ran in and around the picturesque hamlet. Church steeples rose above a cozy business district. Dozens of mom-and-pop shops lined the main drag. The town's old west ambience was a reminder of its nineteenth-century founding during the gold rush era.

Sonora—population about two-thousand—was the biggest town in sprawling Tuolumne County and a gateway to Yosemite National Park and two other national forests. KVML's claim as the *Voice of the Mother Lode* was slightly exaggerated. In the mountainous terrain, its 250-watt AM signal barely reached beyond the city limits. Though not the smallest station in America, it was in the running. The most frequent comment I would hear about the station was, "I can't find it on the radio dial."

In my eagerness to start a broadcasting career, I was unconcerned about the strength of the signal or the station's future prospects. Very dim. Timber and tourism were the county's main industries. But labor turmoil put a huge dent in the economy. A strike had shut down Pickering Lumber Company, the area's biggest employer. Facing hard times, KVML owner Ralph Bowen was interested in hiring a salesman who could announce, rather than an announcer who could sell. He alluded to economic troubles, but I didn't press him for details. Ralph wasn't hiding anything. He was simply a tight-lipped, pocket-protector engineer. His nature was to solve problems, not talk about them.

Ralph's personality, religion and politics made it difficult for him to win the hearts and advertising dollars of a lot of Sonora merchants. Active in a small fundamentalist church, he was an Old Testament kind of Christian—harsh and judgmental of Tuolumne County businessmen who didn't live up to his standards. Financial hardships aside, he refused to solicit advertising from certain businessmen.

I kept my transgressions secret. For now, I was "on the wagon." In months to come, however, my iniquities would test his forgiveness of sinners.

KVML offered me eight-five dollars a week, plus commissions. It was about a third of my potato chip salary. The shortfall didn't bother me. I was brimming with confidence. My sales talents would make up the difference. So blinded by childhood dreams, I disregarded the risks of leaving a secure job, selling our home in North Hollywood and relocating the family in a mountain town where we didn't know a soul.

I won over Glenda with a sales pitch that pursuing my dream would make me a better husband and father, not to mention the benefits of raising our children in a small town. Moreover, the sacrifice was brief. KVML was a mere stopover on the way to rock and roll disc jockey stardom. Inspired by my own bullshit, I turned in the keys to my potato chip truck and headed to Northern California.

The family remained in North Hollywood for a few weeks to close the sale of our house. It had sold quickly, thanks to an assumable VA loan. Meantime, I stayed in a boarding house owned by the town's "gossip queen." A lifelong resident, she gave me names and histories of the county's drunkards, deadbeats, and loose women. My name would eventually be added to her list. For now, the Don Drysdale incident was like being hit in the head by one of his fastballs. It kept me dry for awhile. A good thing, too. I needed my fragile sobriety to keep food on the table.

Selling KVML ads required more skill than hawking Bibles, books, bouncing chairs and brushes. Merchants were reluctant to advertise on a station they couldn't find on the radio dial. Nor did they listen to KVML when finding the frequency. Fully automated, the station featured toe-paralyzing oldies dating back to the 1940's. The liveliest was *The Stripper*. Ralph considered dropping it because of the suggestive title.

The elevator music was intermittently interrupted by too few commercials and too many public service announcements. ABC News ran at the top of the hour, local newscasts at noon and six, and Paul Harvey commentary twice a day. The only other breaks were religious programs and Don McNeil's Breakfast Hour, network radio's last variety show. Since automation had replaced disc jockeys, my dreams of being a record-spinning star were dashed. All the clever patter that I collected was for naught.

Before the family's arrival, I found the best rental we could afford. It was a two-bedroom shotgun house that was half the size of our North Hollywood home. Glenda was justifiably distressed to see the asbestos-shingled shanty, one of three rentals adjacent to a cow pasture on a narrow road five miles from an improved highway. I promised her a better home when commission checks increased.

Meanwhile, we adapted to rustic living amazingly well. Deer and wildlife were abundant in the hills around us, and a creek located less than a mile away was stocked with rainbow trout. Glenda and the kids fished there nearly everyday during the summer. On work breaks I joined them—often wearing a coat and tie.

Though automated, FCC regulations required the station to be manned during broadcasting hours to monitor equipment and maintain logs. Someone was also needed to handle the minor mechanics of switching to network newscasts and other programs. The station was too small to be a network affiliate. News programming was picked-up via KGO in San Francisco. My shift was sign-on to noon. I spent the time writing and recording commercials, and scheduling sales appointments.

Afternoons were devoted to soliciting new accounts. Driving around the county, I kept the dial on KVML for as far as the signal reached, listening to the joyful sound of my voice delivering commercials that I recorded earlier in the day. Advertisers fell into categories of small, tiny and miniscule. It was not unusual to spend two hours selling fifty-dollars worth of radio spots to a *Dairy Queen* to earn a seven-dollar commission.

Although my disc jockey dreams were on hold, KVML satisfied my childhood fantasy of being a play-by-play sports announcer. As a kid, I spent many hours giving vivid accounts of my own athletic feats of running for game-winning touchdowns, hitting home runs and winning championship prizefights—all in the confines of my bed-room. Announcing imaginary feats prepared me to do a pretty good job as a football and basketball play-by-play broadcaster for the Sonora High School Wildcats.

But even before the opening kick-off of football sea-son, a career-altering event had taken place at KVML. The station's only other fulltime employee quit, leaving no one to gather and report news for our two local newscasts. The departure caused a crisis. The sponsored newscasts were vital to the station's financial survival. Ralph didn't do on-air work, and I was the lone remaining *Voice of the Mother Lode*.

"Have you ever done news reporting?" he asked. I hadn't done anything in a radio station before. But I didn't want to admit my résumé was a sham. It didn't make a dif-ference. Ralph appointed me "News Director."

Putting together a newscast was a complete mys-tery to me. I figured somebody handed radio newsmen a script and they read it. My ignorance was compounded by another problem. United Press International had repos-sessed KVML's wire service machine, our only source of state and regional news. Finding material to fill two news-casts seemed an impossible task.

I knew it was inappropriate to make up stories, even though later events in the national media disabused me of the belief that it never happened. The second option was to blatantly plagiarize Sonora's eight-page *Union-Democrat*. But it wasn't available until late afternoon, which didn't help me with the noon newscast. The last alternative was to go out and find stories. This was problematic. I didn't know where real reporters found stories. My predecessor once took me around the police beat. He had also left behind a list of news sources. It was an inauspicious start to a journalism career. But away I went.

My beat covered the Sheriff's office, the Police Department and the California Highway Patrol. I jotted down names of everybody arrested, and reported details of assaults, burglaries, thefts and fender-bending traffic accidents. The town's two funeral parlors furnished names of the newly departed, along with a list of survivors that included the immediate family, nephews, nieces, dogs, cats and livestock. On slow days, I hoped a lot of people died. Ralph banned the use of "in lieu of flowers." He didn't want to alienate Sonora's biggest florist, who was a regular KVML advertiser.

Regardless of the number of funeral notices, traffic accidents and crime reports, finding ten minutes of news each day was an awesome task. Hence, my newscast was filled with public service announcements and news releases. Most were read verbatim. There was, for instance, a convoluted notice giving a parade route that marched west to north to east to south through downtown Sonora. Hearing my report, Ralph pointed out it would have been simpler to say the parade was going to circle the Town Square.

Steadily, though, my judgment and writing skills improved. A *Broadcast News Stylebook* had been left behind by UPI. It was my first journalism textbook, teaching me the old radio adage, "Tell'em what you're going to tell'em, tell'em, and tell'em what you told 'em." It was a better lesson than the bare-bones stories written by my predecessor, which had not been very helpful.

For weeks, he repeated the same story word-for-word. "KVML talked to Mr. Momyer at Pickering Lumber Company today. He said there is no change in the strike."

That was his complete account of an issue affecting the pocketbooks of everybody in Tuolumne County. I gave listeners a more comprehensive report. In a burst of journalistic creativity, I wrote, "KVML talked to *Frank* Momyer at Pickering Lumber Company. He said there is no change in the strike."

Encouraged by my enterprise, I soon reported, "KVML also talked to representatives of the Sawmill Workers Union, and they report no change in the strike." I was on the road to becoming a newsman. I began reporting underlying issues that caused the labor discord, as well as the obstacles to settling the dispute.

An addiction to newsgathering was taking hold. I would grab the *Union Democrat* each day to see what I missed. Significant omissions were stories of government meetings and court proceedings. So I added the courthouse and City Hall to my news beat. To spice up newscasts, I got Ralph to buy me a portable tape recorder to do interviews and provide tape-delayed, on-the-scene reports. In the aftermath of major national stories, I did man-on-the-street interviews.

My newscasts began sounding almost professional as I became comfortable in my role as the *Voice of the Mother Lode*. I covered meetings of the City Council, County Board of Supervisors, School Boards and other government entities. Trips to the courthouse taught me how to track criminal and civil cases, read docket sheets and gather information from interrogatories, affidavits, and depositions. I became familiar with judicial procedures and protocols, and learned the rudiments of real-estate title searches. Working at a station where the wire service machine was repossessed made me a newsman out of necessity. Gradually, I gained confidence in my skills as a reporter.

The lessons I learned in Sonora were the most important of my investigative reporting career. They formed the foundation of my education as a journalist. All news is local. Tuolumne County's issues and government record-keeping were not much different than what I found in Baton Rouge, Miami, Boston and other metropolitan areas.

As the *Voice of the Mother Lode*, I was also introduced to live remote broadcasts in Sonora. In addition to play-by-play and occasional in-store promotions for advertisers, I did live reports from events like the annual county fair.

Every politician in a hundred mile radius came there to solicit votes and be interviewed on KVML. The highlight was the crowning of *Miss Tuolumne County*. We carried the pageant live, including a marathon talent show that seemed to feature every child who took tap dance lessons, played a musical instrument, sang a song, or otherwise had an inclination to go on stage. A formidable challenge was describing juggling acts. "Now it's up, now it's down. Oops, now it's on the floor."

The surrounding mountains were a backdrop for movies and TV shows, and brought moderately famous celebrities to town. During production of *Lassie* episodes, I arrived with my trusty tape recorder to interview Jon Provost, who played Timmy, and to get a bark or two from Lassie, the nation's most famous female impersonator.

My all time favorite "Hollywood" interview in Sonora was with Smiley Burnett, the movie sidekick of my childhood idol, Gene Autry. After the interview at the grand opening of a new supermarket, we talked about the ups and downs of his drinking career. Sober for several years, he enjoyed talking about his misadventures, as well as those of his friend, Gene. I was amazed that he openly discussed an affliction that I tried so hard to conceal. I was having too much fun to jeopardize my job by getting drunk.

In addition to my on-the-job training as a reporter, I took flying lessons—a broadcasting benefit called "bartering." Radio stations swapped ads for merchandise and services from advertisers who were unlikely to spend hard cash. Ralph let me barter flying lessons at Columbia Airport, the nation's only air field offering stagecoach service.

Columbia is a restored Gold Rush settlement. Visitors arriving by air could arrange a stagecoach ride into town.

Flight instructor, Lennart Strand, rarely advertised. Hence, he accumulated a decade worth of radio spots in our trade deal by giving me lessons and taking me as a passenger in my capacity as an "airborne reporter." I taped eyewitness accounts while soaring above fires, ground searches for lost hunters and other mishaps in adjacent national forests and parks.

Noteworthy were my attempts to track the legendary Abominable Snowman. Every so often, a hunter, hiker or resident claimed to have sighted a six-foot tall, howling beast scampering through the woods. As in the Loch Ness monster stories, the reports coincided with the beginning of tourist season. As KVML's intrepid journalist, I taped stories from two thousand feet, intoning something to the effect, "I don't see any sign of the creature, but in this heavily forested area he could easily be hiding."

Twenty air miles from Columbia airport across the Stanislaus River canyon is a county made famous by Mark Twain's short story, *The Celebrated Jumping Frog of Calaveras County.* The annual Jumping Frog Jubilee attracts "thoroughbred" frogs and owners from across the country. Before the 1963 jubilee, I climbed into the PA-11 and made the short hop to a grass airstrip at the Calaveras County fairgrounds. It would have been just as easy to drive. But that didn't have the exhilarating effect of landing my plane and taxiing up to frog jumping headquarters where I recorded interviews with promoters and competitors. The result was a three-minute feature for my newscast.

For the hell of it, I sent the tape to an ABC radio show called *Weekend West*. The five-minute program ran each Saturday. Surprisingly, I got a response from ABC programming executive, Ted Toll. "Very nice handling of the frogs," he wrote. "I've got it tentatively spotted for 9:30 network airing Sat., the 18th." The letter caused my knees to get weak and my bladder to contract. Not only did he like the piece, the network was paying me twenty-five dollars. It was my biggest broadcasting thrill to date.

In my three-plus years in Sonora, I stopped drinking for varying lengths of time. But Ralph Bowen discovered my secret eight months after we moved to Sonora when he learned of a two-day bender I went on over the Thanksgiving weekend. He said I could clean up my act by attending his holy-roller church. I pledged to be there on Sunday. I did, in fact, show up. But only once.

Ralph believed my promise of "never again." Glenda knew my pattern. Six months passed before I decided "One drink won't hurt me." They both knew that I reneged on my promise. But in the absence of catastrophes, they avoided a confrontation. As KVML's only fulltime employee, I had exceeded Ralph's expectations. Our newscasts were better than ever. I got good reviews for my high school play-by-play. And most importantly, I sold a lot of radio spots. Why rock the boat? Still, disaster was just a few sips around the corner. On main street, in fact.

Glenda either went with me to a downtown tavern, or came to fetch me home. Whichever, we had a loud argument that carried onto the street. A cop appeared. I knew him fairly well and it seemed appropriate to say, "Fuck off." He warned that I was in danger of being arrested and I said, "You don't have the guts to arrest me." He did.

At the jailhouse, friends poured coffee down me until I appeared sober enough to be released. I was charged with public drunkenness. Since no bad deed went unnoticed in Sonora, Ralph was waiting at the door when I reported to work. He launched into a harangue so fierce that I began packing my things. "What are you doing?" he asked.

"I thought I was fired."

"No, no. This is a final warning, though. Don't let it happen again."

The following Sunday night, I showed up at Sonora's only AA meeting. My attitude was better than in North Hollywood. However, I was still in the trial stage of sobriety. The fellowship seemed like cut-rate group therapy, and the Twelve Steps were some kind of voodoo. My brain shut down at the mention of a "Higher Power." Therefore, I took a cafeteria approach, nibbling at parts and ignoring the rest.

I attended meetings for a year, and my life improved. Maybe it was by osmosis. As with my trial sobriety in North Hollywood, we were able to buy a home, a better car, take vacations and avoid household disturbances. But ambition made it difficult for me to enjoy sobriety. My early disc jockey fantasy had been supplanted by a dream of being a famous journalist. To that end, I sent out job inquiries and got a response.

KUBA, a 5000-watt station in the Sacramento Valley town of Yuba City, contacted me about a job as News Director and play-by-play announcer. The station's sportscaster resigned only days before football season. I was invited to do a live audition of Yuba City High School's opening game of the season. I drove more than a hundred miles for the Saturday night tryout. The station owner was a former play-by-play announcer. He stood over my shoulder ready to step in if I screwed up. Midway through the first quarter, I saw him give a thumbs-up to my color commentator. By halftime, he had left the stadium. I was offered a job the following day.

Giving Ralph notice was like a marriage breakup. He raged about my ingratitude. I reminded him of my contributions to KVML. Sales increased, newscasts improved and the station was in better financial condition than ever. He said those were the reasons I should stay, intimating that I might someday be a part-owner. I may have ended-up owning the station outright. A coronary facilitated Ralph's early trip to the Pearly Gates.

I felt bad deserting him. And in view of future tragedies that beset our family, I can understand why Glenda has occasionally speculated that staying in Sonora could have saved us from future heartaches. Perhaps. But I can't brood over what might have been. One of AA's earliest lessons is accepting that the past is gone forever.

Two unrelated events prior to my departure from the *Voice of the Mother Lode* foretold the perilous future. The first was a two a.m. call from the Sonora Police Department informing us that our son had driven a car into a ditch. I told the cop he dialed the wrong number. Mike was only eleven years old and asleep in bed. He told me to check. Mike was gone. He had slipped out of bed, taken the car keys and silently backed down a winding driveway so steep that visitors had sometimes gone over the side. He then drove five miles before crashing into a ditch. Thankfully, he escaped injury.

The second ominous episode before leaving Sonora related to my sobriety. At a going away luau, friends served a spicy punch. Most likely, it was a virgin mixture. I drank the beverage without asking. And like Jesus turning water to wine, I turned the punch into booze in my mind. Feeling no effects, I decided my alcoholism was cured. Not only was I bidding farewell to Sonora, I no longer needed those damn AA meetings.

In September, 1965, I arrived in the "The Prune Capitol of the World," a distinction shared by the northern California Twin Cities of Yuba City and Marysville. Actually, they were twins in name only. Yuba City received a major facelift in the aftermath of a disastrous flood on Christmas Day, 1955. Thirty-eight people were killed when levees gave way near the confluence of the rain-swollen Yuba and Feather rivers. Reconstruction gave Yuba City the facelift. Across the bridge, ugly sibling Marysville showed all of the wrinkles and blotches of old age.

Marysville was a Gold Rush crossroads for fortune seeking "Forty-Niners" in the mid-1800's. A hundred years later, it was a crossroads for migrant farm workers. Before and during extended planting and picking seasons, hundreds of laborers arrived in the area. Many stayed to loiter along a bar-lined Marysville skid row. The downtrodden area exacerbated the downtown deterioration that began when merchants and businesses relocated to Yuba City's newly constructed shopping centers and office complexes.

My move to KUBA was a modest step up the career ladder. Eighty thousand people lived in the agriculturally rich counties where farmers grew peaches, almonds, rice, tomatoes and plums for prune processing. America's digestive tract was protected by three nearby missile silos. Strategic Air Command B-52's and high-flying SR-71 spy planes—known as "Blackbirds"—flew out of Beale Air Force Base.

Gathering news in the twin cities was much the same as in Sonora, but with a wider choice of stories. I made rounds to cop shops, attended government meetings and reported "breaking news." A clattering news wire made it unnecessary to fill newscasts with obituaries, news releases and mountain searches for illusory creatures.

Instead, I reported about real life political creatures who worked fifty-miles away in the Capitol City of Sacramento. I got my first taste of statewide politics traveling with Governor Edmund Brown on a campaign swing through Northern California. It was less than thrilling. At a dozen stops, he repeated the same speech to a few somber Democrats. He laughed at a potential rival who had not yet announced his candidacy. On the plane, Brown held up a magazine cover.

"Who is going to vote for this smiling sonofabitch?" he lightheartedly asked reporters.

Many people. The opponent was Ronald Reagan. In contrast to Brown's mind-numbing speeches, I watched the future President excite hundreds of cheering supporters at a "Prune Capitol" Republican rally. The enthusiasm presaged Reagan's political future.

Local GOP operatives arranged for me to interview the actor/politician at a late night fundraiser. By the time I arrived, he had retreated to a private dining room and instructed aides to keep people away while he and wife Nancy recuperated.

My escort interrupted the couple's rest break with a reminder of our interview just as their meal was being served. For Reagan, it was like a summons to a movie set for a scene. His weary demeanor changed in an instant as he walked over to shake hands.

"Sure. Let's move out of everyone's way."

I immediately displayed my political naiveté. "Are you now officially a candidate for Governor?" I asked. It was stupid to think he would officially announce his candidacy in an interview with an obscure Northern California radio reporter. But being a nice guy, he sidestepped the question, rather than say, "Of course I'm a candidate, you dumb shit. Why do you think I'm talking to you when I'm about to collapse from exhaustion?"

At the time, my political views were superficial at best. I was a Democrat because daddy said there was no other political party. Anyway, objective reporting is a myth. Journalists write stories based on life experiences, cultural backgrounds, education and eyesight. At KUBA, I started developing reasoned political views that tilted to the left.

I was influenced in large part by seeing societal ills first hand, such as migrant worker abuses and poverty. Nearby ghetto-like labor camps were the underbelly of agriculture. Already paid low wages, migrants were assessed outrageous rents for shacks with no running water or electricity.

I also saw first hand the gloom of farm workers in my daily stops at the Marysville Police Department. Because of the volume of arrests on skid row, a makeshift courtroom was set up inside the jail to avoid stinking up the courthouse. A judge conducted daily proceedings. He imposed sentences that were practical and compassionate. If a drunk showed symptoms of DT's, he was sent to the county penal farm to get medical attention. If still able to navigate, he was usually cut loose after paying a small fine, which was determined by the amount of money in his pockets.

Most of these poor souls were white male Americans, rather than blacks or Hispanics. Illegal immigration had not yet become a big issue in the country. Regardless of their race, creed or color, I never envisioned being in the same drunken condition. Yet, the jailhouse crowd became occasional drinking companions after I decided to test my theory that a punch concoction consumed in Sonora cured my alcoholism.

I don't recall what led me to uncork the bottle. I do remember forays into low class bars on Marysville's skid row. My choice of pals gives credence to a hypothesis that alcoholics search for places where they can find low-bottom drunks and say, "I'm not as bad off as these guys." My benders were infrequent in the Twin Cities. I avoided serious escapades and stayed out of jail. An injustice really. Enabling cops gave me breaks, even escorting me to an all-night café for coffee after I was pulled over for driving on the wrong side of a median, causing cars to swerve to avoid head-on collisions. By dodging jail, divorce or getting fired, I believed my worst drinking days were over.

I didn't spend enough time at KUBA to truly test the delusion. After eighteen months in Yuba City, I moved forty miles north to KPAY in Chico to head a staff comprised of a second reporter in the main newsroom, a correspondent in the Butte County seat of government in Oroville and two part-time reporters in outlying communities, known as stringers. This was my first News Director job in which I actually directed somebody. But I was a traveling man. In less than a year, I was on the road again to Baton Rouge—a city, state and radio station I knew nothing about.

WJBO manager "Ravin' Dave" Davison recruited me as News Director and anchor of a statewide public affairs program. I had been recommended to him by my station manager in Yuba City, who had recently moved to Louisiana. The salary and perks in Baton Rouge were better than any during my six years in broadcasting. And the Capitol news beat was appealing. I was long past reporting on the leaps of jumping frogs and giving airborne accounts of mythical mountain monsters.

Glenda strongly opposed the move to Baton Rouge. It was two thousand miles from her momma and daddy, who like my parents, had moved to Southern California. I convinced her that moving to Louisiana was an important step up the career ladder. But even before we unloaded a U-Haul trailer at our new residence, Glenda's sense of foreboding came to pass. Our new neighbors welcomed us with a six-pack of beer.

From then until my perceived epiphany in a rundown halfway house in 1971, I descended into alcoholic madness.

—

Five years after hitting bottom, sobriety led me on a remarkable journey to Boston from a gutter in New Orleans. It was amazing that "I got here from there."

I tried to convince myself that I was now a big success—professionally and personally. But I was bullshitting the bullshitter. I was not the guy I thought I was.

CHAPTER TWELVE

REAL REPORTERS DON'T DO HAPPY TALK

WCVB was owned by Boston Broadcasters Incorporated — a mix of television executives, academics, local businessmen and silk-stocking professionals. In a controversial 1972 ruling, the Federal Communications Commission stripped the *Herald Traveler* newspaper of its valuable Channel Five license and awarded the permit to Boston Broadcasters, which had made unparalleled promises to operate in the public interest. The FCC decision was based on ancient allegations of inappropriate conduct in the initial approval of the license fifteen years earlier. The dispute centered around a secret agreement that was purportedly formulated at a 1957 luncheon meeting between the Commission Chairman and a lawyer representing the *Herald Traveler*. Losing the TV station sent the publishing company spiraling into bankruptcy. Boston Broadcasters prospered.

For ten years, WCVB lived up to its *New York Times* "best TV station" accolade. But in 1982, Boston Broadcasters decided to collect the spoils. The station was sold for $224 million—the highest price ever paid for a local TV station at the time. The sale was pivotal in broadcasting history. It launched a nationwide seller's market.

Big corporations began acquiring local stations and consolidating them into media conglomerates. The FCC soon abandoned limits on the number of license permits that a single corporation could own. Money-changers took over television.

Before Boston Broadcasters succumbed to the temptation of big profits, many hours were devoted to public service such as town hall forums on volatile issues like school desegregation. The station was noted for original programming, hard-edged newscasts and incisive commentaries. Dr. Timothy Johnson, the founding editor of *Harvard Medical School Health Letter*, and Harvard legal scholar Arthur Miller were contributors to newscasts. Both became expert commentators for ABC News.

The creation of an investigative team was another WCVB innovation. Only after the fact did I learn it was impractical to rake muck under the guidance of a five-member committee. Each had a different concept of the station's investigative reporting goals.

Bill Poorvu preferred polite exposés. He once opposed my plan to film a recalcitrant grand jury witness playing daily rounds of golf after claiming that ill-health prevented him from testifying. Bill considered the tactic underhanded.

Professor Oscar Handlin suggested stories in committee meetings that were akin to abstract dissertations. Phil Balboni favored reports on systemic abuses ripe for editorials. Larry Pickard wanted segments to fit in his magazine show. Jim Thistle supported exposés that didn't overburden his newsroom resources.

Me? I just wanted to be a "real reporter." Boston was the "big time," and I was eager to impress other journalists with my digging and interviewing skills. However, it was a bad time to establish bona fides for serious reporting. TV news was changing. My obsession with legitimacy did not bode well for the future.

The Investigative Unit never reached its potential. I don't mean to snivel, but there was shared blame. WCVB promised me a staff of a second reporter, a researcher and a fulltime producer. But even before I arrived, plans for the highly-touted unit were scaled back. My staff consisted of a former wire service reporter who had never before worked in television. She was a one-exposé wonder, uncovering only a single story that qualified as investigative. I had veto power after interviewing her in Miami. However, I didn't have the guts to alienate the committee by suggesting she was under-qualified.

This was the first of several mistakes I made in Boston. In retrospect, I see that I was a victim of "Peter's Principle"— the theory that promotions ultimately elevate people to levels of incompetence. I was a good reporter. However, I failed to accept my limitations as a producer.

My reporting partner quit in less than a year—a casualty of a committee blunder and my inadequacy as a mentor. Before leaving, we worked together on the Investigative Unit's debut exposé. It was an eight-part series about the Boston Police Department's cover-up of widespread misconduct by off-duty policemen working on private security details. The jobs were an important source of supplemental income for cops.

Especially galling to cops was the well-founded suspicion that my information came from the department's much-despised internal affairs division. Indeed, the former head of the section slipped me a trove of documents. He was outraged at top brass for concealing and/or glossing over the results of his division's investigation.

The Police Patrolmen's union loudly complained about the series. Cops took out their anger on the station's reporters. Their phone calls were unanswered, tips from previously friendly detectives stopped, and police quit cooperating with WCVB at crime scenes. I got hints from the newsroom to ease up. The reaction foretold the future.

In response to creation of an investigative unit, WCVB's cross-town rival formed a bigger unit, called the *I-Team*. Westinghouse-owned WBZ created a seven-member investigative department. The on-air correspondents, Alan Lupo and Wally Roche, were disheveled, ink-stained newspaper journalists whose New England accents immediately identified them as hometown boys. They were the antithesis of TV personalities.

I was downright handsome compared to Alan and Wally, even with my oversized jowls and droopy eyelids. That is not saying much. As a "real journalist," I rejected hair spray, makeup, cosmetic succors, and/or surgical scalpels.

When a casual acquaintance at a social gathering learned of my job for the first time, she asked, "Are you actually on TV?" Acknowledging that I was left her dumbfounded. "You look so ordinary."

I endured yet another blow to the charisma in a newspaper article that was mostly complimentary of my muckraking talents, but under-whelmed by my appearance. The writer described me as looking "more like an insurance agent than an investigative reporter." The insurance man was not identified. Presumably, he was ordinary looking.

Anyway, I was well aware that TV folks were supposed to look like TV folks and took no offense to the portrayal. If my muckraking show closed in Boston, maybe I could get a job selling insurance.

After my first teammate left me, I was given latitude in selecting a replacement. So long as it was a woman. I hired a young reporter named Michal Regunberg. She had built an impressive record of enterprise reporting at the Springfield, Massachusetts *Union*. We worked together well and for the next three years, our unit held its own against WBZ's bloated *I-Team*. It seemed, though, that the two investigative units were in competition to produce the most boring exposés in a city known for sensational scandals and spectacular crimes such as the Brink's robbery.

Focusing on government corruption, I exposed a City Hall bid-rigging scandal in a 1977 document-heavy story that earned a regional Emmy. In fact, it was the first ever New England Emmy. Investigative Reporting happened to be the initial category at a pretentious televised award's show hosted by talk show host Phil Donahue.

It was my chance to do an exposé about our self-congratulatory conceit. Instead, I muttered insipid clichés. Other winners delivered the same vacuous acceptance speeches, thanking co-workers, spouses and concubines. I love awards, but hate award ceremonies.

Notwithstanding the Emmy and a few other prizes, the Investigative Unit's stories failed to excite newsroom producers—mainly due to my lack of production skills, which I failed to acknowledge. I was too eager to get my face on television. I failed to realize that my on-camera narrations were a poor substitute for creative visuals. The handicap was most obvious in a 1978 series revealing what was then one of the biggest income tax swindles in IRS history.

"This is a story about the world of high finance, foreign bank accounts, coal and diamond mines, real estate and movie investments," I reported. "The characters include Broadway producers, hucksters and fast moving lawyers. The story is also about a king-sized attempt to avoid pay-ing federal income taxes."

The exposé had all the elements of an interesting yarn. Among the tax avoiders were Elvis Presley, *Candid Camera*'s Allen Funt, model/actress Margaux Hemingway, and NBA basketball stars Earl (The Pearl) Monroe and Spencer Haywood. In my hands, the story resulted in widespread yawns.

The nine-part series exposed $250-million in phony tax shelters promoted by a Boston law firm and two gadabout Broadway producers. For rich investors, the deal seemed too good to be true. They invested $20-million in cash, signed loans for another $80-million, and were promised five dollars in tax write-offs for every real dollar put into the scheme. The shelters were supposedly risk free because the loans were executed as "non-recourse notes"—meaning that they didn't have to be repaid if the investment projects failed. Prosecutors later described the scheme as "a thinking man's crime."

Following my series, a federal grand jury returned indictments against the promoters stemming from $100-million in tax shelters related to a failed coal-mining operation near Gillette, Wyoming. The venture never got off the ground. Or under the ground. Miners would have needed to dig to China to produce enough coal to justify the investments. The mining operation failed and investors took their five-to-one tax deductions. But rich folks were in for a costly disappointment.

Congress plugged the loophole in the 1976 Tax Reform Act. Salesmen faced the prospect of losing millions in commissions and tried to circumvent the new rules by backdating contracts. The artifice was discovered and six promoters of the scam were indicted. Two pled guilty. However the "thinking man's crime" was not a "thinking prosecutors" case. They so confused the jury that the remaining defendants were acquitted. Even so, clients were forced to pay back taxes, plus interest and penalties.

My story was not a "thinking viewer's" exposé. But it was an important story, and like climbing a mountain, I did it because it was there. My primary source was a private detective. Promoters had screwed him out of a fee after he checked their offices for wiretaps and listening devices. Owing me a favor, the stiffed dick provided thousands of internal documents identifying clients, the amount of their investments and the particulars of how IRS rules were skirted. I didn't ask how he got the material. But under laws now protecting privacy, we both would have been in big trouble for using the material.

The *Boston Globe*, *Newsweek*, NBC, ABC and other news organizations followed up on my reports and gave WCVB credit for uncovering the scheme. But I got flack from colleagues for reporting the tangled tale. Mike Taibbi, a good friend and later an NBC correspondent, said it was not a TV story. He would have given the material to newspaper buddies. Then Chicago muckraker, Peter Karl, was more explicit in criticizing the series. "You're a good reporter, John. But goddamn, your stories are boring."

Boring is television's unforgivable sin. And unbeknownst to me WCVB was about to embrace happy talk. In a 1978 meeting of department heads, company President Leo Beranek asked a rhetorical question with an ominous subtext. "If we are the best local TV station in the country, why are we still Boston's number two rated newscast?"

The significance of the question soon became clear. An all-out drive was launched to rectify WCVB's also-ran status. The most visible change was at the anchor desk. The husband and wife anchor team of Chet Curtis and Natalie Jacobson consistently won the silver medal. But in the quest for gold, Chet's seat was taken over by Tom Ellis.

His chatty, show biz style built ratings—first at Boston's CBS affiliate, then at WABC in New York City. Critics, however, unfairly labeled Tom a lightweight. Regardless, he attracted viewers, making WCVB the city's most-watched newscast. I gained a bit of anchorman insight a day or so after receiving one of my New England Emmy nominations. Tom stopped me in the newsroom, hand extended.

"Congratulations. We did it." I was flattered that he even noticed the nomination and started to thank him before he interrupted me. "The rating's book is in and we're up two points. You were a big contributor to the team." Awards be damned. Those numbers were the life blood of Tom's world and for that matter, most TV anchors.

To win rating's battles, "viewer friendly" stories—a code for superficial—became a catch-phrase. WCVB's newscasts had more substance than its competitors, but still featured an abundance of lively "cross-talk" between anchors. Natalie Jacobson was a team player, but often appeared uncomfortable with the chitchat. Half-jokingly, she once told me that on her final newscast before retirement, she planned to interrupt the prattle saying, "Cut the bullshit, Tom, and read the news."

Natalie never got that chance. Tom followed the path of ratings-oriented anchor people. Offered a better deal, he moved to a rival station. She retired in 2007, her reputation intact as one of the nation's most respected local anchors.

Even before Tom's arrival, WCVB was retreating from its commitment to keep the Investigative Unit independent of deadlines and pressures. I was stripped of my department head status, and the unit became part of the newsroom. However, I still answered to a five member committee. The prosaic public policy investigations they favored put me at cross-purposes with newsroom producers.

I soon encountered the scourge of TV investigative reporting—the length of my exposés. "How long is it?" was the first question when I told producers a story was ready for air. No matter the length, no matter the topic, no matter the magnitude of the story, their reaction was usually the same, "Too long, can you cut it down?"

For the most part, I ignored them at the expense of my popularity. Producers were only pacified on those rare occasions when a story had a little sex and sensationalism, like my report on the abuse of power by the state Attorney General in carrying out a Sarah Palin-like vendetta against his daughter's ne'er-do-well boyfriend whom he accused of kidnapping after the young couple's two day romantic tryst in plain sight of friends.

The story was sexy enough that I was asked to do a follow-up. Still, there were many instances when I should have complied with requests to trim the length of stories. Instead, I was intent on doing it my way—an inappropriate reaction caused by my red-neck insecurities in Boston. I never felt I belonged in the environment.

Before leaving, though, my final exposé brought considerable attention to "the best local TV station in America." The story was also a defining moment in my attitude toward the criminal justice system. The frame-up of mobster Anthony Accetturo five years before, combined with other events in Florida, had raised caution flags about the reliability and fairness of many lawmen. But that was not as bad as it gets.

I saw a sordid brand of "justice" in Boston that taught me to always be skeptical when dealing with cops and prosecutors. The lesson was the basis of my contrarian reporting of law enforcement stories throughout my career. My dubious attitude earned me a reputation as a friend of criminals. In reality, I was a friend of justice.

Myles J. Connor was a notorious New England lawbreaker, whom I would never have invited into my home without first stripping the walls of art and hiding the family jewels, assuming I had valuables. Son of a police sergeant,

Myles was a popular New England musician prior to July, 1965, when he sounded a sour note.

He and his wife were caught stealing antiques from an unoccupied mansion in Maine. A deputy tried to arrest them. Connor pulled a gun and they fled. He didn't get very far before being caught. A few days later, he escaped from the lock-up by carving a bar of soap into the shape of a pistol, blackening it with shoe polish and forcing a jailer to unlock his cell. Swimming across a river, he hid in the woods for four days—surrendering only after his mother pleaded with him on a loudspeaker.

This was the opening chapter in a novelistic criminal career that put him on the front pages of New England newspapers for four decades. Connor was released on bail, but skipped after being accused of a series of art thefts at Boston area museums. In April 1966, he was cornered near Boston University. In an exchange of gunfire, he shot a State Police Sergeant in the groin and a barrage of bullets severely wounded him.

He survived, was convicted of attempted murder, and sentenced to prison. At notorious Walpole penitentiary, he was a model inmate, accruing college credits and ingratiating himself with influential pointy-heads, who helped him get an early release.

Billed as the *President of Rock and Roll*, Myles resumed his music career at a Boston area nightclub. But he carried the weight of having shot a cop, making him a target of constant surveillance – and maybe even entrapment.

In mid-1974, FBI agents arrested him in the company of two men who possessed stolen Andrew Wyeth paintings. Connor claimed they had contacted him to authenticate the art. No matter. He was accused of receiving stolen art. That's when his career took a bizarre turn.

To extricate himself from his latest difficulties, Connor came up with a bizarre plan to steal a rare Rembrandt and trade it for freedom. Because his short stature and flaming red hair made him easily recognizable, Myles paid cohorts to do the job. To finance the scheme, Connor masterminded a bank robbery. Three months after the bank heist, his hired hands walked into the Boston Museum of Fine Arts and fired a shot into the ceiling. When everybody dived to the floor, the *Portrait of Elizabeth Van Rijn* was grabbed from the wall. The 1632 Rembrandt was then valued at $3-million. In January 1976, a deal was struck for the return of the painting.

Following a series of mysterious telephone calls and a movie-like rendezvous with a motorcyclist in a dark corner of a restaurant parking lot, *Elizabeth Van Rijn* ended up in the trunk of a car driven by a state cop. The following day, the U.S. Attorney, the State Police Commissioner and the acting director of the Museum of Fine Arts jointly announced that a "public-spirited citizen" arranged the return of the painting.

The "public-spirited citizen" was hustled into a federal courtroom two days later. Connor received a four year sentence in the Wyeth case, which amounted to a slap on the wrist for a convicted felon. The plea bargain allowed him to serve time at his old stomping grounds, Walpole State Prison. Inmates there greeted him as a returning hero. They admired his resourcefulness in "outsmarting" lawmen. In reality, he outsmarted himself. FBI agents and other lawmen have long memories. And when Connor pulled off another scheme that obtained his release from prison, it backfired.

Among his admirers was one of Walpole's most dangerous inmates, a mentally deranged vicious killer named Tommy Sperrazza who occasionally signed letters, "Manson," in tribute to California's imprisoned lunatic. Sperrazza was a suspect in numerous homicides, including the murders of two teen-aged girls who disappeared after witnessing him kill a man outside a Boston bar. The girls' bodies had not been found.

Looking again for keys to the prison gates, Connor approached Sperrazza with an absurd proposal. If Tommy would tell him the location of the bodies, Myles promised to hijack a helicopter following his release and fly into Walpole to facilitate the killer's escape. Nobody in their right mind would believe such a proposition. But according to prison psychiatrists, Sperrazza was legally nuts. He drew a map for Myles.

The victims, Karen Spinney and Diane Webster, were buried in western Massachusetts, more than a hundred miles from the scene of the murder. Norfolk County District Attorney, William Delahunt—a U.S. Congressman as this is written—made a deal with Connor. In September,

1977, he led investigators to the girls' remains. Myles was paroled after serving only one year of his sentence.

However, lawmen decided it was time for payback. FBI agents first gathered evidence to charge him with bank robbery. The case was weak and a jury acquitted Connor, even though he admitted to me that he was guilty. There is a law enforcement maxim, "If you can't catch them on the swing, catch them on the slide."

Immediately after the innocent verdict, Connor was linked to the murders of the two girls. The chief witness was none other than Sperrazza. He said Connor gave him a primer in how to kill the victims—a remarkable claim for a guy believed to have murdered a dozen people or more. Myles barely knew Tommy outside of prison. Nor did he have a motive to commit the murders.

Enter on the scene John Connolly, the rogue FBI agent convicted two decades later for his dealings with informants. Connolly promised Sperrazza all sorts of rewards if he linked Connor to the murders, including financial aid for Tommy's family. If he didn't cooperate, the agent threatened to file charges against the murderer's wife and place their children in a foster home. Sperrazza's decision didn't require a lot of thought.

I first met Myles Connor in July, 1980, at Boston's Charles Street Jail. I listened for three hours as he proclaimed his innocence in the murder case and rationalized nearly every crime he ever committed. At the same time, he boasted of being a "master thief" and connoisseur of art. He also admitted to the bank robbery that financed the Rembrandt theft. Myles was not an innocent lamb being taken to slaughter.

As much as he enjoyed top billing, Connor was less important to my reporting than the characters recruited to testify against him. The focus of my research was the excessive rewards and inducements given to jailed criminals in return for testimony in high-profile trials—a tactic I would describe in my series as a "bounty hunter system of justice." Witnesses like Tommy Sperrazza had more reasons to lie than tell the truth.

I started digging into allegations of witness buying by prosecutors in 1979 after two men were found innocent of Boston's notorious "Blackfriars Massacre." Five card-playing friends—one a former investigative reporter—were shot to death during an after-hours robbery at a downtown discothèque.

Lawmen were under intense pressure to find the killers. And within days, the two defendants were identified by a dope-addled heroin addict desperately trying to get out of jail for his next fix. His trial testimony revealed that prosecutors made little or no effort to corroborate his statements. Instead, he was moved from Boston to Bermuda and provided methadone so that he could testify. The case collapsed when the witness confessed under cross-examination that he was lying.

While gathering background on the Blackfriar's case, I contacted Earl Cooley, the court-appointed attorney for Myles Connor. Cooley was a partner in Hale & Dorr, one of the nation's best known law firms. His clients included the Boston Celtics basketball team and a list of Beacon Hill bluebloods. A federal judge had assigned Cooley to defend Connor in the bank robbery trial, stating that Hale & Dorr had an obligation to accept more court appointments. With Cooley at his side, Connor was acquitted.

The prominent lawyer was a reluctant courtroom warrior at first. However, he evolved into a fierce advocate after seeing obvious misconduct by FBI agents and prosecutors in deals with witnesses. Following the robbery trial, Cooley agreed to also defend Connor in the murder case in state court. When I first contacted him, he recited a litany of abuses and arranged my no-holds-barred jailhouse interview with Connor.

My October, 1980 exposé titled *Witness for Hire*, set off a firestorm even before it aired. Aware that my Connor interview would be part of the series, prosecutors filed a motion to prevent WCVB from reporting the story. Connor's trial was three weeks away. A motion was filed claiming my report would jeopardize the prosecution's right to a "fair trial"—a flip-flop rationale since it is the defendant who is guaranteed a fair trial.

Nevertheless, the trial judge issued a prior restraining order to block the series from airing. It was overturned by an appeals court on the same day, prompting the judge to deliver a withering attack on WCVB and postpone the trial for three months.

The prior restraint litigation brought more attention to the series than all of my previous Boston stories combined. However, the publicity was a dilemma for "the best local TV station in America." I had been fired six weeks earlier. For image sake, I was asked to keep quiet about the shutdown of the investigative unit, a decision that management said was irrevocable. As a reward for my silence, I remained on the payroll work free until the controversy subsided.

So while the media portrayed us as courageous protectors of the First Amendment, I made no effort to dissuade reporters of our heroics. Nor did I reveal that WCVB's ratings obsession contributed to the uproar. My series was ready for air in late August. It was delayed until October. A ratings month.

By the time Myles Connor got his day in court, I had been recruited by ABC *Close Up* in New York to expand the scope of the *Witness for Hire* series. Hence, I sat through much of his trial. We were the only video crew covering the proceedings and may have influenced the outcome.

Sitting next to the photographer, I told him when to turn on the camera. No matter how subtle our movement, the jury looked our way and seemed to become more focused on the testimony. I believe cameras should be allowed in courtrooms. Based on the Connor trial,

I believe the equipment should be out of sight of the jury.

I don't know if cameras had an impact, but I was surprised when the jury returned a guilty verdict. Earl Cooley was shocked. He methodically dismantled the prosecution's case and the line-up of witnesses whose mug shots belonged on Post Office walls.

Close Up now faced the prospect of defending a career criminal convicted of murder. It was an uncomfortable position. But the whole point of the documentary was to show the outrageous deals made with murderers and thieves to obtain convictions. If defense lawyers were to offer tangible rewards for favorable testimony, they would be indicted for witness tampering.

Myles Connor was a criminal. However, I believed the murder rap was a frame-up. And an appeals court agreed. The conviction was overturned based in large part on issues that I raised in the *Witness for Hire* series. The same witnesses testified at a second trial. But the verdict was innocent.

I had a lot of misgivings about taking up a banner on Connor's behalf. But I believe perverted justice needs to be exposed, no matter the notoriety of defendants. And as usually happens to career criminals, Connor got his just due. He ended up in federal prison following a conviction in Illinois on drug charges.

Midway through a fifteen-year sentence, Connor tried to beat the system again by hinting that he had inside information on the biggest art theft in the nation's history.

In March 1990, burglars breached the security alarms at Boston's Isabella Stewart Gardner Museum and got away with $300-million in rare paintings. The theft had earmarks of a Connor-planned crime, even though he was tucked away in prison.

This time, he failed to earn a get-out-of-jail-free card. The art has never been found. Connor served the full sentence before returning to Boston, perhaps to live a less adventuresome life. It wouldn't surprise me if investigators occasionally peek at his walls, hoping to see Gardner Museum art.

Law enforcement abuses I uncovered in Boston were not unique to the city. I found a pattern of win-at-any-cost justice by both state and federal lawmen throughout the country.

The *Close Up* documentary, titled *When Crime Pays*, aired in June, 1981. Afterwards, my future was cloudy. A new manager was running the *I-Team* at WCVB's competing station. He had chased away the investigative unit's two ugly duckling on-air reporters. The two disillusioned journalists returned to the newspaper business. Rationalizing that I was prettier and more adaptable, I set up a lunch with the new leader. I thought we were making progress toward a job offer when he asked an odd question.

"Since you have a lot more experience than me as an investigative reporter, what happens if we disagree on your approach to a story?"

"I guess we will try to find a common ground," I answered.

It must have been the wrong answer. I never heard from him again. Just as well. Watching the *I-Team*'s superficial stories, I realized it would have been impossible to find a common ground. TV investigative reporting was in freefall in Boston, as well as other major cities around the country.

Before my job hunt, I heard grumbling at gatherings of Investigative Reporters and Editors that topflight muckrakers were being forced to do superficial consumer oriented and/or "viewer friendly" stories. It was evidence of an insidious trend away from television's post-Watergate attempts at hard-edged investigative reporting.

Perhaps it was time for me to pursue my dream of being a rock and roll disc jockey. An oldie playing oldies. Fortunately, John Spain interceded by promising me great things if I returned to Baton Rouge. It was a giant step backwards in a business that measures success by market size.

But more disturbing was my fear of revisiting the horrors of my past.

CHAPTER THIRTEEN

PAST, PRESENT AND FUTURE

I've been asked many times why I continue to attend Alcoholics Anonymous meetings after nearly four decades of sobriety. There are many reasons, none of which relate to a burning desire to pick up a drink. But one reason I go is Peggy.

With my career on hold in March, 1981, I was working as a part-time reporter for a small syndicated news service when my daughter, Sherri, called in near hysterics. My son, Michael, had been arrested in a New Orleans suburb as he fled the scene of a vicious rape. I tried to calm Sherri, though barely able to control my own emotions. After hanging up, I did what eleven years of AA meetings taught me. I called another alcoholic.

Peggy's office was two blocks away. We attended the same meeting in a Boston suburb and rode the same train into the city most days. Educated at one of New England's "Seven Sisters" Ivy League colleges, she was as different from me as could be. But we shared a bond that defines Alcoholics Anonymous. Regardless of backgrounds, members have deep-rooted obligations to one another.

Hearing the agony in my voice, Peggy told me to meet her in ten minutes at the gate of Granary Burying Ground, a historic 250-year-old cemetery that serves as a quiet refuge in the midst of Boston's downtown hubbub. Sitting on a bench near the burial tomb of Paul Revere, I unleashed my grief over narcissistic failures as a parent and my inability to show Michael the kind of love he needed as a child.

She listened patiently and non-judgmentally. Her willingness to drop everything and rush to my side personified the Higher Power that is the essence of AA's success. I haven't seen Peggy in more than twenty-five years. But others like her give me good reasons for my continued presence at meetings.

The decision to return to Louisiana after a nine year absence stirred painful memories. Michael and I both entered the speed lane to self-destruction in Baton Rouge. During the 1960's, it was a city that tolerated people like me. My alcoholic lunacy went unnoticed at watering holes where drunkards were then commonplace. So with the forbearance of drinking buddies and buddettes, I let the good times roll—*Laissez les bontemps rouler* as the Louisiana motto goes.

As my self-indulgences increased, so did my disconnect with the family. Being a husband to Glenda, and a parent to Michael and his sisters was less important to me than the booze. I sporadically caught glimpses of my insanity, but dulled reality with another drink while trying to attain the feeling of exhilaration that first triggered my alcoholism.

My introductory swig came from a blood-spattered pint bottle of whiskey hidden in my parents' bedroom closet in a box containing the belongings of a distant relative who was killed in a traffic accident. Seeing dad pack away the stuff, I became obsessed with the bottle in the box. Then one night the most fetching girl in my seventh grade class was babysitting in an apartment next door. I wanted to keep her company but didn't have the nerve to ask. Instinctively, I associated the whiskey with bravado. After a few sips, I was bold enough to go calling on my classmate. I was eleven-years-old.

Precise memories of early encounters with liquor are a characteristic of most alcoholics. Many spend years—even lifetimes—trying to recapture the elusive sensation that makes us believe we are bigger, stronger and better looking. My search inflicted heartbreaking damage on Glenda, the kids and my parents.

Michael was the most visible victim. My return to Louisiana would facilitate reconciliation with him and his sisters, Patti, Sherri and Terri. Among sobriety's greatest reward is forgiveness by those we love.

The Baton Rouge homecoming also provided an extraordinary career boost—in large part because of transgressions by Brother Jimmy Lee Swaggart. *Give Me That Big Time Religion* aired ten months after I moved back to Louisiana, earning me a third Peabody medallion. I soon covered my walls with other prestigious prizes for all sorts of exposés.

In March, 1987, a Holy War broke out among men of the electronic cloth. The first shots in the religious mêlée were fired when spiritual mini-mogul Jim Bakker confessed to baptizing Jessica Hahn by injection. Unable to find a Biblical reference for the ritual, she threatened to share the innovative baptism technique with the world. To protect his patent, Bakker paid the young lady $260,000. Cynics described the fee as hush money. However, Jessica didn't hush.

When the *Charlotte Observer* first revealed Bakker's sin, the scandal caused a gaggle of self-righteous preachers to descend on his $100-million religious empire, lusting for leftovers. The preacher invasion was instigated under the guise of saving the organization—particularly from a take-over by Jimmy Swaggart, who was held in low regard by brethren of the electronic church. Swaggart preached under the same International Assemblies of God banner as blubbering Jim Bakker, causing speculation that he had first dibs on the fallen evangelist's assets.

Considerable chattels were at stake. The Reverend Bakker and his wife, the late Tammy Faye, were proprietors of *Praise the Lord* cable network, known as *PTL*. The couple had begged their way to success on TV programs emanating from *Heritage USA*, a ministry-owned religious retreat in Fort Mill, South Carolina.

Located a few miles from Charlotte, the complex featured a luxury hotel, campgrounds, gift shops, restaurants and the world's biggest water slide. The backslide by Bakker had now jeopardized the domain. And as it teetered, the late Jerry Falwell led vulture-like preachers on a mission to pick the bones.

The Baton Rouge brother denied a role in a religious coup. But Swaggart's wife, Frances, surreptitiously helped disenfranchise Bakker. Learning of the sexual indiscretion from *PTL* insiders, she and others in the Swaggart ministry were among the *Observer*'s sources. And when the scandal erupted, Brother Jimmy slipped into a pair of steel-toed brogans and metaphorically stomped on the balls of his whimpering competitor. In the spirit of *Old Testament* vengeance, he piously condemned Bakker at news conferences, on television newscasts and in fiery sermons.

The ranting provoked an ominous warning from Norman Roy Grutman, a New York lawyer hired by Falwell to expedite the removal of *PTL* from Bakker's lustful hands. Grutman was a curious choice. A few years before, he successfully defended *Hustler* magazine in a libel case initiated by Falwell. The pastor took offense to a cartoon suggesting he was a motherfucker. Literally. Now retained to represent an odd alliance of preachers, Grutman unloaded on Swaggart in appearances on national news programs.

"We're going to be compelled to show that there is smellier laundry in his hamper than the laundry in Reverend Bakker's," Grutman threatened.

There was no inkling yet that the Baton Rouge homeboy had an uncontrollable zipper. So the warning seemed peculiar to me, the self-professed Swaggart "expert." Brother Jimmy seemed unfazed by Grutman's comments. During a Los Angeles news conference in Los Angeles where he was conducting a crusade, he continued his thrashing of Bakker and also took potshots at hallucinating televangelist, Oral Roberts. The aging faith-healer had recently claimed that a 300-foot tall Jesus told him to build a gigantic medical center at Oral Roberts University in Tulsa, Oklahoma. Or die.

"We've got one brother that's perched up in a tower in Tulsa and telling people that God is going to kill him if they don't send money," Swaggart told reporters. "We've got this played-out soap opera down in South Carolina, all in the name of God. It is a sorry spectacle."

Maintaining that his ministry was "as pure as the driven snow," Swaggart made a statement that later caused belly laughs. "I married my wife when I was just a kid. She's the only woman I've ever kissed in my whole life." In Jimmy's defense, it must be pointed out that he was never accused of kissing the whore.

For the benefit of newsmen, Swaggart compared his Louisiana lifestyle to that of Jim and Tammy Bakker. "I have a house that has two bedrooms. It has a big steep roof, big porches. It looks a lot bigger than it is. It's got two bedrooms, a big living room, a small dining room, a kitchen and a tiny den that I'm going to make bigger. That's it."

He was being overly modest. His Acadian style residence was not a tract home. The master bedroom measured nearly a thousand square feet. Front and rear balconies overlooked twenty acres of immaculately landscaped lawn inside an eight-foot cedar and brick fence topped by razor ribbon. Security guards manned the entrance to a circular drive leading to the preacher's parsonage. Another two-story home on the estate was occupied by son, Donnie, and his family. The shanties and accouterments were eventually offered for sale for more than $3 million. Jimmy's distortions re-enforced my belief that he created his own reality.

In addition to his Bakker-bashing at a news conference, Swaggart scheduled satellite interviews with local TV stations around the country. WBRZ was invited to participate with a caveat that I not participate. So I wrote a list of questions. One dealt with litigation disclosing Jimmy's gangster-like threats to break the legs of a guitar-picker who was involved in romantic liaisons with a Swaggart family member. I didn't intend to report the affair. But if the issue was raised, I wanted his response on tape.

To my amazement, he denied any knowledge of the lawsuit when my surrogate asked the question. His aides were also taken aback by his answer. They knew I could flash documents on the screen to prove he was a liar. Therefore, minutes after the interview, a ministry official called WBRZ and said Jimmy misunderstood the question. He promised to make Swaggart available for another interview after returning to Baton Rouge the following week. I could even ask questions.

Before the meeting, the ministry asked that WBRZ General Manager Richard Manship, News Director John Spain, and the station's lawyer be present. It was a strange request, but we complied.

Ministry minions were waiting for us in a conference room when we arrived. Jimmy was nowhere in sight. At our insistence, the gofers went to fetch him. Suspicious that our conversations were being recorded, I said rather loudly. "It's a damn shame that the world's leading evangelist doesn't have the courage to meet us face-to-face."

Moments later, Swaggart entered the room loaded with a bundle of resentments, though he greeted me like an old friend. It had been four years since *Give Me That Big Time Religion* and our last personal contact. I had retired from Swaggart bashing. But almost immediately, he asked why I continued to attack him. When? I wanted to know. He avoided my question. It turned out that his biggest resentment related to the Peabody.

"It was based on lies," he said. I suggested he complain to the judging panel. And besides, I thought the documentary was extremely fair. Anyway, there was a half-hour of tense back and forth between us before Jimmy retreated to his "good old boy" persona.

"Now that we've had this conversation and understand each other, I want you to become a ministry Prayer Partner," he said laughingly.

"After raising $5-million by attacking me as Satan, you should make me an honorary partner," I replied.

"It's probably closer to $10-million, John," he said, wrapping his arm around my shoulders in a bear hug. Cheerfulness notwithstanding, he refused to do the promised on-camera interview.

Two days later, I traveled to the Holy War battleground. I was eager to know the weapon that attorney Roy Grutman planned to use against Jimmy. The lawyer arrived by private jet the night before a scheduled Jerry Falwell news conference at *Heritage USA*. Curiously, he came directly from the airport to the Charlotte hotel where I staying. Putting me at the top of his to-do list seemed strange. However, it didn't take long for me to surmise that the Swaggart weapon he planned to use was in my possession.

Somebody, Falwell perhaps, must have suggested that I could neutralize Jimmy's rhetoric. Grutman was now desperately looking for information to back-up his threat to expose Swaggart's "smellier laundry." Apparently, I was his best hope. But I had not dug deep enough into Jimmy's hamper to detect an odor.

After returning to Baton Rouge, I produced a report titled, *The Holy Truth*. The central theme of the thirty-minute segment was Swaggart's hyperbole relating to the Bakker scandal, as well as the misrepresentations he made at the Los Angeles news conference about his lifestyle. Jimmy was not happy with my reporting. Four days later, I was permanently expelled as an honorary Prayer Partner. During Sunday services, he described me as "a snake and a reprobate." He also claimed that an unnamed college professor overheard me say, "I'm going to put that SOB out of business and I'll use any tactic I can."

Accustomed to Brother Jimmy's flights of fancy, I didn't bother to respond to the crazy remark. Still, I didn't know he was totally nuts until a February 17, 1988 call from a *Nightline* producer telling me the preacher had been caught consorting with New Orleans' prostitutes. I waited for a punch line. He was serious. I went into denial.

"Can't be. I would be the first to know if he was screwing around."

"But there are pictures."

"Oh."

Despite the ostensible existence of photographs, I expected an explanation. Perhaps Jimmy was on a mission to save a harlot. But I soon learned something was terribly amiss at the ministry. The televangelist and his family had made an early morning flight to the Assemblies of God headquarters in Springfield, Missouri. They returned late that night. As Jimmy descended the steps of the ministry jet, the stricken looks on the faces of his staff and family told me these were desperate hours. Questioned by WBRZ producer Dorothy Taylor, Swaggart's lips moved. But before any sound emitted, son Donnie grabbed Jimmy's arm and guided him to a car. The Springfield meeting was a rehearsal for Swaggart's televised performance-for-the-ages confession.

The International church's thirteen-member Executive Presbytery was then comprised of middle-aged to elderly men. Most were raised in deeply religious families in the cloistered confines of small churches. Pictures of Jimmy standing next to a hooker outside Room 7 of the Travel Inn in a squalid section of the New Orleans suburbs were passed through the hands of church overseers. Given the Assemblies narrow view of fleshly sins, the indiscretion may have caused some leaders to become palsied with outrage. In a matter of months, two superstar televangelists preaching under the Assemblies banner had been caught with their britches down.

Explaining his presence on the wild side, Swaggart told of an obsession with pornography that had begun as a teenager. He assured his brethren that he never penetrated the orifices of the tainted woman. He was only there to masturbate. For uptight churchmen, it was a crash course in what they considered kinky.

Brother Jimmy told them of passionately praying for deliverance from his whore-peeking obsession—just like the young man he depicted in his booklet, *that Thing*. Despite fervent prayers, the Lord only gave him enough strength to resist consummating the illicit relationships. His anguished wails were so loud that Frances became alarmed. Waiting in an office adjoining the conference room, she banged on the door.

"What are you doing to my husband?" Sadly, he did it to himself.

The Presbytery was in no mood to excuse Swaggart's misconduct. The Elders ordered him to leave the pulpit for one year. The famed televangelist would disclose the penalty three days later during his memorable TV confession. Though followers inside the sanctuary appeared forgiving, ministry income took a nosedive. Lost revenue prompted Jimmy to hurry his rehabilitation. He announced that a sixty-day absence from the pulpit had cured him of unseemly erections. It was show time once again.

Anticipating drama, Geraldo Rivera came to Baton Rouge for Brother Jimmy's renaissance. WBRZ carried Geraldo's talk show. Consequently, I was assigned to be his escort and pew mate. As we took our seats at Family Worship Center, ushers told me that Donnie Swaggart wanted me to leave or move to the balcony. Geraldo went with me. The commotion caused all eyes to be on him. In the balcony, people lined up for autographs.

The evangelist's return to the pulpit lacked the melo-dramatics of his departure. When he suggested that he had kicked the hooker habit, followers applauded, shed a few tears and prayed. But not nearly as enthusiastically as before. A woman stood and spoke in tongues. A member of the congregation interpreted the gibberish, saying in effect that Jimmy was going to be okay. Something must have been lost in translation. The preacher would be caught again in the company of another whore in Palm Springs, California.

Following Jimmy's announcement of his return to the pulpit, Geraldo was eager to get an exclusive interview for his Monday show. We located Swaggart at a restaurant where he was having lunch with his family. As he left, he answered Geraldo's questions in a straightforward man-ner. I kept my mouth closed. Good thing, too.

As soon as I tried to ask a question, he walked away. We did not speak for another ten years. Geraldo's interview was the centerpiece of his show the following day. The ministry's lawyer and an Associate Pastor of Family Worship Center were guests on the program. I was also on the program, but didn't have much to contribute.

Jimmy Swaggart is more than a career footnote. For years, I have received Swaggart-related calls from print, radio and television journalists seeking my "expertise" about the rise and fall of the preacher. I was quoted in magazine articles and books. I also continue to get calls relating to the life and death of drug smuggler Barry Seal. Both men played important roles in my career. But other lesser-known characters in the muckraking Nirvana of Louisiana were just as significant in terms of my investigations of systemic abuses.

WBRZ gave me the luxury of one hour of prime time to tackle complicated issues rarely reported by television stations. To make the reports coherent, I reverted to my first lesson after becoming a "journalist" at the 250-watt *Voice of the Mother Lode* in Sonora, California. "Tell'em what you're going to tell'em, tell'em, and tell'em what you told'em."

In my quest to be a "real reporter," I had forgotten the axiom until the bane of broadcasting jogged my memory. A consultant for *Frank Magid Associates* reminded me of the tenet. The Magid group and other consulting firms are blamed for reducing television news to a potpourri of superficial headlines. In my case, though, a Magid consultant reminded me that viewers didn't take notes during my documentaries. I needed to constantly reinforce my narrative by putting into context what I told'em. Applying the principle, I collected a fourth Peabody for an exposé titled, *The Best Insurance Commissioner Money Can Buy.*

"Every once in awhile an example of investigative reporting in its purest, most absolute form comes to the fore," the judges stated. "This is the type of reporting that uncovers damaging facts, makes them publicly available and leads to decisive action."

The exposé deserved a Peabody, as well as an equally prestigious Columbia DuPont award. The "decisive action" that followed my revelations was an investigation that sent Louisiana Insurance Commissioner Douglas Green to prison. Also convicted were owners of Champion Insurance Company, the state's third largest automobile insurer before it collapsed and left behind $100-million in unpaid claims. My report revealed that Green concealed the company's financial shenanigans. Why? Because ninety percent of his campaign finances, nearly $3-million, came from Champion.

Prior to the insolvency, I asked Green on-camera about money laundered into his campaign by Champion surrogates. "Don't you think it's strange that a third-year law student at LSU would loan $45,000 to the campaign and you don't even know him?" Green's answer exemplified why I considered the state a muckraking Mecca.

"No. This is Louisiana."

At least he was more forthcoming than predecessor Sherman Bernard, whose incompetence I dealt with in a previous Chapter. The Green exposé was a spin-off of Bernard's ineptitude. Before Green's election as the "reform candidate," I produced a documentary disclosing that Bernard had protected other insurance companies by overruling employees. An example was his approval of a license for an under-funded prepaid dental care plan. Tipped that Bernard and his family received $10,000 in free dental care from the applicant, I asked him about teeth-for-tat. He denied opening his mouth for the dentist until I lifted a dental chart from a file folder.

"Come to think of it, I don't know if the bill was paid," he backtracked. "My wife takes care of things like that."

Confronting Bernard with the dental chart was actually the cheap trick of a BS artist. It was my personal chart—not his. Dental charts all look the same from a distance. My ploy accomplished its purpose. Believing I had his dental records, Bernard called later to say his wife forgot to pay the bill.

The dental ruse was part of a wider investigation of regulatory corruption in which I revealed a quid pro quo arrangement of $50,000 in "campaign contributions" to Bernard. The "pay to play" scheme allowed thieves to loot the assets of a small New Orleans insurance company. In the same manner as the dental plan approval, Bernard ignored the recommendations of his staff.

Compared to Doug Green, Bernard's pay-off was a pittance. I became suspicious of the "reform Commissioner" after learning that he sacked a department official, who questioned the solvency of Champion Insurance Company. The premise for firing was weak. He had used official stationary in a letter to Champion inquiring about a fender-bender claim filed by his son. Poor judgment, but not a firing offense.

My curiosity was the beginning of a muckraking "perfect storm." In a matter of weeks, Bernard allies were giving me leads on Champion's secret campaign contributions. Armed with the information, I played a game of "I'll show you mine, if you show me yours" with then Assistant Attorney General, Winston Riddick.

He was a friend I first met in the 1960's when he was Louisiana's Deputy Superintendent of Education and chief legal counsel to the department. In addition to a law degree, he had a Doctorate in Education from Columbia University. Prior to researching Champion's shenanigans, I didn't realize Winston had moved to the Attorney General's office. He was defending the state in litigation involving the firm. In a trade-off, he showed me his and I showed him mine. Mine was evidence that the insurance company was headed toward a financial disaster.

A former Champion executive told me that the insurer placed a daily dollar limit on amount of claims it paid. He said the company was falling behind at a rate of $40,000 a day. If true, the shortfall was ruinous, even for a company collecting $100-million a year in premiums. "But what is the proof," I asked. The man's response was one of those a moments that investigative reporters treasure. He reached into a briefcase and produced copies of six months of records that confirmed the amount of claims received each day, and the amount approved. The daily deficit averaged almost exactly $40,000. He had provided me a smoking cannon. And when the smoke cleared, Champion was declared insolvent.

Following my exposé, Governor Buddy Roemer asked for a briefing on the burgeoning scandal. He was a Harvard MBA graduate, and someone who promised to bring big changes to Louisiana. However, his top advisors said Champion was no big deal. By his own admission later, he dropped the ball. Winston Riddick did not. He aggressively led an investigation that resulted in indictments and convictions.

By May 1989, my reputation as a muckraker had soared nationally. My picture appeared on the cover of *Washington Journalism Review*, now called the *American Journalism Review*. Looking as cocky as I felt after all the awards, I leaned behind a TV monitor, elbows propped on the console, a near smirk on my face. Swaggart's tear-stained image was on the screen beneath me, his features contorted in agony of confessing his sins to the Almighty. The magazine profile exceeded my own threshold for bullshit.

Brother Jimmy's "one of the finest investigative reporters in the world" description was reprised. The author wrote that Swaggart acknowledged "what many inside television news already believed."

It was nice to read the accolades of fellow journalists. But I recognized—at least on most days—that my success was largely due to geography and the fortuitous circumstance of working for WBRZ. Louisiana had been very good for me.

And very bad. The magazine article reported both extremes. Governor Edwin Edwards depicted me as a "derelict gunslinger." A local lawyer said, "He has hurt a lot of good people with his outright lies. I hope the bastard fries in hell." The attorney may have lacked objectivity. He handled a $12-million libel suit relating to my Barry Seal story. The case was thrown out of court.

After years of attending AA meetings, I was not reticent in disclosing the seamier elements of my life and the impact that my alcoholism had on others. Still, I cringed at reading details in a national magazine. "He was arrested at least a half-dozen times for alcohol-related offenses and hospitalized three times for treatment. His thirty-five-year-old son, the oldest of nine children and stepchildren is serving a life sentence in Louisiana State Prison for aggravated rape—an offense Camp links to his son's problems with drugs and his own problems with drinking."

A phrase in *Alcoholics Anonymous* states, "We will not regret the past, nor wish to shut the door on it." The so-called Big Book from which the fellowship derives its name was written in 1939 by an ex-drunk known the world over as "Bill W." It is a guide to sober living. I don't believe I'm committing heresy in saying that I deeply "regret the past." Otherwise I would be devoid of a conscience.

I interpret the word, "regret," to mean not dwelling in the past. It is necessary for me to remember with "regret" that Mike and his sisters were witnesses to appalling incidents like my arrest on Christmas Eve, 1969, when I went into a drunken rage in our home. I don't dwell on the image of Glenda and the children bailing me out of jail on Christmas morning. Nor do I recycle other insanities. However, I cannot afford to forget those times when alcohol controlled my life.

Although Alcoholics Anonymous put my life on a different path, personal problems didn't end at the doorways of meetings. Fifteen years after my second wife helped me out of a New Orleans gutter, we were divorced. Details from my perspective would be unfair. We have conflicting opinions of what went wrong. Suffice to say there were irreconcilable differences, and I caused much of the discord.

Following the separation in January, 1985, I moved to a vacant mobile home I had bought for my parents ten years before. Momma had moved to an apartment. Her leftover furnishings in the trailer consisted of a bed, an old couch and a chest of drawers. My dining table was an overturned cardboard box. I found a rusty dinette chair outside. In an ironic coincidence, the same week I moved out of the "big house," I was featured on the cover of the Baton Rouge *Advocate*'s Sunday magazine.

At the break of dawn on Sunday, I waited at a nearby convenience store for the newspaper delivery, eager to find out what kind of impression my bullshit made on the young reporter. Returning to the trailer, I fixed a bowl of cereal and sat down at the cardboard box to read of my renown as a muckraker. It was too bad there weren't pictures of my elegant quarters as evidence of my award-winning success.

After a decade in big time television in Miami and Boston, the article implied that Baton Rouge was fortunate to have its own mini-Mike Wallace. My alcoholism and recovery were also part of the story. Overall, the article was flattering. But the marital break-up took the luster off my professional achievements.

My first marriage ended because I was a drunken bum. This time, I couldn't blame whiskey for the mess in my personal life. I tried to justify the separation by telling myself that it was unhealthy for our adopted sons to live in an environment of household tensions. Moreover, I had provided them opportunities they would not have had otherwise. My rationale provided little comfort. The stark reality of the divorce was I failed to fulfill my commitment as an adoptive father. I needed to quit kidding myself.

After a few weeks in the trailer, I rented an apartment. Sixteen-year-old Rob came to live with me. Ed, who was thirteen, stayed with Patricia. The boys never seemed traumatized by the separation. However, I may be playing mind games. Children are always affected by divorce.

Regardless of how we see ourselves in the milieu of sobriety, our adherence to AA's Twelve Step principles are compromised by the excuses we make. "We" meaning me. Rather than self-justification, I try to remember to move forward and "do the next right thing," a mantra recited by members of the fellowship. The failure to correct faults, foibles and misdeeds can be deadly.

Alcoholism doesn't respect achievements or position, as personified by Baton Rouge's former Mayor—an AA friend. He succeeded in accomplishing what I once tried to do. He drank and drugged himself to death in a seedy hotel not far from the curbside perch where I sat in 1971. The tragedy is haunting.

When I returned to Louisiana, Pat Screen was midway through the first of three terms as East Baton Rouge Parish's Mayor-President. A former LSU quarterback and high school All-American, he was a rising star in politics. Many predicted he was destined to become Governor or U.S. Senator. Pat was a brilliant political tactician. Law school classmate, James Carville, considered him a mentor. Both were foundering in legal careers before teaming together in politics. Carville took lessons he learned from Pat to a national stage as a key strategist behind Bill Clinton's election as President.

Investigative reporters are supposed to avoid getting too close to potential targets of exposés. Based on an AA bond of friendship, I recused myself from digging dirt in the Mayor's office. Pat and I attended meetings together, had long discussions about his road to sobriety and occasionally competed in tennis. Despite the best efforts of everyone who knew him, he could not stay sober for more than a few months.

In the fall of 1995, Pat checked himself out of a rehab center. He was last seen in Baton Rouge on a game day in the Tiger Stadium parking lot. The next week, his wife, Kathy, received a telephone call inquiring about a credit card he used at a New Orleans hotel. She and a priest hurried there to bring him home. They arrived too late. Pat was dead from a lethal combination of alcohol and drugs. He was fifty-two.

James Carville and I are only casual acquaintances. But he was aware of my AA connection to Pat. On the way home from the funeral, he called me at CNN on a cell phone and asked a question for which there is no single answer. Why? Pat seemed to have everything to live a sober life for. I broaden Carville's question to include other AA friends who die drunk. Why him or her and not me?

I doubt that Pat wanted to kill himself. But like all addicts, self-destructive impulses become uncontrollable after the first drink, first snort or first hit. In Alcohol-ics Anonymous meeting rooms, I have heard the harsh and detached response by members that "Some must die to keep others sober." No doubt, drunken deaths have a sobering effect on all of us. The only difference between Pat's last bender and mine is that I survived. I don't know why. Maybe that Power we talk about in meetings wanted me in a certain place at a certain time. In retrospect, some destinations seem clear.

I met my present wife, Annette, at an AA meeting. It was a surprise introduction for both of us. I was research-ing the links between her estranged spouse and Governor Edwin Edwards. She was shocked to discover an investiga-tive reporter in her refuge from the publicity surrounding her ex- husband's disappearance. He was a heavy drinker and my guess is that at the outset of a grand jury investiga-tion, he took an alcoholic's escape route from problems by slipping out of town to live with a girlfriend in New Jersey. He died of cancer before the FBI could deliver a witness subpoena.

Although Annette and I occasionally attended the same meetings, I avoided questioning her about the fed-eral investigation. After we became friends, it took awhile for romance to bloom. The last thing she wanted was to be part of a love triangle. And the last thing I wanted was to be a two-timing, two-time loser. But stuff happens.

We were married in December 1986, two years after my marriage break-up. I was nearing my sixteen-year AA anniversary. She was five years in recovery. The marriage added three more children to my progeny, bringing the total to nine. Donna was twenty-two, Dawn twenty-one, and Ken Jr. was nineteen. They were too old to adopt, but over the years they adopted me.

By 1989, I was happy and content in Baton Rouge. I expected WBRZ to be my final career destination. Why would I want to leave a newsroom that gave me so much support? Then as happens when we become satisfied with status quo, CNN executive Ed Turner called. The network was putting together a big investigative team.

Ed read the *Washington Journalism Review* article about my muckraking prowess. He said my name was at the top of his recruiting list. I was fifty-three-years old. So I told him I was too old, too good, too well paid and too happy at WBRZ to consider an offer. Later that day, I mentioned the phone call to Annette. "What did you tell him?"

"I'm too old, too good, too well paid, etc. etc." As a psychotherapist and member of our society of former boozers, she had dual insights of my split personas—the egomaniacal reporter and the not-so-mild-mannered recovering alcoholic. The latter didn't always remind the former that being a hotshot muckraker was only a TV role I played. Annette sometimes put our conversations on pause while waiting for what she called "the real John" to appear. It usually didn't take long.

Moving to Atlanta was appealing to her. She graduated from the University of Georgia, and her aging mother still lived in Athens. Moving, though, was problematic. A big obstacle was the legal chaos in my personal life. Patricia and I had failed to reach a final resolution on alimony, child support and division of property.

Making matters worse, I dug myself deeply in debt by investing in an AM radio station in a small town near Baton Rouge. Owning a radio station was a fantasy of mine ever since my first broadcasting job in Sonora, California. Unfortunately, ownership turned out to be something different than I envisioned. Bankrupt different.

Despite pending court dates related to the divorce, a dying radio station and other quandaries like my employment contract with WBRZ, Annette suggested that I at least find out more about CNN's investigative team. She was right. I might need a change.

The Insurance Commissioner documentary was followed by an exposé of Louisiana's Alcohol Beverage Control agency. The story was okay. It got the head of the agency fired and even won an Investigative Reporters and Editors award. But I was in one of my what-do-I-do-now funks—a mindset that often followed the completion of projects. In the past, stories always came along to rejuvenate me. But after seven years in Baton Rouge, I felt as if I were repeating myself. Maybe I should talk to CNN.

As a big-frog-in-a-little-pond, I acted like a jerk when Ed Turner first called. Fortunately, he wrote a nice note asking that I reconsider his proposal. I didn't know it then, but Ed was an ex-drunk and probably recognized the megalomania that periodically plagues alcoholics. Anyway, he offered a face-saving excuse for me to contact him and arrange a visit to CNN. I don't know what I expected, but the network failed to live down to my expectations.

CNN's world headquarters is located in a pair of fourteen-floor buildings separated by an enclosed atrium that adjoins the Omni Hotel. Touring the newsroom, I sensed the energy of young producers, editors and technicians who staffed state-of-the-art facilities. China's Tiananmen Square protests then dominated the news. And CNN's reporting outshined all its competition. The network was at the threshold of establishing itself as an important international news organization.

Ed Turner had big ideas for expanding its investigative reporting capabilities. He planned to recruit TV's best muckrakers for a thirty-member team. I was offered the position of Senior Investigative Correspondent. After he outlined his vision, I was ready to move to Atlanta. There was, of course, the matter of money. I set a target salary of $125,000 a year—fifty thousand more than I my base salary at WBRZ. I was willing to consider anything over six figures. Subconsciously, I must have had an extraordinarily inflated opinion of myself. When Ed asked what it would take to bring me to CNN, I heard a strange voice say, "$175,000."

Where did that come from? I knew the network's cheapskate reputation. Ed blinked, but he didn't kick me out of the office. After several weeks of negotiation, we agreed on $135,000, plus relocation expenses, yearly raises and other perks.

WBRZ's News Director John Spain knew of my discussions with CNN from the beginning and agreed to release me from my contract. Like me, he believed I had an opportunity to take Louisiana's style of muckraking to a national forum. Maybe even the world.

In September, 1989, I took my mini-Mike Wallace act on the road. Unfortunately, it didn't work out as we had hoped.

CHAPTER FOURTEEN

IT SEEMED LIKE A GOOD IDEA AT THE TIME

CNN's decision to create television's biggest investigative team caused a stir in the news business. This was a huge investment for an organization known for frugality. Nine years before, Ted Turner's 24-hour cable network had been greeted with belly laughs—labeled the *Chicken Noodle Network*. But his "joke" was becoming a worldwide brand name. Its growth had taken a heavy toll on ABC, CBS, and NBC. The so-called Big Three broadcast networks could boast of celebrity journalists, but CNN made them peddlers of second-hand news.

Ted's ownership of the Atlanta Braves, a victory in America's Cup as a yachtsman, and his other ventures and adventures had made him the nation's highest profile entrepreneur. Known as "the mouth of the South," he was famous for unpredictable antics and outrageous opinions. Playing the role of unsophisticated maverick, he took pride in picking the pockets of New York and Hollywood titans.

"I was cable before cable was cool," he bragged.

In an atmosphere of informality during CNN's early days, employees were not surprised to see Ted have breakfast in the company cafeteria wearing pajamas. The network operated like a "Hey, kids, let's put on a show" episode of *Our Gang* comedies. Key newsroom positions were manned by people recruited from local stations. Twenty-something kids arrived straight out of college as Video Journalists—a network term for glorified interns. Hoping to break into big-time TV, they worked cheap. To fill twenty- four hours with something resembling news, the fledgling network picked up stories from local stations that subscribed to CNN's video news service.

In fact, my first real awareness of Ted's folly was a result of the arrangement. While I was unemployed in Boston in 1981 and struggling to pay bills, a $300.00 check arrived in the mail from CNN. The surprising windfall was a talent fee for carrying my WCVB *Witness for Hire* series. Not be-ing "cool," our neighborhood didn't have cable. I had no idea the reports aired nationally. The windfall was certainly timely. I needed money to clean an overflowing septic tank. Thankful for the cash, I considered sending a résumé to the nascent network. But I expected CNN to soon go out of business. Who is going to watch news all day and night?

But the network survived. And eight years after my dire prediction, I was hired under the impressive sounding title of CNN's "Senior Investigative Correspondent." I arrived in a blaze of glory. Much smoke was blown in the direction of my derriere in newspapers and trade publications. The word, "legendary," was even attached to my name. Fortu-nately, I was sober long enough to laugh. Even though I was a pretty good muckraker, WBRZ gave me the time and resources to take investigative reporting beyond the su-perficial. And besides, Louisiana rascals frequently made my job easy.

In September 1989, my new boss, former *Close Up* Executive Producer Pamela Hill, had not yet signed a contract to lead the *Special Assignment* unit. I had worked for Pam as a freelance reporter at ABC, so I guess she was okay with Ed's decision to hire me. Pam was married to *Times* Op-Ed columnist Tom Wicker. They lived on Manhattan's Upper East Side, and she wanted to work out of CNN's New York bureau, rather than Atlanta or Washington. An agreement was finally worked out for her to commute between all three bureaus.

Following my earlier freelance work at *Close Up*, Pam inadvertently did a huge favor for me—though I didn't think so at the time. Instead of hiring me fulltime, she opted for a British producer with a more worldly résumé. The snub was providential. While I racked up awards in Louisiana's happy-mucking ground, *Close Up* and other documentary units at the Big Three networks faded to black—victims of *60 Minutes'* success.

The popular CBS show is responsible for the demise of long-form investigative reporting by the Big Three. Conceived by Don Hewitt in 1968, *60 Minutes* became television's most watched show. Its success sounded the death knell for single subject network documentaries. *Close Up*, NBC's *White Paper* and *CBS Reports* received critical acclaim and won journalism prizes, but the ratings sucked. Magazine shows soon proliferated, leaving the real reporting to PBS's *Frontline* and other off-brand networks.

Investigative reporting in local markets also suffered from *60 Minutes* success. Station executives expected newly hired muckrakers to bring in viewers. However, most substantive stories lacked pizzazz. And enthusiasm for hard-edged investigative journalism diminished. The number of stations committed to developing "truth squads" dwindled, putting TV muckrakers on journalism's endangered species list.

The irony of *60 Minutes'* reputation is that many of its exposés were a result of smoke and mirrors. Although the show's producers and researchers uncovered a few original stories each season, the program was notorious for taking credit for the work of other journalists. Nonetheless, *60 Minutes* did it better than anyone else.

In recent years, gray hair and wrinkles have been visible on *60 Minutes* correspondents, as well as its viewers. The show has tried to attract a younger audience with more celebrity profiles and the promotion of controversial books, including some that are released by CBS-owned publishers. The loss of journalism toughness at CBS caused internal turmoil. The Dan Rather controversy over his George W. Bush reporting was the most publicized. Also notable was the departure of investigative producer Lowell Bergman. His battles over a *60 Minutes* exposé was the basis of a film, *The Insider*. The veteran journalist resigned after the network watered down his a segment exposing *Brown & Williamson's* manipulation of addictive ingredients in cigarettes.

The accuracy of the story was never an issue. But CBS was threatened with litigation because Bergman's primary source, former *B&W* chemist Jeffery Wigand, had signed a confidentiality agreement before leaving *Brown & Williamson*. He later testified in a landmark case that cost "Big Tobacco" hundreds of millions of dollars.

At CNN, I had visions of the network restoring some of *60 Minutes'* early nastiness. Introducing Pam Hill as a speaker at a convention of Investigative Reporters and Editors a few months after the *Special Assignment* team was recruited, I gave brief résumés of the staff. I went on to say that "Only a genius could devise ways for us to fail." We didn't totally fail. But we fell short of what I imagined when leaving Louisiana.

A major shortcoming was CNN's inability to clearly define our network role. We engaged in endless experimentation. Important stories were haphazardly positioned in daily newscasts. To overcome the problem, we produced prime time magazine shows under titles such as *Impact*. But the impact was negligible. An infamous exception was a disastrous 1998 nerve gas "exposé" that is the subject of another Chapter. The story accelerated the network's retreat from high-risk investigative journalism.

Prior to the nerve gas fiasco, *Special Assignment*'s setbacks were symptomatic of the same trend that led to the demise of serious investigative reporting elsewhere. Although CNN was the originator of twenty-four hour news, producers acted as if twenty-five hour days were necessary for our stories. Like my experience in Boston, nearly everything we produced for daily newscasts was considered too long, regardless of the content. And attempts to have mandated time slots failed.

I must add that *Special Assignment* correspondents— me included—contributed to the problems. When asked to keep stories within certain time limits, we ignored newsroom producers. Our collective attitude was, "I don't need no stinking time limits."

In terms of experience, skills and academic backgrounds, the thirty-member investigative team was extraordinary. Several of us had won dozens of journalism awards. Our younger journalists were setting sail on successful careers. Harvard, Yale, Princeton, Dartmouth and Tuscaloosa High School were among the fine education institutions represented in the unit. As a representative of the demographic of small town radio reporters, ex-drunks and low-life trailer trash, my insecurities ran rampant—a condition that I concealed with a constant flow of bullshit.

Special Assignment correspondents shared at least one thing in common. We were never accused of being television's pretty faces. Genetically-bald Art Harris described us as looking like the cast of *Star Wars*. Art was a former freelance writer for the *Washington Post* and other publications, including *Penthouse*. We first met while sheet-sniffing at the New Orleans motel where Jimmy Swaggart's ministry went limp.

Prematurely-wrinkled Brooks Jackson came to CNN from the *Wall Street Journal*. His specialty was politics and campaign finance. He has since established FactCheck. org.—a non-partisan blog that keeps tabs on media inaccuracies, campaign commercials and promises made by politicians. Like Art Harris, he had no previous on-air experience.

Nor did *Special Assignment* correspondents, David Lewis and Brian Barger. David, the son of New York *Times* Op-Ed columnist Anthony Lewis, previously worked as an investigative producer for ABC. Brian was a former wire service reporter, who received journalism awards for stories dealing with political turmoil in Latin America.

Mark Feldstein was the only correspondent besides me recruited from local television. A tall, skinny, Harvard graduate, he had been a friend for years. Because of his gaunt appearance and thick spectacles, news managers advised Mark early in his career to forget about on-camera reporting. Ignoring the advice, he went on to win two Peabody awards as an in-your-face muckraker at stations in Tampa, Florida and Washington D.C. He is now a journalism professor at George Washington University and a frequently quoted critic of television investigative reporting—or the lack thereof.

Rounding out *Special Assignment*'s on-air staff was former NBC political expert Ken Bode. Bespectacled and carrying a slight paunch, he was an inside-the-beltway Washington reporter and former host of PBS's *Washington Week in Review*. Like Mark, Ken left CNN for academia. He is a professor at DePauw University.

Ken's longtime NBC producer, Jim Connor, came with him to *Special Assignment*. Martin Koughan—one of television's best investigative journalists—was the first producer to join the unit. Marty formerly worked for CBS *Nightly News* and *60 Minutes*. In recent years, he produced a variety of freelance documentaries.

The unit's initial senior producer was Alan Weisman, another *60 Minutes* alumnus. Early on, Ted Turner pissed off Alan by enforcing a smoking ban in all network bureaus. Tired of traveling, he decided to quit—CNN, not cigarettes—and remain close to his New York home where he could light up anytime he damn well pleased.

Alan's successor as Pamela Hill's second in command was John Lane. In a long career in television, he served as Vice President of the news divisions at both CBS and NBC. Despite our radically different backgrounds—my years in Baton Rouge versus his years in New York City—John and I shared a bond that made us fast friends. He plugged the jug six years before my 1971 sobriety date.

In addition to well-known producers, *Special Assignment* was staffed by young people who became "better knowns." Peter Bergen emerged as one of the country's foremost experts on Osama Bin Laden. He arranged a *Special Assignment* exclusive interview with the terrorist leader three years before Bin Laden's name was etched into America's consciousness. Peter is now a book author and consultant on terrorism issues.

Bill Smee, a young Yale graduate recruited to the unit from CNN *Headline News*, now heads the video division for on-line *Slate Magazine*. My Whitewater producer, Matt Saal, is an Executive Producer at MSNBC. Latecomers to the investigative team included former *Close Up* and CBS *48 Hours* producer Kathy Slobogin, and longtime NBC journalist James Polk. His Watergate stories in the 1970's earned Jim a Pulitzer Prize. As of 2008, he and Kathy held senior positions at CNN.

Researchers included Ken Shiffman, more dogged at digging out information than anyone who ever worked with me. Ken moved up the CNN ladder to become a Senior Producer of network documentaries. The unit's technical and support staff was also loaded with talent, including Mike Haley. He was my video editor in Baton Rouge. Pam Hill's top video editor at *Close Up*, Ken Warner, followed her to CNN.

All the talent recruited to staff the investigative team was a radical departure from the network's prudent past and didn't go unnoticed. Under the headline, *CNN Goes for the Gold*, a quizzical article was published by *Columbia Journalism Review* asking why "some of America's top reporters gave up great jobs to join an untested *Special Assignment* projects unit at the nation's fourth network?" Pam had an answer.

"This is a rare opportunity to build a unit we hope will set a standard for television journalism in the 1990's."

In the same article I predicted that the unit "would pioneer techniques in telling complicated stories, giving lie to the oft-repeated comment in newsrooms that it's a great story but too complex for television."

Pontificating in the nation's most prestigious journalism magazine was a long way from the potato chip truck I parked in Los Angeles when I set out to become a rock and roll disc jockey at the *Voice of the Mother Lode*. Considering all the alcohol-related interruptions in my odyssey, arriving at this destination seemed beyond the pale.

Regardless, Ivy League colleagues and others in *Special Assignment* were unperturbed by my shady past. What surprised them most was one of the secrets of my sobriety. I didn't take myself too seriously. Like many clowns and comics, my sense of humor—often inappropriate—was honed as a defense against sobbing. I had laughed my way through many of the lowest points in my life.

Special Assignment made its CNN debut in March, 1990. To mark the event, Pam Hill bought me a new necktie. She said it was a good luck ritual, rather than a comment on my redneck tastes. We shopped at Barney's, the Madison Avenue clothing store for shoppers claiming the ability to discern between Parisian designer garments and rip-offs sold on the sidewalks of New York. She selected a $125

Hermès, tempting me to knot the tie with the label exposed. I rarely paid more than twenty bucks for a tie.

The necktie was a metaphor for Pam's uncompromising production standards. She didn't spare the expense. Her New York network style caused gnashing of teeth among the penny-pinching executives accustomed to the ways of the *Chicken Noodle Network*. But she had a mandate from Ted Turner to raise the network above its local news roots.

Most journalism purists oppose production techniques that incorporate music, dramatic pauses in narration, slow motion and other imagery tricks in news stories. Painfully, I had learned there was no reason to bore the hell out of people with tedious investigative stories that lacked visual creativity, or were so complicated that viewers failed to comprehend what the hell I was trying to say.

Tedium led to my unemployment in Boston. In the boonies of Baton Rouge I began to enhance exposés with a bit of zing. Pam added new dimension to investigative stories. Her techniques softened my harsh approach while maintaining substance.

I got a head start on other *Special Assignment* correspondents by reprising a five- year-old WBRZ exposé about the hypocrisy of college athletics. *Prisoners of the Game* focused on the pervasive greed of colleges in pursuit of TV money. Four ten-minute segments aired concurrent with the NCAA's 1990 Final Four basketball championship. The series revealed abuses in recruiting and educating so-called student-athletes or more accurately, athlete-students. In effect, players were low paid entertainers.

Our investigation of graduation rates at major universities disclosed an abysmal record, especially among black basketball players. Promises of a good education and/or dreams of professional careers in the NBA and NFL materialized for only a few.

Moreover, athlete-students were asked to live by NCAA rules that encouraged cheating. Then LSU basketball coach Dale Brown was a relentless critic of the NCAA policies that often seemed irrational. He said what other coaches avoided saying out of fear of retribution. He called the NCAA "a joke," repeating sharp criticisms that were part of my Baton Rouge documentary. Brown maintained it was unrealistic to expect athletes from the lowest income neighborhoods to resist the temptations of perks offered by fans and alumni. He advocated monthly allowances to discourage under-the-table payments.

The segments were repeated multiple times during CNN's twenty-four-hour news cycle. Reaction inside the network ranged from hostility to apathy. *Special Assignment* had caused lingering resentments by filling positions with so many from outside CNN, and "cherry-picking" the best producers from inside. We were seen as overpaid interlopers. And Pam's production style was criticized as too arty for the minimalist approach of producers who struggled through the days of *Chicken Noodle Network* budgets.

However, a lot of network producers soon began copying Pam's style.

I was not altogether thrilled with all the *Special Assignment* innovations, such as heralding our stories with an opening audio montage and photographs of correspondents. For my picture, artistic director Consuelo Gonzalez marched me along New York City's Sixth Avenue with a photographer skulking about like paparazzi. I could barely keep a straight face, realizing that bystanders were wondering, "Who the hell is this guy?" The end product was a head shot of me gazing off into the distance.

For our premier story, I was transported by limousine from Manhattan to a New Jersey high school gymnasium that Pam rented for the night. Producers, cameramen, lighting and sound technicians, and a teleprompter operator scurried about to make me look good. Then it was "lights, camera, and action."

Wearing my *Hermès* necktie, I pranced around the gymnasium like an actor on a set. It was not an ideal setting for a "real reporter." But I enjoyed every minute of the attention. Despite all the showbiz energy, my on-camera narration could just as easily been shot in a studio. Pam, however, didn't take shortcuts. The expense of renting a gymnasium and bringing in an army of folks for a few minutes of narration was not extravagant by her standards.

I had already learned about Pam's New York way of doing things during my brief freelance stint at *Close Up*. To gather material for a documentary, I traveled with an entourage that consisted of a director, producer, associate producers, a cameraman and sound technician. It was then an eye-opening experience for a yokel like me.

Special Assignment's fancy production didn't bother journalism traditionalists like Steve Weinberg, the former Executive Director of Investigative Reporters and Editors. In a 1990 article in *Columbia Journalism Review*, he said good things about our early stories. At the same time, he speculated about future obstacles.

"Despite the superb work of Camp and some of his colleagues at this stage, there are as many questions as answers about the Special Assignment effort. Will the unit have financial support only if CNN remains profitable? If Special Assignment segments have no appreciable effect on ratings, will Turner want to continue paying what are bound to be large bills? Will the unit practice a genuinely different kind of journalism or wind up doing formula pieces? Will the Special Assignment staff break news or be relegated to rehashes? Will the journalists there be doomed to the also-ran status of television investigative reporting, where findings are not validated unless they appear on the front page of the New York Times or Washington Post?"

Each question eventually came into play in determining the success of *Special Assignment*. And its downfall. At the outset, everything seemed rosy. I had enough stories in my repertoire to get us started. Old stories are only rehashes when reporters fail to substantially advance topics. *Prisoners of the Game* gave a broader perspective on college athletics than my earlier Baton Rouge documentary. The CNN series gave an account of problems that plagued big time college athletics ever since TV dangled cash in front of winners. In the absence of substantive reforms, the charade that athletes are in college to be educated continues as a basis for investigative stories.

As *Special Assignment* producers and correspondents completed early projects, I reported two of the investigative unit's first three stories. The second was a rip-off of *The Best Insurance Commissioner Money Can Buy*, my WBRZ exposé that helped send Louisiana's top regulator to prison. In the same vein as *Prisoners of the Game*, insurance exposés are ripe to be rehashed and updated on a frequent basis. And should be. Twenty percent or more of the average American family's disposable income is spent on insurance coverage of health, life, auto, property, etc. Yet, the industry's ties to regulators get little attention in the mainstream news media, television or print.

Titled *Mad as Hell*, the CNN version of my earlier report exposed the incestuous relationship between the nation's Insurance Commissioners and the industry they are supposed to oversee. Companies are exempt from federal regulation. Fifty states have fifty different sets of statutes. Worse, Insurance Commissioners go through revolving doors from regulatory jobs to high-paying positions in the industry and vice versa.

Accompanied by a *Special Assignment* camera crew and producers, I went to the 1990 annual convention of the National Association of Insurance Commissioners in Las Vegas. The industry had picked up most of the half-million dollar tab for the privilege of rubbing elbows with regulators. Outnumbered fifteen to one by insurance executives and lobbyists, Commissioners were entertained at plush receptions and parties. For the first and possibly the last time, a television crew was given almost unlimited access. The video documented the wet-kiss-on-the-lips love affair of insurers and their overseers.

By late fall, *Special Assignment* had begun cranking out stories every month. However, my reporting got side-tracked in November by a freedom of press controversy. It stemmed from CNN's defiance of a federal judge's order to delay the airing of tape-recorded telephone calls between imprisoned Panamanian Dictator Manuel Noriega and his defense team. The U.S. Justice Department recorded and transcribed several of General Noriega's conversations while he awaited trial in Miami on drug trafficking and money laundering charges. Taping of attorney-client discussions is prohibited.

My dead Baton Rouge pal, Barry Seal, had been among the first to link Noriega to the Colombian drug cartel. At the time, the General was a CIA "asset" and escaped scrutiny. In the same way as Iraq's Saddam Hussein, Panama's heartbreak of psoriasis poster boy was a U.S. friend of convenience prior to his regime devolving into a dictatorship. Demonized by former friends, he was indicted by a federal grand jury in Miami. Just how pro-active he was in cocaine trafficking remains questionable.

Regardless, President George Herbert Bush launched "Operation Just Cause" in December, 1989. Twenty-four-thousand troops invaded Panama to capture the saber-rattling strongman, who turned meek during the invasion and sought refuge in the Vatican Embassy. Noriega surrendered three weeks later and was transported to Miami to stand trial. He was eventually convicted based on the testimony of an array of convicted dope smugglers who were trying to save their asses from long prison sentences. Guilt or innocence aside, the trial was a replay of the abuses in my *Witness for Hire* series in Boston. Prosecutors gave outlandish deals to criminals in return for dubious testimony.

My involvement in the story began after a young correspondent for CNN's Spanish language network acquired copies of audio tapes of Noriega's calls that were routinely recorded by the Bureau of Prisons. The tapes were slipped to Marlene Fernandez by former Panamanian diplomat Jose Blandon. I'm not violating confidentiality in revealing his identity. He has since been identified as CNN's source in newspaper stories and court testimony. As a former Noriega confidante, he was recruited by DEA agents and prosecutors to identify voices on the tapes and evaluate the conversations. Unbeknownst to the feds, Blandon made his own copies of the recordings. Pam assigned me to work with Marlene to authenticate the tapes. The daughter of a Bolivian diplomat, she was unfamiliar with the subtleties of the U.S. justice system.

Based on past experience, I was reasonably certain that lawmen were barred from listening to attorney-client discussions under any circumstances. To make sure I was correct, we began a whirlwind series of on-camera interviews of legal experts, beginning with New York University law professor, Stephen Gillers. He confirmed the prohibition of monitoring lawyer/client discussions, saying the tapes could jeopardize the prosecution of the case.

A day after interviewing Gillers in New York, Marlene, *Special Assignment* producer Kathy Slobogin, a camera crew and I flew to Miami. I had arranged interviews with Noriega lawyer, Frank Rubino, former Assistant U.S Attorney Dick Gregorie and Neal Sonnett, the President of the National Criminal Defense Lawyers Association.

Before entering private practice, Gregorie was one of the Justice Department's top drug prosecutors. He successfully prosecuted the traffickers indicted in Barry Seal's Nicaraguan sting operation. After hearing excerpts of the tape, he agreed with Gillers' assessment that the recordings could damage the government's case.

A couple of hours later, Neal Sonnett described the tapes as an appalling violation of Noriega's rights. Following the Sonnett interview, I made what turned out to be a costly goof. I accidentally hit the record button when turning off the tape machine. The excerpts we brought to Miami were erased.

Already an hour late for the Rubino interview, I asked him to be patient while arranging for an Atlanta producer to play the original tape over the telephone. The quality was terrible. But when I played the tape for Rubino and a Spanish-speaking paralegal, they could understand enough to confirm it was authentic. The lawyer said he planned to report the violation to the trial Judge. I was now confident we had information that exposed government overstepping in an extremely high-profile case.

After returning to Atlanta, we made plans to break the story in a Wednesday evening newscast. But early Tuesday afternoon, I received a call from Rubino asking us to delay the story until he filed motions in court. He feared the on-camera confirmation of the tape could be interpreted as a waiver of Noriega's attorney-client confidentiality. I explained that the focus of our story was government misconduct, not defense strategy. As a courtesy, I agreed to inform CNN's legal department about his request for a delay.

Given clearance to run the segment by our chief counsel, I told Rubino we planned to air the story the next day. He threatened to seek a restraining order. I again apprised CNN's lawyer of the threat. He recommended we beat Rubino to the punch by running the story early Wednesday morning before the courthouse opened.

After an all-night session writing a script, gathering archival video and editing the piece, the story ran in a seven a.m. newscast. By hastening the release of the report, I did something I've since condemned. I was rushing a story to air to protect a scoop. Knowing Rubino's relationships with Miami reporters, I failed to exercise caution, even though nobody else possessed the tapes. The decision would prove costly in the end.

Exhausted after the report aired, I headed home to get some sleep. My snooze was interrupted by CNN President, Tom Johnson. He said the Justice Department denied recording any attorney-client conversations. The denial may have been based on the fact that the quality of the audio in our report proved nothing. We considered using the original tapes, but decided it would misrepresent what happened in Rubino's office as he and the paralegal strained to hear the audio. Tom told me to hurry back to the office.

As soon as the federal courthouse opened Wednesday morning in Miami, Rubino followed up on his threat by seeking a restraining order. Trial Judge William Hoeveler scheduled a hearing for the next day. Until now, I had only limited contact with Tom Johnson. Earlier in the year, he succeeded Burt Reinhardt, CNN's President since the network first signed on. The two men were opposites.

From my seventh floor office, I could see Burt at his desk one level below. He never seemed to leave. I was told that he regularly swam laps at CNN Center's health club. It must have been on my days off, or while I was on the road. We were introduced during my first visit to CNN, but the conversation was so brief I figured he didn't give a shit about hiring me or creating an investigative team. When *Special Assignment's* staff was finally assembled, Burt made a brief appearance at a celebratory reception. He departed so quickly, a breeze was created in his wake.

In contrast to Burt, Tom Johnson was gregarious to the point of distraction. When major stories broke, he roamed the newsroom like a commanding General. Following Tom's retirement, he publicly disclosed a battle with clinical depression for most of his adult life—a possible explanation of our odd encounters over the years.

Ted Turner hired Tom for much the same reason as Pam Hill—to boost the image of the "Chicken Noodle Network" as a reputable newsgathering organization by paying top dollar to high-profile media executives. His résumé was certainly impressive. He was a former publisher of both the *Los Angeles Times* and the Dallas *Morning News*. As a young man, he worked for Bill Moyers in Lyndon Johnson's White House press office and afterwards was an executive at Lady Bird Johnson's Austin, Texas television station.

To the surprise of CNN lawyers, Judge Hoeveler issued a temporary restraining order and directed the network to cease broadcasting excerpts until he reviewed the tapes. The ruling set off a series of Atlanta meetings involving Tom Johnson, corporate eagles, legal beagles from private firms and members of the *Special Assignment* team. Even as the court hearing took place, we were putting finishing touches on a follow-up report.

The Justice Department's denial of our disclosure required a response. The second story contained audible portions of the tape, as well as an on-screen translation of the conversation and the identity of the participants. Senior Producer Marty Koughan was now assigned to the story, along with another producer from CNN's Spanish network.

While editing was being completed for the five p.m. newscast, network lawyers were in Judge Hoeveler's courtroom trying to overturn the restraining order. As the newscast deadline approached, I sat in a conference room with CNN executives and lawyers from inside and outside the network. Tom sat at the head of the table. He asked the advice of Washington attorney Stuart Pierson, a First Amendment expert on retainer to review *Special Assignment* stories. Citing a Rhode Island prior restraint case, he believed we had a basis to defy the ruling if the judge ruled against us. Thirty minutes prior to air time, one of the attorneys called from Miami.

Not only had Judge Hoeveler refused to lift the order, he demanded that CNN immediately turn over the tapes for his inspection. It was nut-cracking time. Tom looked around the room for dissent.

"If anyone believes we should delay the report, speak now." There was silence. He called the newsroom and gave the go-ahead.

Watching the newscast in the conference room, everyone cringed when the story was introduced by anchor Bernard Shaw with words to the effect, "Today, a federal district court Judge in Miami, Florida ordered CNN not to air secret recordings of Manuel Noriega's discussions with his legal defense team. Fuck you, Judge."

Federal judges do not react well to violations of their orders. Many have God-like complexes. From high above, they exercise absolute authority over their courtroom domains. The network's defiance angered every God-like judge in the country, as well as Hoeveler. He immediately cited CNN for criminal contempt. When attorneys later tried to overturn his ruling at the appellate level, they were treated like court jesters.

In my opinion, Tom made the right call but made a tactical error. The news media must abide by the nation's laws. However journalists must have broad freedoms to expose government misconduct without interference from the courts. Judge Hoeveler's restraining order shielded prosecutors, who were under intense pressure to convict General Noriega in order to justify the invasion of Panama.

Failure to obtain a conviction would have been a huge embarrassment to the Bush Administration. In an unprecedented act of U.S. aggression, hundreds of Panamanian civilians were killed, thousands lost their homes, businesses were destroyed and looted, and the small nation's economy was thrown into chaos. President Bush promised billions to rebuild. Congress delivered only a fraction of the sum.

CNN may have avoided the court's wrath by handling the story in a more circumspect manner. My eagerness in jumping the gun before Rubino could get to the courthouse was our first mistake. Failing to include comprehensible audio in the initial report was the second. And third, Bernard Shaw's lead-in should have provided a rationale for defying a court order. Marty Koughan and I asked Tom Johnson to do an on-camera interview explaining the network's position. He said it was inappropriate for him to be part of the story. He became part of the story anyway.

As happens in prior restraint cases, the news media jumped on the story. CNN's defiance prompted hundreds of stories and scores of editorials. With the exception of right-wing politicians and salivating radio performers, most commentaries supported the network's decision. "Oddly, federal judges aren't so concerned with probing the potential invasion of the defendant's rights," the *New York Times* wrote. "Hastily, they assail CNN for its reports that brought the problem to light in the first place. It's a textbook case of shooting the messenger."

Many editorials took the same tone. But widespread support for CNN didn't sway Judge Hoeveler. Three days after our story, FBI agents showed up at CNN headquarters in Atlanta demanding that we turn over the tapes. Although agents didn't have search warrants, I instructed a *Special Assignment* researcher to keep the recordings outside the building until an appeals court overturned Hoeveler's ruling. That never happened.

Throughout the controversy, we continued to gather information about the conduct of prosecutors and investigators. Marlene's confidential source, Jose Blandon, claimed to have witnessed abuses over and beyond the taped conversations. However, we had to be very careful in using his information. Like men and women who cheat on spouses, secret sources are betrayers of trust. As symbolic lovers, muckrakers are complicit in helping them cheat. Blandon betrayed the prosecution team. Hence, his trustworthiness was questionable. The tapes were indisputable. His other accusations lacked documentation.

In conversations with Marlene, Blandon claimed to be present at a meeting in which prosecutors coached a witness to commit perjury. Elements of the story such as the time and place could be independently verified. Other parts of the tale had to be accepted on faith. As a show of faith, I wanted an on-camera interview giving exact details.

Blandon was then in the Witness Protection Program, living under a false identity in the Texas Panhandle. Over his attorney's objection, he agreed to an interview so long as his identity was concealed. I traveled to Texas with Marlene, three producers, a camera crew and a lawyer. The arrival of FBI agents at CNN had triggered paranoia. Consequently, the lawyer escorted us as a matter of precaution.

To avoid drawing attention to Blandon by hauling TV equipment into his Texas home, we met at a motel. For more than an hour, Marlene asked questions in Spanish. I rephrased them a half-dozen times for inconsistencies, warning Blandon of my personal rule in keeping his identity confidential. If he lied or misled us, the agreement was void. He steadfastly insisted that he was telling the truth.

On the basis of the interview, we prepared a report to reinforce earlier stories of prosecutorial misconduct. I got preliminary legal approval for the segment from the lawyer assigned to review *Special Assignment* stories. But Steve Korn, head of CNN's legal department, wanted additional corroboration. Irritated by his caution, I contacted Blandon's Dallas attorney. Though cordial, he had previously refused to talk to me about the case. So I tried an old ploy by telling him the allegations were going to air on CNN the next day, regardless. That got his attention.

"I would advise you to be very careful in checking those facts," he said. Asked if he was saying the Blandon story was untrue, my question went unanswered. "That is all I'm going to say."

The ominous tone of his voice was enough for me to back away from Blandon's allegations. A good thing, too. We subsequently determined that his information was inaccurate. The former Panamanian official's motive, if any, for falsely alleging misconduct is a mystery. He very well may have misunderstood the discussions.

In early December, the Noriega tapes story took a strange turn. Marlene was mugged in a corridor outside her room in the Omni Hotel at CNN Center. Producer Marty Koughan suspected a link between the assault and the story. He angrily accused the network of failing to protect her. Tom Johnson ordered him to take a few days off to cool down. Marty interpreted the demand as his being pulled off the story. The dispute led to his departure from CNN—a significant setback for the *Special Assignment* Unit.

Marlene's return to Washington triggered another bizarre event. She inadvertently left copies of the tapes in her hotel room. The tapes were taken to lost and found by a maid. When someone noticed the CNN label, the network's head of security was contacted. He was a retired FBI agent and saved his old pals the trouble of enforcing a subpoena. "Hey guys, you know those tapes you wanted......"

In reality, the recordings were much to do about nothing, a technical violation of Noriega's rights. After CNN finally turned over the tapes to Judge Hoeveler, he dismissed Rubino's motion to throw out the case. And in April 1992, the General was convicted and sentenced to forty years in prison. His conviction was based almost entirely on the testimony of Latin American drug criminals, who were given sweetheart deals by prosecutors. Compared to several of his accusers, Noriega was a fine fellow. If he belonged in prison, it was in Panama for offenses committed against fellow countrymen.

Following the trial, I reported a one hour *Special Assignment* documentary titled, *The General's Price: The Full Story*. Watching the show fifteen years later was eerie. On a smaller scale, the Panama invasion looks like a preview of what happened in Iraq.

Retired General Frederick Woerner described "Operation Just Cause" as a needless waste of human lives and property. He spoke with authority as the former head of SouthCom, the command that encompassed Panama. Woerner was transferred because of a moderate stance toward Noriega. In an interview for our documentary, he contended that Military Police could easily have arrested the dictator with a show of force at Fort Amador, the U.S. installation that Noriega drove past nearly every day.

"I think it was absolutely predictable that the policy we put in place would ultimately lead to an incident that would justify a military intervention," he said.

The incident justifying an invasion was the shooting death of a U.S. Marine by Panamanian soldiers. The Marine had failed to stop at a check point. But in the same vein as George W. Bush's Iraq war, the mainstream media failed to investigate the weak premise for the Panama invasion. Nor did reporters pay attention to the casualties and heavy damage inflicted on a country that historically has acceded to U.S. interests. The pointless invasion was the basis for the film, *Panama Deception*, winner of the 1993 Academy Award for Best Documentary Feature.

It took four years to resolve CNN's contempt of court citation. Miami lawyer Robert Dunlap received a temporary appointment as Assistant U.S. Attorney to lead the investigation. I was subpoenaed in September, 1993 and testified to the aforementioned sequence of events. Outside the grand jury room, Dunlap sarcastically remarked to my attorney that I "held the CNN line." But there was no "line," other than the freedom to expose prosecutorial misconduct.

In November, 1994, CNN was found guilty of criminal contempt. Tom Johnson was given a choice. Risk a huge fine or pay $85,000 in court costs, grovel before the judge and air a scripted retraction multiple times. Tom chose option two. The assessment was a high price to pay, but only represented a fraction of the legal fees paid to outside lawyers who defended CNN. Judge Hoeveler wrote the retraction, which stated in part:

"The court held CNN in contempt because CNN broadcast tape recordings of General Manuel Noriega's telephone conversations with his attorney in November 1990. CNN's broadcast of these recordings violated an explicit order of the United States District Court not to broadcast. On further consideration, CNN realizes that it was in error in defying the order of the court and publishing the Noriega tape while appealing the court's order. We do now and always have recognized that our justice system cannot long survive if litigants take it upon themselves to determine

which judgment or orders of the court they will or will not follow, etc."

I respect judicial authority, however, I considered Judge Hoeveler's mandated statement to be total bullshit. Our culpability was rushing to air to beat the competition. It was a mistake, but one common in the news business. The real issue in this case was CNN's freedom to expose governmental misconduct based on the cliché of "the public's need to know." We simply lost a battle of wills by pissing off a judge.

Contrary to popular belief, the news media's Constitutional protections are more by implication than law. First Amendment privileges of freedom of press and speech are further limited by judicial decisions that have placed restrictions on what we can and cannot report. It is "a chilling effect," to use another cliché often repeated by journalists.

Tom Johnson was certainly chilled. More than once when we came face-to-face he jokingly said, "You're the guy who got me in trouble with Judge Hoeveler." I assumed the remark was in jest. But in September 1995, I learned the extent of his trauma.

In fear of Judge Hoeveler, he killed a well-documented story disclosing that a key witness in the Noriega case was secretly paid $1.3 million for his testimony. The payment was concealed from defense attorneys in violation of what is known as the "Brady rule," which requires prosecutors to disclose all exculpatory evidence, including details of lucrative deals that motivate witnesses to testify.

The witness for hire against Noriega was Ricardo Bilonick, Panama's former "Ambassador at Large." In return for his testimony, he received a reduced sentence in a drug case, his family was placed in the Witness Protection Program, and he was allowed to keep $3-million in assets he accumulated by shipping twenty tons of cocaine into the United States. That part of his lucrative deal was disclosed to Noriega lawyers.

However, prosecutors failed to reveal an outlandish scheme that earned Bilonick another $1.3-million. To facilitate his cooperation, the government secretly agreed to reduce the prison sentence of a Colombian cocaine smuggler named Luis (Lucho) Santacruz. He was a half-brother of the leader of the notorious Cali cartel. Santacruz had nothing whatsoever to do with the Noriega case.

A longtime source of mine got cross-ways with prosecutors and gave me documents outlining the remarkable arrangement. I laid out details for Pam Hill. She told me to pursue the story. But when it was ready to go, Tom Johnson spiked the exposé because of his fear of irritating Hoeveler. "Even if angels stood at your side, the judge will think it's payback." he said. The response prompted me to do something that may cause straitlaced journalists to shudder. I stuffed the documents in a plain brown envelope and mailed the material to a Noriega lawyer. It was no doubt a violation of a journalistic principle, though I don't know which one.

In the five years since the tapes controversy, I stayed in contact with Noriega's co-counsel, John May. He kept me abreast of the appeals process. We hit it off as friends, which is surprising given his comment when we first met.

"I don't know if I want to talk to you. The only source of yours I'm familiar with was murdered by a Colombian hit team," he said, referring to drug smuggler Barry Seal. I didn't detect a smile.

Anyway, I mailed the documents to John because I strongly objected to the "win at any cost" tactics of prosecutors. He shared my belief that the integrity of the criminal justice system was as important—if not more so—than the guilt or innocence of defendants. He knew what to do with the documents. The *Miami Herald*, *Washington Post*, *Newsweek*, and *60 Minutes* revealed Bilonick's lucrative deal with the Cali cartel. At the same time, John May and Frank Rubino filed motions for a new trial. However, the revelation that prosecutors indirectly helped the Cali cocaine smuggling operation in order to induce a witness to testify failed to influence Judge Hoeveler. He refused to grant a new trial, ruling that disclosure of the deal would not have changed the trial's outcome.

Noriega served twelve years in a U.S. prison. Following his release in 2008, he was extradited to France to stand trial in a money-laundering case. He will face charges in Panama. If he ever gets there.

Tom Johnson may have been bothered that other news organizations broke a story that he rejected. Shortly before

Christmas 1995, he was sitting in the reception area of his office when I stepped in to wish him Happy Holidays.

"I guess we should have aired your report," he blurted out, a non sequitur in response to my greeting. Tom's handling of the stories foreshadowed a bleak future.

The furor caused by the Noriega tapes had at least given *Special Assignment* a bit of recognition. Otherwise, we were reporting in a vacuum. In my radio days as the *"Voice of the Mother Lode,"* people complained they couldn't find our little station on the dial.

I now heard complaints from sources that they couldn't find our investigative stories on the network. The unpredictable placement in newscasts of *Special Assignment* exposés ensured the anonymity of our correspondents. It was as if we had joined the Witness Protection Program. Nobody knew us. The impact of our stories was negligible.

I was disappointed when my best CNN stories went unnoticed. An example was a series exposing the illegal practices of one of the North America's biggest medical waste disposal companies. Titled *Dumping on Small Town America*, we uncovered safety violations, as well as bribery of a Missouri mayor who approved a dump site in his town.

The medical waste series allowed me to display interviewing skills and the bullshit tactics that formed the foundation of my muckraking success. The President of a Canadian-based company had agreed to an on-air interview. But when we arrived in Toronto, he had a change of heart and offered instead to give a written statement. Not wanting to throw away the money spent to fly a producer, camera crew and me to Canada, I performed my BS act for producer Bill Smee. I explained to the man the difficulty of using the text of a written statement in a TV story.

"Since we are in the business of pictures, I may have to use an Interpol mug shot," I told him. Bill looked at me incredulously. He knew of no such photo. That's because we didn't have a mug shot. Nor did I say we had one. But one must exist. Research disclosed that he served time in Australia in the biggest bankruptcy fraud in the country's history.

After mentioning the "mug shot," the businessman excused himself. Ego and vanity were about to trump good judgment. I told Bill that he would now do the interview. And he did. On-camera, he conceded after unloading medical waste in South Carolina, company trucks hauled watermelons north. He also admitted paying an inflated price to the Mayor of a Missouri town for a waste site. As an added incentive for allowing the town to be dumped on, the Mayor was rewarded with a high-paying job.

Journalism ethicists can judge my tactics in getting the interview. Regardless, it was a good story that barely caused a ripple. I saw additional evidence of *Special Assignment*'s invisibility following an exposé of a not-for-profit organization operating under the official sounding title of the *National* Association of Chiefs of Police (NACOP)—not to be confused with the *International* Association of Chiefs of Police, the world's largest organization of police executives.

NACOP's membership was comprised mainly of Police Chiefs in one-traffic-light villages, small-town cops, security guards, part-time deputies, school-crossing guards and "honorary members" willing to contribute a few bucks for faux-police credentials. But because of name confusion, its Executive Director was often quoted as an authoritative source on law-enforcement issues. His police background consisted of working a few months as Chief of a three-man police force in a tiny Illinois town.

The *National* Association of Chiefs of Police was in the fundraising business. It collected money to support the fledgling American Police Hall of Fame in Miami and massage the egos of its members. The *International* Chiefs of Police repeatedly tried to discourage reporters of using the faux-police organization as a source.

Long after my *Special Assignment* story exposed the charade, journalists seemed unable to distinguish between "national' and "international." Obviously, they didn't watch CNN. But neither did most people. The gullibility of network and local reporters in relying on NACOP's "expertise" was amazing.

But it was symptomatic of the decline of television news.

CHAPTER FIFTEEN

AT LEAST I GOT A NEW FACE

My disparagement of television reporters is not about them. It's about their bosses who, too often, are corporate ghosts cloaked in greed. The threshold for enterprise reporting has sunk under the weight of rating pressures. The sad result is that most politicians, government officials and private citizens at the vortex of public issues believe that journalists are dim-witted, both those in TV and print. What other explanation is there for devious statements that can be easily discredited with a little bit of research, and/or underhanded actions that can be exposed by a modicum of investigation. Because reporters are considered stupid, malefactors lose their fear of exposure.

After twenty-five years at local radio and television stations, I was stunned by the slipshod reporting of veteran network correspondents. I soon realized there was no venue for in-depth stories on the Big Three networks unless reporters were lucky enough to produce segments for *Nightline*, *60 Minutes* or other magazine shows. My first awakening to this sad state of affairs occurred during the 1992 Presidential campaign.

Pam Hill volunteered to oversee the production of "a landmark series of six prime-time specials," titled *Democracy in America*. Three of the documentaries focused on public policy issues, two were in-depth investigations of

President George H.W. Bush and Arkansas Governor Bill Clinton, and one program profiled their running mates. Seven CNN correspondents and a team of *Special Assignment* producers and researchers were assigned to the project.

At the last minute, a third candidate entered the campaign. And by the luck of the draw, I was assigned to do the digging on Ross Perot. By far, he was the strangest. Perot's rise from horseback-riding paperboy to billionaire mogul was legendary. Beyond wealth, he was best known for liberating two employees from a Tehran prison at the outset of the 1976 Iranian hostage crisis. The mission was the subject of a book and a film. I don't recall if I read the book beforehand, but I saw the 1986 movie, *On Wings of Eagles*.

Other than skimming newspaper and magazine articles that reported Perot's self-aggrandizing publicity stunts, I knew little else about him, which is the best way to start an investigative project. I had no opinions about him one way or another. I soon discovered that there was much to learn about the Perot myth.

The plain-spoken Texan—journalists are required to describe all Texans as plain-spoken, even if they are mute—announced his candidacy February 20, 1992, on the Larry King show. The program was a favorite venting venue for Perot's grandiose claims. Most went unchallenged. During this appearance, he told Larry that he had heard the cry of American masses demanding a leader of his skills. He wouldn't just "tinker with the engine" under the hood, he would fix the thing altogether.

To ensure that Perot heard fellow citizens correctly, a 1-800 number was flashed on the screen for people to register their support. The next day, he claimed that telephone lines were jammed by thousands of calls begging him to rescue the nation in the same manner he saved his jailed employees in Tehran. Perot's response was to establish the Reform Party. In some ways, it was the face of angry white men. White women, too.

I missed the Larry King interview. And so did Bill Smee, the producer assigned to work with me on the project. We watched a videotape in awe. By the end, Bill and I were ready to rush to the ballot box and cast our votes for Perot, even though neither of us was particularly angry. Perot sounded great. As we soon learned, Perot's shtick on the Larry King show was pretty much the full range of his political acumen. He accused other candidates of speaking in sound bites, while doing nothing but.

Despite his often-stated criticism of federal spending, Perot was a prime beneficiary of government programs. The source of his fortune was Electronic Data Systems (EDS), the nation's biggest processor of Medicare and Medicaid claims. The big surprise for us, though, was learning undisclosed details of the "dramatic rescue" that became the basis of On Wings of Eagles. Finding the real story was relatively easy.

The fable revolved around an EDS subsidiary that handled data processing for Iran's Social Security system. Newspaper articles disclosed that in 1980, a federal court in Dallas awarded Perot's company $20-million in a breach of contract lawsuit against Iran. The trial took place at the same time fifty-two Americans were held hostage in the U.S. Embassy in Tehran. Defense lawyers claimed the revolution prevented them from calling important witnesses. Tough luck. The judge refused to delay the trial.

"It was a slam-dunk, 100 percent win," Perot declared in my CNN interview. Given public opinion, EDS may have won if Jesus testified for the defense.

The litigation was my research's starting point. It was linked to the most spectacular public event in Perot's biography. Several publications had reported stories during the trial. But many depositions, affidavits and other relevant documents were unavailable until the appeals process ended. I assumed that dozens of reporters would be rummaging through the files in the wake of Perot's candidacy. When I arrived at the federal archives in Fort Worth, Texas, I was surprised to discover that the records had not been inspected in years.

Tucked away was background information raising questions about the integrity of the company that made Perot a billionaire. The files offered insights of EDS business practices that had resulted in the jailing of Iranian-based Perot employees. Even though scores of U.S.

businesses were operating in Iran at the outset of the Islamic revolution, EDS employees were among the only U.S. citizens imprisoned. Why? Court files revealed that Perot's company was target of a bribery investigation. To obtain a $40-million contract, documents disclosed that EDS-Iran agreed to a partnership with Abolfath Mahvi, a close associate and distant relative of the Shah.

Despite royal connections, Mahvi was barred from government-related business activities due to his involvement in illegal arms transactions. To circumvent the blacklist and protect the company from allegations of making improper payments, EDS funneled money into a charitable organization—the Abolfath Mahvi Foundation.

"These foundations were essentially bag-holding operations," said John Stempel, a former American Embassy official in Tehran. "They were focused on, particularly by the secular elements of the Revolutionary coalition, as centers of corruption." The retired diplomat didn't mince words in my interview. He described Abolfath Mahvi as a notorious Iranian bagman.

I contacted the Iranian to get his response. Mahvi was then residing in Geneva, Switzerland and agreed to an on-camera interview. Luckily, my flight to Geneva was delayed at the gate in Atlanta. While waiting to board, I checked my office for messages. Mahvi had called to cancel. Former EDS executives advised him against the interview. I had talked to several ex-employees. Most refused to comment on the record. An exception was Paul Bucha, the executive in charge of EDS's Iranian operations.

"Did we succumb to pressure? We succumbed to the realities of life," he said. "We wanted his help, we needed his help."

EDS lawyer Tom Luce also defended dealing with a purported "bagman" partner. "What was eventually worked out was a very proper, above board arrangement with a prominent Iranian businessman to perform legal and proper services in Iran," he said. "To avoid even any appearance of impropriety, what was done was put money in that foundation."

Regardless of claims of propriety, the transactions seemed to contradict Perot's claims of uncompromising integrity. Indeed, two EDS executives ended up in jail in a bribery investigation, necessitating the renowned rescue attempt. In the movie, Perot was portrayed by Richard Crenna. His character is shown greeting employees after a team of Vietnam veterans incited a prison riot to facilitate their escape.

It is true that Perot recruited a rescue team led by retired Lieutenant Colonel and military hero, Arthur (Bull) Simons. After visiting the jail, Simons decided the mission was too dangerous to undertake. The prison gates were actually broken down by revolutionaries to free political prisoners. According to John Stempel, EDS executives Paul Chiapprone and Bill Gaylord escaped with 10,000 other inmates, walked to the Hyatt Hotel in Tehran and joined

Perot for a steak dinner prior to being transported in a motorcade to the Turkish border. Facts be damned in Perot's version.

"Those people that did the rescue did a heroic, unselfish, incredible thing to do what they did and bring everyone out without a scratch on anybody. Now that's the story. If somebody in the State Department, who was probably hiding under his desk during the whole time and whining for his mother, wants to claim credit for this, give it to him."

My one-hour interview with Perot two months after he announced his candidacy allowed me to view what proctologists see everyday. He angrily reacted to any questions that challenged the carefully-nurtured Perot myth. In fact, my audacity in digging into his background almost cost me the opportunity to even ask the questions. The campaign's newly-hired spokesman tried to cancel the interview. Former Chicago newspaper editor Jim Squires, whose brief exposure to Perot is proof that assholism is contagious, called me on the eve of the scheduled meeting.

"Our people say you are asking very unfriendly questions." When I acknowledged talking to former employees, he expressed concerns about the Iran litigation. "Lawyers handled all aspects of the case. It would be unfair to expect Ross to know details."

Squires volunteered to make EDS attorney Tom Luce available to discuss the case. In turn, I promised not to ask questions about the lawsuit. Fair enough. During the interview, however, Perot continually brought up the subject. An hour with the bantam rooster was akin to paying penance for past sins. He was evasive, hostile and accusatory in answering the most mundane questions.

"You said you wanted a profile of my life. I just thought I would come in and we would talk about a cross-section of my life. We're into minute details, which I will be glad to get for you or have people make available for you if you really want them."

It is no wonder that I felt a sense of déjà-vu sixteen years later when Vice Presidential candidate Sarah Palin promised to get back to Katie Couric with answers to rather simple questions. Perot was fighting mad in avoiding answers.

"If you really want to know, rather than just throw dust in the air like gorillas do when they fight, go over to EDS....." The simian metaphor was followed by a lesser creature. "You're off on an absolute rabbit chase is where you are, but you love being there. So, I've got to bring you back to reality." Then he visited the insect kingdom. "All you want to do is find, if it's at all possible, to find one mosquito somewhere. Well, there are no mosquitoes."

I wondered what Perot would do if a foreign leader pissed him off. "Hand me that red phone. I'll fix him."

Mine was one of the last in-depth Perot interviews with anyone asking questions more challenging than those of Larry King. That's not necessarily a criticism of Larry. He asks what viewers would ask. Anything more edgy angered Perot. Unlike Harry Truman, he wanted to avoid the kitchen altogether. So when serious media scrutiny began, he shocked followers by withdrawing from the race in mid-July, claiming his family was a target of "dirty tricks." He was vague about the nature of the tricks.

Perot's absence was only temporary. In a bizarre turnabout, he re-entered the race six weeks later. It is not surprising that the campaign adopted Patsy Cline's country song, *Crazy*, as its anthem. Perot ultimately invested $65.9 million of his own money to get 18.9 percent of the vote. Many political pundits believe he cost George Herbert Bush re-election. A different view is held by Bill Clinton. He believes Perot cost him a majority vote. Being elected by a plurality weakened his Administration from the beginning.

During Perot's short-lived retreat, I was assigned to profile Bill Clinton's Vice Presidential running mate, Al Gore. It was like trading a fudge sundae for Brussels sprouts. Maybe I missed something. But from my standpoint, Gore was as boring to an investigative reporter as people characterized him. If there was anything to hide, his daddy, Albert Gore, Senior, certainly didn't know it.

My supposition is based on an incident at the Tennessee home of the late Senator, who once sought the Vice Presidency. To connect the ambitions of father and son in my *Democracy in America* segment, I wanted video of Albert, Senior watching his son's nomination at the Democratic Convention. We brought along a videotape for that purpose. However, the VCR in the Gore's home was broken.

"We'll go get Al's," he said. "Al" lived across the hollow about a quarter-mile as the crow flies.

Behind the wheel of his car, the eighty-five-year-old Gore was transformed into a NASCAR driver. We sped down the driveway, raced over a twisting road and zoomed past Secret Service agents at the gate of "Al's" home with barely a wave. The elder Gore remained in the car, giving me free rein to roam the house in search of a VCR. Had I found porno tapes, marijuana or other incriminating items, it would have been CNN's big campaign scoop. But the residence was as prosaic as the public perception of its owner.

Ross Perot's comeback occurred too late for inclusion in our "landmark" *Democracy in America* documentaries. Therefore, he got prime time treatment in a series of lengthy segments. His asshole buddy, Jim Squires, was quite unhappy with my reporting. Writing of his Perot experiences in a newsletter for Harvard's Neiman Fellowship, he called me an investigative reporter "wannabe." At least I was trying.

—

A day after the Presidential election, I sent Pam a memo proposing a plan to overcome *Special Assignment*'s invisibility. The random and unpredictable placement of our stories in CNN's twenty-four-hour cycle had diminished the impact of important exposés produced by our unit. Newsroom apathy toward investigative stories was an insult to our reporters and producers. So to make stories easier to promote, I suggested we have mandated time slots in CNN's Monday newscasts, historically a slow news day. I cleverly suggested we name our Monday reports the *Monday Report*. Pam liked the idea. And so did Ed Turner. He paved the way to implement the plan.

The segments turned out to be too much of a good thing. Newscast producers were coming under increased pressure to keep stories short and visual. The "viewer friendly" disease had invaded CNN. Consultants warned the network that attention-deficit remote control surfers switch channels in seconds if bored.

"Less is best" did not bode well for *Special Assignment* reports that required background and context. We tried to set informal time limits on stories of six to seven minutes. Instead, our segments sometimes ran ten minutes or longer, and reinforced the belief of the newsroom that we were arrogant and uncooperative.

Failure to cooperate led to conflicts that were compounded by egotism—mine, for example. Questioned by a newsroom producer about the fairness of one of my stories, I didn't bother to explain that the purpose of exposés is to expose, which made the reports inherently unfair.

"How long have you been an investigative reporter?" I asked. "I've been doing this kind of reporting since you were in grade school." Or words to that effect.

I don't recall reciting a list of journalism prizes. Regardless, the humble face that my wife referred to as the "real John" was well hidden. I needed more lessons in learning AA's underlying principle of humility. And I knew where to go to for emergency ego deflation. In addition to my home AA group, I helped start meetings in CNN Center.

The *Monday Report* that caused the flare-up was the kind of investigative story that kept my muckraker adrenalin flowing. It disclosed overstepping by the U.S. Customs Service in an elaborate sting operation known as *Exodus*. As I recall, a Congressional staffer suggested I investigate the flagrant entrapment of two men caught in a Customs' sting operation of arms dealing—a legal but sinister business. Agents had lured two German buyers to the United States by misrepresenting the legality of the merchandise being offered for sale. The men were secretly videotaped buying today's equivalent of B.B. guns.

The arrests were announced with great fanfare. Then Attorney General Richard Thornburg portrayed them as "merchants of death." In reality, it was the first arms venture for both buyers. Neither had been in trouble with the law before. Because of the unsavory tactics of investigators in assuring the victims of the sting that the deal was lawful, the charges were thrown out of court. The case led me to other *Exodus* abuses.

One target was a retired Egyptian Air Force General hailed as a hero in his country. He was considered a close friend of the U.S. military. Responding to an ad in a weapons magazine, he was entrapped by agents who repeatedly vouched for the legality of a sale. By exploiting his lack of understanding of American slang, investigators elicited incriminating statements.

"There was a lot of talking, mostly by the government," an irate federal judge said in dismissing the charges.

Exodus was not limited to arms sales. A California electronics salesman was secretly videotaped finalizing the sale of an obsolete supercomputer to a Belgium informant—a snitch being paid a bounty for ensnaring suspects. During negotiations, he told the seller that the computer was Paris-bound. But at a final secretly-videotaped meeting in an Orlando, Florida hotel room, the informant said the computer was actually being shipped to an embargoed Eastern European country. On camera, the salesman backed out of the deal. It was too late.

Agents stormed his hotel room as he explained the turn of events to his lawyer in a telephone call. Again, the arrest was portrayed at a news conference as ensuring the safety of U.S. citizens. And again, the charges were ultimately dismissed.

At news conferences following *Exodus* arrests, Attorney General Thornburg, U.S. Attorneys and Customs officials regularly overstated the importance of spurious arrests. Journalists dutifully wrote down the names and allegations, but rarely questioned the propaganda. Bloated cases made front page headlines. After being tossed out of court, verdicts were reported in the back sections of newspapers alongside obituaries. Television reporters completely ignored the outcomes.

There is a reason that law enforcement agencies inflate the significance of cases, which are only slightly more serious than gays cruising airport restrooms. It's the money. Budgets are allocated based on statistics and/or favorable publicity. Cops, prosecutors and law enforcement officials see nothing wrong with overstating the charges. Gullible reporters act as flacks—cozying up to cops just like I did in Miami.

The Customs exposé was one of an array of solid stories reported by me and other *Special Assignment* correspondents. However, the *Monday Report* failed to survive. Admittedly, some stories were complicated and downright boring. Most, though, were deserving of whatever time it took to explain the issues.

Unfortunately, we couldn't compete with video such as Rodney King being battered senseless by Los Angeles cops. The beating of the black man aired so many times on CNN that we joked about including the video in all our exposés. In retrospect, I think Rodney King's famous question was appropriate for us to ask in working out differences with newsroom producers. "Why can't we all get along?"

In 1994, CNN's documentary unit merged into *Special Assignment*, increasing our staff to fifty people. Added manpower allowed us to experiment with prime time magazine shows. But weekly programs meant meeting deadlines, a problem for a spoiled reporter like me. For years, I had worked at my own pace. I was also accustomed to picking and choosing my stories.

Adapting to collaborative reporting was a challenge. My muckraking fervor had already diminished in the wake of CNN's resistance to exposing the Whitewater scandal as the political ploy it was. My stock in trade was contrarianism—not for the purpose of being ornery or controversial, but rather to corroborate for my own satisfaction the truth of collective conclusions of "lemming journalists" like those reporting the Whitewater farce. But CNN was content to follow an agenda set by major newspapers, sensationalism and disasters.

Following the April, 1995, domestic terrorist bombing in Oklahoma City, I went on a hunt for militia nuts with Matt Saal, the producer who joined me in the search for right-wing crazies in Arkansas. We found more loonies in the boonies of Montana and Idaho—like the guy whose home security system consisted of a twelve-year-old son patrolling on the roof with a twenty-two-caliber rifle. The windows below were protected by pyramids of soft drink bottles that would come tumbling down if anyone tried to enter. Matt and I produced reports on the militia that were sidebars to the search for the bomber.

I was almost sixty years old, running around the hills and dales of militia country and competing for air time with young and pretty people who were taking over television news. The end of my on-air career was in sight, but I tried to hang on. As a critic of TV's "blonde" trend, I have to make an embarrassing confession.

I tried to be young and pretty by investing $10,000 to remove genetically sagging jowls, trim puffy pockets beneath the baby blues and squeeze the skin tight around my jaw line. I bought designer suits, Pam-approved neckties, and ate *Lean Cuisine* and broccoli. My fifteen-dollar barber was replaced by a hair stylist. I stocked the bathroom cabinet with a variety of sprays, facial crèmes and other alleged youth-inducing beauty aids. My futile search for a fountain of youth was rather pathetic. Admitting sins of vanity is awkward because of vigorous past denials.

"A facelift? Hell no," I answered curious queries about the slicing and dicing. "I've lost weight, exercised, got a little sun." The new face did help me outlast a lot of friends who were drummed out of the business for being too old and/or too ugly. But a disconcerting result of my long survival was realizing that I was repeating myself. It was the same feeling I experienced in Baton Rouge after seven years of reporting scandals.

Storylines at CNN were like replays of previous exposés. The names changed, though not always. Nearly two decades after I first disclosed the misconduct of Boston FBI agent John Connolly, his snitches came home to roost. My CNN report focused on Connolly's corrupt relationship with Whitey Bulger, the notorious hit man who found a permanent place on the FBI's Ten Most Wanted List.

AT LEAST I GOT A NEW FACE

Following a reprise of the Bulger story, I returned to the land of religious hucksterism.

A *Special Assignment* investigation of televangelist Benny Hinn was a Jimmy Swaggart repeat without sex. The strange little faith-healer wearing a white suit and sporting a weird hairdo administers God cures to the sick and lame. Praying for miracles, he lays hands on his "patients," and with a sweep of the arms, he causes them to swoon backwards into the arms of ministry aides who are positioned to prevent broken necks and skull fractures. Benny can't waste time healing broken bones.

Before taking a dive, believers claim to be instantly healed of ailments ranging from drug addiction to terminal cancer. Those are the easy cases. Benny once claimed credit for raising a man from the dead during a crusade in Africa. Producer Graham Messick and I tracked a few "miracles." We were unable to determine if the African "Lazarus" was alive. Or if he was ever dead to begin with. Whatever, our investigation revealed that most of the people Benny healed relapsed. Sometimes, into the grave.

Doctors and researchers concede that faith can play a big part in healing illnesses. But Benny's miracles were performed on pre-screened, highly suggestible people who had temporary adrenalin rushes as a result of being on stage before huge audiences. The healing huckster gives hope to many who have lost hope. But the danger of his faith healing occurs when his "patients" stop taking medications and risk serious reactions—including death.

Anyway, Benny Hinn was so confident in his powers that he gave us almost unlimited access to the inner-workings of the organization. His consent followed a lengthy meeting in which I told him we were doing a story on the ministry, with or without his help. The subsequent series disclosed extravagances and misrepresentations. Yet, Benny didn't complain. Instead he promised to make changes. We were invited to revisit him at another crusade. I don't know why. Nothing had changed.

While promising health and wealth in return for a few bucks, he stayed in $1500 a night Presidential Suites, flew across the ocean in private jets, lived in a million dollar home and collected a million dollars a year in salary and perks. In 2008, his expensive tastes made him a target of a Congressional investigation into financial finagling by seven tax exempt television ministries.

Televangelism is a story that keeps on giving. Issues raised in the Benny Hinn exposé and my Swaggart documentary twenty-five years earlier, remain more relevant than ever because of the proliferation of Low Power television stations. LP signals cover about the same radius as the tiny California radio station where my reporting career began. However, access to cable systems increases potential audiences a hundredfold.

Compared to traditional outlets, commercial time on LP stations is usually cheap. Half-hour blocks are affordable for just about any preacher able to say, "Send me money so that you will go to Heaven," be healed of whatever ails you, and see your bank account increase ten-fold. California-based Trinity Broadcasting is the nation's biggest religious network by virtue of its ownership of more low power TV stations than perhaps any broadcaster in the world.

Despite a name similarity, the network is not connected with the Trinity Foundation. Just the opposite. The small Dallas, Texas religious community keeps close tabs on greedy TV preachers who fleece electronic church congregations, including vicars who appear on Trinity Broadcasting Nework. The self-appointed religious cops in Dallas have been a great resource for journalists, even diving into dumpsters to gather material for our CNN exposés of televangelists.

As a sign of the times—hard times, perhaps—Jimmy Swaggart was not among the televangelists identified in 2008 as targets of a Congressional investigation. But as I reported in a 1997 *Special Assignment* series, he is doing okay as a Baton Rouge real- estate mogul selling and leasing millions of dollars of property that the ministry acquired at the peak of his popularity. The city's biggest shopping mall is located on property once owned by the organization. Ironically, given past battles, lessees include the Baton Rouge *Advocate* newspaper—parent company of my former employer, WBRZ.

As this is written in 2009, Brother Jimmy still preaches on television. But instead of the big crusades that once drew thousands, his huge tabernacle is ringed by black curtains to conceal empty seats. He is a shell of the evangelist once described as the most dynamic preacher of the Twentieth Century. His son, Donnie, tries to mimic daddy and does a pretty fine job. However, it's like watching a very good Elvis impersonator.

Before shedding too many tears for Brother Jimmy, keep in perspective that he continues to live in high style. In addition to real estate, ministry-owned radio stations and the sale of Gospel albums are sources of income. He and Donnie still live side-by-side behind gates encircling a $3-million estate. To avoid tax problems, the ministry must continue operating. If it shuts down, IRS rules require the liquidation of assets, payment of taxes, and/or distribution of remaining chattels to similar tax exempt groups.

I interviewed Jimmy in 1997 as part of my CNN report, *Rich in Disgrace*. He retracted his portrayal of me as "one of the finest investigative reporters in the world," the strange critique of me before his infamous 1988 confession to whore-mongering.

"John, I'm going to take back what I said. You're not as good a reporter as I thought you were. You can take the *Sermon on the Mount* and turn it into a conspiracy to overthrow the government." In typical Brother Jimmy fashion, he threw his arm over my shoulder, thus giving my career a bit of symmetry. I had received a more kindly brotherly hug fifteen years before when I traveled with him on a crusade. That was our first encounter. This was the last.

Now travelling familiar paths, I realized I was nearing the end of an improbable odyssey that began at the lowest point in my life.

CHAPTER SIXTEEN

THE NERVE OF CNN

Twenty-four-hour news is convenient. But it's a distortion of reality. And I'm not referring solely to Fox News. There is a four-letter word that distorts what cable news networks report. Live!

In times of crisis and/or disaster, CNN has a greater capacity than any network to go live just about anywhere, at anytime. But the "Breaking News" graphic flashes on the screen for too many stories that range from trivial to insignificant. I've seen CNN use the banner on non-injury accidents, reminding me of newscast fillers I relied on in my first radio job as the *Voice of the Mother Lode* at tiny 250-watt KVML in Sonora, California.

Abuse of the "Breaking News" characterization is really a form of trickery designed to attract the attention of viewers and stop them from surfing away from the network—only a moderate transgression, perhaps, in an era of journalistic irresponsibility by print and broadcasting.

Far more serious, however, is the exaggerated urgency given to "Breaking News" that is truly important, but requires context. Breathlessly, correspondents rush before live cameras with live reports of every sentence uttered relating to ongoing issues. The anchor then asks them to add meaning to their report— instant interpretations, so to speak. Their comments are then followed by more interpretation by the network's huge stable of pundits. Everybody weighs in, but not necessarily with depth. Nuance is rare on CNN—and television in general. The aim of television news is to show conflict.

With a few exceptions, what passes for television investigative reporting as this is written is the kind of enterprise that should occur on a daily basis. Hard-edged, name-calling exposés ended on CNN when the network got caught in the middle of a controversy that damaged its image.

Special Assignment's demise is a story of what happens to television investigative reporting in a corporate environment. A single segment resulted in an epidemic of shriveled balls that swept through the network in 1998.

The virus was spawned by an "exposé" accusing the U.S. military of using nerve gas in a clandestine operation during the Vietnam War. The mission was conducted by an elite commando unit that crossed the border into Laos for the alleged purpose of either capturing or killing American defectors suspected of collaborating with enemy forces encamped in the supposedly neutral country.

Produced by *Special Assignment*, the story was titled *Valley of Death*. It is better known as *Tailwind*, the name given the secret mission. The segment was to be a "holy shit" blockbuster bringing attention to a new prime-time Sunday night program called, *NewsStand: CNN & TIME*.

It was a blockbuster all right, but for all the wrong reasons. Instead of divulging military secrets, the "exposé" revealed the pitfalls of television muckraking. Encapsulated in an eighteen-minute segment were overstatements, injudicious editing, lack of context, and omissions of relevant facts. The fiasco is a paradigm of flaws, blunders and decisions epitomizing the superficial mentality that is an obstacle to serious television investigative reporting. The story also embodied the perils of muckraking in a profit-driven media conglomerate that placed more emphasis on ratings and image than on courage and journalistic principle.

In the face of intense criticism, CNN adopted a policy of appeasement and finger-pointing. Two producers were summarily fired, a distinguished war correspondent was held up to public ridicule and two esteemed executives resigned—one under pressure, the other in protest. All were victims of corporate cowardice.

My role in the ignominy was limited to being a clean-up reporter. However, the story had a profound impact on me, my career and my attitude about the future of television investigative reporting. If a *Journalism Hall of Infamy* is ever created, *Tailwind* will occupy a prominent place alongside Dan Rather's 2004 calamitous exposé dealing with George W. Bush's disgraceful military record.

Although accurate in reporting the future President's dereliction of duty, the CBS story was rendered ineffectual by phony documents provided to a producer by a source in

Bush's National Guard unit. An expert, who examined the material, failed to detect that the documents were counterfeit. The uproar surrounding the story resulted in Dan Rather's departure from CBS in near disgrace. Three executives were forced to resign and a producer was fired.

In 2007, three years after the debacle, Dan Rather filed a lawsuit against the network, asserting that CBS's retreat from the Bush story was a result of White House pressure. He contends the exposé was essentially true, even if the documents were manufactured. The court has dismissed key elements of the complaint.

Like the veteran CBS anchorman and his collaborators, CNN *Special Assignment* producers were victimized by sources, maybe even senility. Given the publicity accorded to their missteps, *Tailwind* deserves a place in my fictional Hall of Infamy in a section called "Overreaction by Television Executives."

Mistakes, misinterpretations and inadvertent omissions are an inherent risk of investigative reporting. However, except for egregious incompetence, plagiarism or fictionalized reporting, the proper response by news organizations should be, "We fucked up, we're sorry, and we will add safeguards to ensure it doesn't happen again."

NewsStand was touted as a brand new program. In reality, it was another version of *Special Assignment's* eight-year quest to create a successful magazine show. Previous efforts aired under the titles of *CNN on Special Assignment*, *CNN Reports*, and *Impact*. The newest incarnation followed the marriage between Turner Broadcasting System and Time-Warner Corporation.

The unveiling also coincided with the arrival of Rick Kaplan as CNN's new President and Tom Johnson's promotion to Chairman of all network entities. Kaplan was a former Executive Producer of two highly successful ABC programs, *Nightline* and *Prime Time*. He was eager for CNN to produce shows of equal quality on a CNN budget, a fraction of what broadcast networks spent.

The only substantive difference in *NewsStand* and prior editions was the backdrop behind co-anchors Bernard Shaw and Jeff Greenfield. Rather than introduce segments from inside CNN studios, they stood in front of authentic newsstands in Washington and New York. The innovation was not exactly revolutionary. But it was cheap. Regardless, the show was promoted as something different, a showcase of the combined resources of "two of the world's leading news organizations."

Time magazine, however, had little to do with preparing the nerve gas exposé. Even so, the magazine shared in the embarrassment after publishing a version of the story under the byline of CNN reporters, Peter Arnett and April Oliver. Peter was a veteran war correspondent on loan to *Special Assignment*. April was the lead producer.

The *NewsStand* allegations related to a 1970 commando raid into Laos by a super-secret Special Forces unit innocuously named the Studies and Observations Group,

SOG for short. Accompanied by more than a hundred Montagnard mercenary tribesmen from Vietnam's high country, the small unit slipped across the border to attack a North Vietnamese encampment. Sixteen SOG soldiers were wounded in the ensuing battle. Montagnards also sustained heavy casualties, including six deaths. Those are confirmed facts. Virtually everything else in the *NewsStand* report is in dispute.

The most visible person caught up in the controversy was Peter Arnett. The high profile correspondent was temporarily assigned to *Special Assignment* to narrate the segment. A Pulitzer Prize winning journalist during the Vietnam conflict, he was a battle-hardened reporter who had covered many of the world's hotspots.

The story centered on two volatile claims—the assassination of U.S. defectors and the ostensible use of the nerve chemical, sarin. According to the *NewsStand* account, the weapon was used during a helicopter evacuation of the commandos after they killed two turncoat Americans. In danger of being overrun by a North Vietnamese regiment, the outmanned SOG troops were shielded by A-1 Sky Raiders, which fired cluster bombs on the encampment during the evacuation. The CNN story claimed that nearly everyone in the camp was killed by nerve gas, known in military parlance as CBU-15. Pentagon officials immediately denied the assertions. Documents were released indicating the cluster bombs contained a non-lethal tear gas. Outraged Special Forces veterans and their commanders also disputed the allegations.

Two days after *NewsStand's* premier show, Executive Producer Pamela Hill summoned me to Washington. "We need you to interview a Pentagon official as a follow-up to April Oliver's report," she said without a hint of alarm.

April was a thirty-four-year-old Princeton honors graduate, who worked for the PBS *McNeil-Lehrer Report* prior to joining our unit. Nine months before *Tailwind*, she produced a CNN exposé that was a precursor to *Tailwind*. Titled *Secret Warriors*, it disclosed other SOG covert activities. She had been researching *Tailwind* ever since.

Working closely with April was Senior Producer Jack Smith, a former CBS Washington bureau chief. The tough-talking Chicago native had an impeccable reputation for integrity. The combined experience of April and Jack gave Pam confidence that the story would withstand scrutiny. She and several key people in *Special Assignment* had reviewed a thick briefing book that contained notes, transcribed interviews and stacks of material relevant to the exposé.

Moreover, CNN Senior Legal Counsel David Kohler cleared the segment and Rick Kaplan gave his approval. All necessary precautions seemed to have been taken to ensure the story's accuracy. The only missing component was a response from Pentagon officials. Repeated requests for an interview were ignored.

In large part, April and Jack were relying on the credibility of two main sources. The most authoritative was retired Naval Admiral Thomas Moorer. Eighty-six-years old and living in a nursing home, he was Chairman of the Joint Chiefs of Staff at the time of the Laos mission. In a roundabout way, he confirmed the allegations made by both identified and anonymous sources who were interviewed by April. CNN critics later claimed Moorer was a dubious source because of occasional periods of senility.

Tailwind's most explosive charges were made by former SOG Lieutenant, Robert Van Buskirk. He was second in command during the mission. In on-camera interviews, he gave vivid accounts of firing into a "spider hole" to kill an American defector. He also told of seeing enemy bodies scattered in the camp after the alleged nerve gas attack. His story was supported in ambiguous fashion by another Special Forces veteran.

But it was Admiral Moorer's interview that gave credence to the story. On-camera, he was vague. "Off-camera," according to Peter Arnett's narration, he was explicit in corroborating the premise of the most incendiary accusation. "Admiral Moorer acknowledged off-camera that *Tailwind*'s target was, indeed, defectors."

In the interview itself, the retired officer's comments were generic. Asked by April if he was morally opposed to using lethal chemical weapons, he said, "I would be willing to use any weapon and any tactic to save the lives of American soldiers."

Absent from the *NewsStand* segment were the denials of several people April interviewed in researching the story. Indeed, the only straightforward denial in the report came from *Tailwind*'s commanding officer, Captain Eugene McCarley.

"I never, ever considered the use of lethal gas, not on any of my operations." The statement was discounted in Arnett's narration. "Captain McCarley told CNN off-camera that the use of nerve gas was, quote, 'very possible.'"

The former SOG leader also contradicted allegations that his troops killed American deserters. "To this day, Captain McCarley denies *Tailwind*'s mission was to kill defectors, saying his orders were to draw enemy troops away from CIA mercenaries in a battle nearby," Arnett reported. Again, conjunctive "but" in the narration made McCarley sound like a liar.

"But several former senior military officials have confirmed to CNN that the village and the defectors were *Tailwind*'s objective," the story stated.

These officials were not identified. Still, the "exposé" seemed solid to me. Van Buskirk's resolute on-camera comments and the acknowledgement by Admiral Moorer seemed to corroborate the disclosures. My only question was whether viewers really cared about a twenty-eight-year-old war story. The My Lai massacre and other U.S. military atrocities had raised the threshold of the nation's outrage to a point that I expected the CNN allegations to go unnoticed. Hardly.

Former members of U.S Special Forces units and the military establishment immediately took dead aim at the network. CNN's own military analyst, retired General Perry Smith, resigned in protest. Then came a worst case reaction. Pentagon officials issued a statement attributed to Admiral Moorer in which he claimed to have been misquoted and/or quoted out of context. Simultaneously, a spokesman announced that Secretary of Defense William Cohen had ordered a full-scale investigation, even though a review of *Tailwind* documents had already disclosed that two forms of non-lethal gas were used during the mission. Neither was a nerve agent.

Coincidental to Pam's assigning me to back-report the story, a former Marine arrived at my Atlanta office with his daughter—a Time Warner employee. Eighteen years earlier, John Snipes was a twenty-year-old crew chief on a helicopter involved in the *Tailwind* evacuation. His chopper was shot down, caught fire and he was trapped inside.

The mission was supposed to be Snipes' final flight before returning home from Vietnam, and he faced almost certain death. Then moments before the helicopter exploded, a Montagnard mercenary pulled him from the wreckage. The memory was so horrifying he broke down during the interview. "You can't forget it. It's been there for my entire life. And it won't go away." It was the first time his daughter saw him weep.

Snipes said he was aware that *Tailwind* was a top-secret mission. However, he was unable to substantiate the presence of defectors in the camp or the use of nerve gas. He only recalled being forewarned that something more potent than regular tear gas would be dropped. "It was some other kind of gas, what they called knockout gas."

Following the Snipes interview, I strapped on my derelict gunslinger's belt and headed to Washington. An abundance of misrepresentations, outright deceit and cover-ups during and after the Vietnam War convinced me that the Pentagon was lying. Why else would they turn down CNN's requests for interviews before the story aired? Only after being exposed did officials emerge from hiding to rebut the report.

A chemical warfare expert was designated to go on camera for the CNN interview, so long as Peter Arnett was not the interrogator. His reporting in Vietnam and in Baghdad during daddy Bush's Gulf War earned Peter the lasting enmity of the military.

In his place, Pam sent me for a high noon showdown with retired Army General Walter L. Busbee, the Army's foremost authority on chemical weaponry. He held the impressive civilian title of Deputy Assistant to the Secretary of Defense for Counter Proliferation and Chemical/Biological Defense. Busbee held undergraduate and post graduate degrees in Chemical Engineering from Georgia Tech.

Facing him down was a graduate of Tuscaloosa High School, Class of '52. My knowledge of chemical weapons was limited to years of sophomoric flatulent warfare. But never fear. I had devoted almost an hour trying to understand scientific papers about nerve gas and other lethal chemical weapons. Despite my crash course in chemical warfare, General Busbee was an odds-on favorite to make me look like a fool. To overcome my ignorance, April and her crack staff of researchers armed me with a list of twenty questions. And like a good TV soldier, I dutifully "grilled" the former General.

The Pentagon official answered in language that was comparable to me of listening to unknown tongues spoken in snake-handling backwoods churches. But whatever he was saying, Busbee sounded confident. To his credit, he didn't say, "You're the stupidest son-of-a-bitch who ever interviewed me."

CNN's retreat had not yet begun. And on the June 14th edition of *NewsStand*, Arnett and I did a team report aimed at bolstering allegations made the week before. Peter's segment added more interviews with *Tailwind* participants, as well as civilian experts on chemical warfare. Most remarkably, April Oliver and Jack Smith prevailed on Admiral Moorer to retract the retraction released by the Pentagon. I reported his latest wishy-washy statement in my segment.

"I did not authorize the use of sarin gas by U.S. military forces during Operation Tailwind in Laos in 1970. As Chairman of the Joint Chiefs of Staff at the time, I had no documents, operational orders, after-action reports or knowledge of the use of sarin. However, later in general discussions I learned of the

operation, including verbal statements indicating the use of sarin on the Tailwind Mission."

Though not absolute, the statement again seemed to corroborate CNN's exposé. In addition to Moorer's clarification, my interviews with General Busbee and with helicopter crew chief, John Snipes, were part of the program. Also included were portions of an interview omitted the previous week that undercut the nerve gas allegation.

Air Force Sky Raider pilot, Art Bishop, stated that he had shown April his contemporaneous entries in a journal that indicated tear gas was loaded on the planes flying cover for the *Tailwind* evacuation. Still, I suspected the military of engaging in "plausible deniability." April said that Admiral Moorer and one of her main confidential sources read the entire script before the *NewsStand* broadcast and suggested only minor changes. My confidence in the story remained unshaken. At least, for a few hours.

The next day, *Newsweek* published a devastating critique of the *Tailwind* story. Reported by Evan Thomas, the article ripped the segment apart. It disputed April's interpretation of several interviews and criticized CNN for omitting denials by SOG participants, who unequivocally contradicted the allegations. The article also attacked the credibility of Robert Van Buskirk, *NewsStand*'s key on-camera source.

According to the magazine, Van Buskirk gave a vastly different account of *Tailwind* in a book he authored—never mentioning the use of nerve gas or the assassination of American defectors. Van Buskirk explained that his revised version of *Tailwind* was a result of repressed memories that emerged during interviews with April.

The recovered memory explanation was another bit of information left out of the *NewsStand* segment. Also omitted was the disclosure of Van Buskirk's past treatment for Post Traumatic Stress Disorder, his history of drinking problems and a German prison sentence for illegally selling weapons.

Following the *Newsweek* story, several other publications drilled holes in the exposé, reporting that two people interviewed on camera were not even involved in the *Tailwind* mission. Military documents later confirmed those disclosures.

April was in denial. She defended the exclusion of Van Buskirk's background, saying that she asked for an hour to report the *Tailwind* story and got only eighteen minutes. The disputed material, she said, would have been included in a longer report. Her unwavering confidence and that of co-producer Jack Smith kept me digging.

In a matter of days, I hop-scotched across the country trying to substantiate the *Tailwind* allegations. But I found nothing but contradictions. In South Carolina, former Sky Raider pilot Jack Keeter disputed April's account of a telephone interview with him. Her notes stated that he confirmed the use of banned chemical weapons in Vietnam. However, the retired Colonel told me that she distorted his comments. He said April made the only references to lethal weapons in their conversation.

In Florida, former SOG Sergeant Denver Minton stated in an on-camera interview that he was directly behind Van Buskirk throughout the *Tailwind* mission, and described the former platoon leader's story as a fantasy. Minton then played an audio tape of air-to-ground communications during the evacuation. Pilots presented the recordings to SOG commandos at a post-mission survival party. The retired Sergeant had kept the tape as a memento of his scariest Vietnam mission. Pilots warned that "bad stuff" was being dropped, but gave no indication that it was a lethal chemical.

Following the Minton interview, I traveled to a Special Forces convention in Albuquerque, New Mexico with two other *Special Assignment* correspondents, a producer and a camera crew. Three SOG veterans of the *Tailwind* mission showed us documents contradicting CNN's exposé. On the final day of the convention, a resolution was adopted condemning the network and the *NewsStand* segment. I had about given up hope of salvaging the story.

Twelve days had passed since *Newsweek*'s exposé of CNN's exposé. The network was being criticized and ridiculed by gloating journalists, radio personalities, military brass and Vietnam veteran's groups. I decided to make one last phone call before giving up altogether. Before the Albuquerque, trip, a crackpot had called CNN. "I almost came out of my seat when I saw that story on TV," he said.

"I figured that stuff was buried so deep in military intelligence, it would never be found."

The caller was a Texas goat rancher who made the startling assertion. He said he led a nerve gas attack on enemy forces in 1970 that was a mirror image of *Tailwind*. Identifying himself as retired Army Master Sergeant Ralph Griest, he claimed to have spent twenty-two years on active duty, including five consecutive years in Vietnam. I figured it was an exaggeration if in fact, he was ever in Vietnam. That length of time in a war zone without a break was implausible. But not as implausible as his explanation.

"I was running around the bush and the rice paddies. I actually had my own little army. I could saddle up my folks and we could go anywhere I wanted to. And you know I paid 'em, I fed 'em, I clothed 'em, slept with 'em, drank with 'em. What better job could you have?" No doubt, Griest was deranged. And I said as much. He was undeterred by my skepticism and kept on blabbing, saying his expertise was in demand in Vietnam. And what was that? He stated cheerfully that he was an overseer of assassination squads.

Now, I knew he was insane. But experience taught me to listen to wacky people. They could be entertaining and sometimes there was even a grain of truth to their tales. So I listened to Ralph's fable of being an advisor in Vietnam to Provincial Reconnaissance Units. I had never heard of these so-called PRU's.

I soon learned they were CIA-connected paramilitary squads comprised of South Vietnamese army troops, local police and bad-ass Vietnamese mercenaries. PRU's were established in 1965 as an operational arm of a pacification and intelligence gathering program called *Phoenix*. Working with American advisors, small teams swept through villages and hamlets capturing and interrogating Viet Cong insurgents.

The mission of *Phoenix* was to destroy the Viet Cong infrastructure by repatriation. Or by other means. Critics alleged that "other means" was a metaphor for indiscriminate murders. Congressional testimony revealed that innocent civilians were killed and tortured, Viet Cong insurgents were tossed from helicopters during interrogations, and long-standing village feuds were settled by falsely identifying old rivals as VC—the equivalent of a death sentence.

American advisors worked with about 4,000 Vietnamese. Military officials blamed the abuses on Vietnamese nationals, claiming that advisors had no authority to intervene. The number of PRU members scattered throughout Vietnam at any given time was fewer than two hundred officers and enlisted men. The chain of command was indistinct and accountability erratic.

In Congressional testimony, Defense Department and CIA officials disclosed that PRU-connected squads killed over 20,000 civilians identified as insurgents. Since success in Vietnam was measured by body counts and cost effectiveness, the program was considered a huge success. But atrocities were so rampant and criticism so loud that American advisors were reassigned in October, 1970.

Before talking to Ralph Griest, I knew nothing about the intricacies of Vietnam warfare. His chatter gave me the impression that he was a walking, talking history book when it came to PRU's. But like characters I met in barrooms during my misspent years before plugging the jug, I figured he was another bullshit artist. I wanted to believe his story—an investigative reporting pitfall that can be dangerous.

My plane-hopping had turned up nothing but flaws in the *NewsStand* segment. Reaction to the report was incredulity. "Nerve gas? Killing our own soldiers? Are you fucking crazy? This is the United States military you're talking about."

Between my first and second conversations with Ralph Griest, a couple of former Special Forces veterans at the Albuquerque convention were less disbelieving than me when I mentioned Provincial Reconnaissance Units. "PRU's were capable of doing just about anything," they said. So I set out to determine if his story had any basis in fact.

April and Jack Smith remained adamant in refusing to concede errors in their reporting. Confidential sources had convinced them that nerve gas was used in Laos following the elimination of American defectors.

My telephone conversations with Griest raised a farfetched possibility. What if the two central allegations were true—the use of nerve gas and the assassination of

U.S. soldiers—but wrong in the specifics. I learned early in my career that trivial errors undermine stories that are otherwise accurate. When a bribe-taking official is described as wearing a brown jacket and it was a shade of tan, color blindness becomes a defense. "How can you believe somebody who doesn't know tan from brown?"

Admiral Moorer and top brass were regularly briefed on secret missions. For the sake of plausible deniability, it was not unusual to keep them in the dark about precise details. The who, when and where of Ralph's story deviated from *Tailwind*. His supposed nerve gas mission took place in Cambodia rather than Laos. And he told of killing four defectors, not two. But he said the only witnesses were seven Cambodians he trained for the operation. Could April and Jack's sources unintentionally have misled them by juxtaposing details of separate missions?

It was an unlikely scenario. However, I was looking for anything to support the *NewsStand* story. And when Ralph agreed to give me proof of his exploits in an on-camera interview, I headed to Texas, realizing that the trip was a desperation measure.

A producer and camera crew from the Washington bureau were sent to work with me. The photographer was Australian-born Mike Marriott, a CBS cameraman during the Vietnam War. He had been April's principle photographer throughout production of the *Tailwind* segment. And based on his experiences during the war, he believed in the accuracy of the story. Mike's Vietnamese wife was his sound technician. The couple had a long association with CNN as freelancers.

Associate producer and researcher Amy Kasarda accompanied the camera crew. A daughter of California college professors, she became a journalist after a short-lived career as a ballet dancer. She had also worked on the *Tailwind* story from its outset.

Joining up at the airport in San Antonio, the four of us loaded equipment into a rental van and a car, and made a late night four-hour drive to the small town of Carlsbad. Early the next day, we followed Griest's directions to a hard-scrabble piece of property ten miles out of town. Passing through a metal gate, we bumped along a rutted dirt road that reached a dead-end in front of a ramshackle hovel. Compared to the shanty, hooches in Vietnam rice paddies were like the Ritz Carlton.

Ralph took up goat ranching after retiring from the military. His herd greeted us by climbing over the hood of the car. Amy's ballet footwork helped her escape the friendly animals. I wasn't as quick stepping around goat droppings that peppered the yard. When the man we intended to interview emerged from the two-room dwelling and ambled toward us with a snarling dog at his side and a beer in hand, I had a sinking feeling that the trip to Texas on a scorching hot June day was for naught.

Ralph looked as if he had barely survived an exploding land mine. His ruddy, weather-beaten appearance and

Texas drawl fit perfectly with the image of an old soldier—one who was rapidly fading away. He was fifty-seven-years old and close to six feet tall when standing straight. But stooped posture added another ten years to his age. I couldn't decide if he was skinny or debilitated.

Inside the decrepit hut, empty beer cans were scattered around, dirty dishes piled in the sink, grease-filled skillets sat on top of the stove and a thick coating of dust covered every exposed inch of the place. Ralph had lived in the seemingly uninhabitable shed since his wife died three years earlier.

He cleared space for us to sit at the kitchen table as goats strolled in and out the open door, nuzzling up to us like house pets. After getting as comfortable as we could in such bizarre surroundings, Griest began displaying his bona fides. Military records confirmed he was a counter-intelligence agent assigned to Provincial Reconnaissance Units in Vietnam for five consecutive years. Picture albums, documents, and memorabilia substantiated his extended PRU tour of duty in Phong Dinh Province.

Despite drinking his breakfast, Ralph was lucid in giving an account of an alleged nerve gas mission that was remarkably similar to the one depicted in the *NewsStand* segment. He claimed the chemical was used to kill American deserters and Viet Cong insurgents encamped a few miles inside Cambodia. I had serious doubts about his claims. But since had we come this far, I decided to record an on-camera interview. Videotape is cheap and we had time to waste before catching a plane home.

Since there was no space inside the hut to do the interview, Mike set up the camera beneath a scraggly tree that offered the only shade on the property. Ralph had no problem with us showing his face on television, but asked me to avoid using his full name. He was concerned about becoming a target of crank telephone calls. I was given permission to identify him by name two years later when he moved to a nursing home.

Ralph said he was stepping forward because he believed that CNN had confused *Tailwind* with a mission he led as a PRU advisor. "After seeing the Laotian program, I said, 'hold it here.' I was in Cambodia doing this same thing, even before that, the Laotian business. I said, 'What in the dickens is going on here?' And so, that's why I contacted you all. I thought maybe you had something mixed up."

What followed was a story more detailed and compelling than the *Tailwind* segment. For nearly an hour, he gave an account of an ostensible operation in which nerve gas was used. He claimed to have crossed the border into Cambodia in April, 1970 to locate, identify and kill U.S. soldiers suspected of collaborating with Viet Cong guerillas. The alleged operation occurred only days before the official acknowledgement of American incursions across the border in pursuit of enemy forces.

According to Griest, he was assigned to the mission by Colonel Lester Conger, a senior PRU advisor in Phong

Dinh Province. Present at the meeting was an American Embassy representative in civilian clothes whose name he couldn't recall. He assumed the man was a CIA operative. However, several months after leaving Vietnam, Griest said he encountered the same man at a Texas military base, and he was wearing a uniform displaying the rank of Major. This would not have been unusual. The roles of military personnel and CIA agents were interchangeable in the *Phoenix* project.

The Cambodian operation was supposedly based on intelligence photographs showing four Americans—known as "long shadows"—unshackled and moving freely inside two Viet Cong encampments about five kilometers apart. Ralph said he led a team of seven Cambodian mercenaries to confirm the men were defectors. If so, his orders were to summon aircraft to dump "knockout gas" on the camps.

"That was a new one on me. The only thing that got me suspicious that something was funny was when they issued us gas masks. PRU advisors, as far as I knew, were never issued gas masks. Neither were the Vietnamese and Cambodians that I advised provided with gas masks."

Prior to the mission, Griest said he trained the "Cambotes" how to use the gas masks and auto-injectors containing Atropine, a nerve gas antidote. The squad was issued Russian AK-47 weapons and outfitted in black pajamas, the trademark garb of Viet Cong rebels moving along trails in Cambodia. The clothing and equipment were stripped of any markings that could be traced to the American military. If killed or captured, the U.S. could deny involvement in the operation.

"We went in what they call sterile. In other words, your underpants didn't have any *Fruit of the Looms* on them."

From an airbase in Phong Dinh's provincial Capitol of Can Tho, he said two black Huey helicopters transported the squad to an area about ten kilometers from the first target. One chopper carried the PRU troops. The other flew cover. At a drop point, he said the squad moved along rice paddies at the edge of the jungle and reached the perimeter of the first enemy camp before nightfall.

"I could surveille them that evening until it got dark and when the sun came up that next morning, I surveilled them some more. And it was very plain who they were."

He claimed the Americans stood head and shoulders above twenty or more enemy troops. When I asked what, besides height, led him to believe they were Americans, he dropped a bombshell.

"They were immediately identifiable. They weren't Russians. They weren't Chinese. They weren't anything else. They were black Americans, period."

My skepticism reached its zenith. Not even the CIA would order the assassination of black soldiers. The most vociferous opposition to the war came from Civil Rights leaders and other prominent blacks. Muhammad Ali, then

Cassius Clay, refused the draft three years earlier. He took the position that Vietnam was a war against people of color. His example ignited a wave of draft avoidance by many young African-Americans, who described Vietnam as a subtle form of black genocide.

My disbelief of this strange story didn't faze the retired, beer-swilling soldier. He dispassionately explained how he directed aircraft to the target area where cluster bombs armed with nerve gas were dropped.

"In about forty-five minutes the planes were overhead and they dropped it at just about, not ground level, but it was about twenty or thirty meters above, in air bursts. The only forewarning I got was their call sign 'we're two minutes away.' That was the cue for us to put on our gas masks." According to Griest, no insignias were displayed on the aircraft to designate the country of origin. But he said pilot lingo made it evident they were Americans. When the planes passed over, Ralph said troops in the camp were exposed to a barely discernible colorless mist.

"I could see them. They were down on their hands and knees throwing up. And then they were going into convulsions and died. I'm positive they were dead."

If there is any truth to the story, what Griest witnessed defies explanation. In 1970, the American military did not possess non-lethal chemical weapons that caused temporary unconsciousness. Ralph said that's why he concluded nerve gas was dumped on the camp.

"I had seen in training pictures in the states, what they do to goats and animals and things like that. Once they issue you those syringes of atropine, I knew darn good and well that it was no knockout gas. It was damn nerve gas." Convinced that everybody in the camp was killed by the chemical, Griest said his squad moved to the second target where two unguarded African- Americans were moving freely around the camp.

"Same scenario, gas and everything. And we sit around about another fifteen minutes and made sure we could see all the folks out there on the ground in convulsions. And then they laid still and we extracted as quickly as possible out of the area to our pickup point." Griest said Huey helicopters returned the squad to Can Tho airfield.

"Once I'd gotten back to Can Tho, the Province Senior Advisor picked me up himself in his own jeep and took me directly to province headquarters. About five or ten minutes later, the agency man came in. And they asked me basically what I've told you." Ralph said the only record of the mission was a handwritten "after assault" report. It was handed to Colonel Conger and the man he thought to be a CIA operative. End of story.

The tale sounds preposterous, the ramblings perhaps of a drunken old soldier. But he wasn't a run-of-the-mill wacko. Military records disclosed an impeccable career. Nor did he portray himself as a hero. In fact, he neglected to mention two Bronze Star decorations for gallantry. I learned of the citations by reviewing his military dossier.

If he was lying, I can't imagine his motive. There was no evidence he had axes to grind. By the same token, I never found evidence to support the story. He forewarned that I wouldn't.

Do I believe the story? I believe Griest believed what he was telling me. The tried and true method that one source begets sources who beget other sources was ineffective in investigating his tale. Too much time had passed. Colonel Conger died in a 1972 plane crash, and Griest couldn't remember the name of the CIA operative/military officer. He vaguely recalled a surname that I ran past a former CIA employee assigned to the Saigon Embassy in 1970. He recalled someone with a similar name—a military officer working as a liaison to the Phoenix Program. He couldn't be sure.

The Pentagon steadfastly maintains there were only four known American collaborators during the Vietnam War. That may be the semantics of differentiating between defectors, deserters and collaborators. Hundreds of soldiers went AWOL in Vietnam never to be seen again. Some remained after the U.S. withdrawal.

There is also a history of radio distress calls by American voices in Vietnam that resulted in ambushes during medical evacuations and other operations. Because of such occurrences, Griest said he had no qualms about killing turncoat soldiers.

"They were deserters. Plus the fact they could operate a radio, a captured American radio and they could divert choppers and Medivacs into other areas and then shoot them down."

My inspection of only a few hundred declassified military and CIA records obtained under a Freedom of Information request has references to desertion and suspected collaboration. The most intriguing was a classified Phoenix report of "Possible identification of four captured U.S. Servicemen." There were no other details. The document was dated April, 1970, the same month of Ralph's alleged mission.

In November, 2002, the Pentagon disclosed that rockets containing sarin were test-fired in 1967 in the dense rain forest of Hawaii's Upper Waiakea Forest Reserve to determine the effect of chemical and biological weapons in a jungle-like climate and environment—conditions similar to Vietnam. Presumably, the weapons were tested for a reason. Throughout the war, the military maintained stockpiles of the nerve chemical on Okinawa 1400 miles from Saigon.

Following my on-camera interview with Ralph Griest, I stayed in contact with him until his death in a Colorado assisted-care facility. Not once did he waver from his story. As I gathered more information, I tried to trap him with pop quizzes about his career and personal life and an arrest in New Mexico that was a case of mistaken identity. He had a perfect score answering questions that were embarrassing to him, such as his reduction in rank in 1964 for insubordination. Ralph was also quick to say, "I don't know" when asked questions outside his limited area of expertise, or beyond his recall.

I'm not suggesting that CNN should have aired the Griest allegory under a "Breaking News" graphic, or any time before it was corroborated. But to use a term coined by *Comedy Channel* faux commentator, Stephen Colbert, the story reached a level of "truthiness." My whine is that CNN didn't care if the tale were true.

The videotapes of the Griest interview were transcribed, stashed away, and I was told to forget the nerve gas story. Testicle-challenged executives just wanted *Tailwind* to go away—along with the people responsible for the segment. Twenty-five days after *NewsStand*'s disastrous debut, CNN President Tom Johnson fired April Oliver and Jack Smith. He also announced the resignation of Pamela Hill. The reasons were stated in a *Tailwind* critique.

"A decision was made by CNN to broadcast accusations of the gravest sort without sufficient justification and in the face of substantial persuasive information to the contrary."

The report was co-authored by CNN General Counsel David Kohler and Floyd Abrams, one of the nation's leading First Amendment lawyers. It was released so hastily, a speed typist may have been recruited to put it in final form. Kohler was an anomalous critic. He gave final legal clearance for the segment.

I agree there were serious flaws in the "exposé." But April Oliver, Jack Smith, Dave Kohler and others reviewing the supporting material believed the story to be accurate. The sources were considered reliable, particularly Admiral Moorer.

But faith in sources can be perilous. Oftentimes, journalists unconsciously discount exculpatory inconsistencies. A firing offense? In the imperfect craft of investigative reporting, mistakes are bound to happen. Indeed, CNN's post mortem admitted as much on its first page.

"Our central conclusion is that although the broadcast was prepared after exhaustive research, was rooted in considerable supportive data, and reflected the deeply held beliefs of the CNN journalists who prepared it, the central thesis of the broadcast could not be sustained at the time of the broadcast itself and cannot be sustained now."

"Now" was a Monday morning meeting of quarterbacks. The admission that April and Jack did their best but reached the wrong conclusions was certainly not a sufficient reason to ruin careers and reputations. They were casualties of an inordinate level of journalistic cowardice. Rather than retract and apologize for imperfect reporting, April and Jack were hauled to a sacrificial altar. It was a rush to judgment to protect the network's image.

Peter Arnett, the on-camera face of *Tailwind*, survived the initial cleansing. But not without insult. His minimal involvement resulted in a sharp public rebuke from Tom Johnson, who said it was unconscionable for a reporter to front a story that he failed to research. The statement was remarkable in its ignorance. Television correspondents consistently parrot the work of producers. If all news personalities did their own reporting, *60 Minutes* would only be on the air about once a year.

Nobody knew this better than Tom's co-executioner, Rick Kaplan. As a former Executive Producer of ABC's *Prime Time* and other personality-driven news programs, Kaplan supervised high-profile journalists who were often parachuted into stories at the last minute. Yet, he made no effort to defend Arnett. Nor did he defend producer Jack Smith—the man who years before, gave him one of his first television jobs.

Worse, Jack found out he was fired in a *Special Assignment* conference call. Despite a promise by Tom Johnson that Jack and April would have a chance to review the critique, the hatchet fell without so much as a courtesy call. It was like Rudy Giuliani's wife hearing at a news conference that her husband was divorcing her for another woman.

"This is a corporate whitewash," Jack bitterly complained. "This is a cave to the military establishment, to the secret army which is one step away from the secret police." An overstatement perhaps, but not altogether wrong.

Another Kaplan mentor and longtime confidante also left CNN in the wake of *Tailwind*, but voluntarily. John Lane had planned to retire a year earlier. But when Kaplan became the network's top news executive, he persuaded him to remain as a consultant. John was not consulted about the purge and resigned in disgust.

Given my self-righteous attitude, I should have quit. It would have been an appropriate symbolic gesture. But I was offered a new two year contract boosting my income well over $200,000. To hell with symbolic gestures. I was a hypocrite.

But money notwithstanding, two years was a long time to spend with people I judged to be eunuchs. Fortunately, CNN relieved me of the burden. Five months after the *Tailwind* housecleaning, I was told not to come to the office anymore, although I would remain on the payroll at full salary until the end of my contract. To rephrase military jargon, I was a "collateral beneficiary" of *Tailwind*.

To everyone's surprise, Rick Kaplan elevated an old Chicago friend to head *Special Assignment*. She was the only producer in the unit I failed to get along with. We had worked together in Costa Rica on a story about child prostitution. It was a disaster. My disagreement with her approach to investigative reporting was so intense that for the first time in my career—sober—I walked off the job. I flew back to Atlanta, vowing never to work with her again. Now I was working for her.

Adding insult to *Special Assignment*, a Washington producer from outside the unit was assigned the task of scrutinizing our stories to ensure they were "fair and balanced," the laughable slogan of Fox News. The guy knew nothing about investigative reporting. Moreover, he was

scared shitless of making a mistake. Investigative reporting is not about being fair and balanced. It's about revealing truth. I came, I found, I exposed. If I'm wrong, demand a
retraction, sue me. Reported in context, bad guys get
their say. Being fair and balanced requires a suspension of
belief.

A few days after Kaplan chose his pal to head the unit,
Senior Producer Jim Connor delivered the news that I was
fired as of December 31, 1998. He accompanied me to
Human Resources where I was told that CNN planned
to fulfill my contract. Alone with Jim in the elevator afterwards, he asked how I was feeling. I smiled, pumped
my fist and let out a whoop. Leaving was a relief. The
network had abandoned high risk reporting and adopted safeguards to minimize the possibility of offending
anyone.

A CNN news release stated that I left the network to
"pursue other interests." My interests included acting like
a Republican by living in a gated community in the North
Georgia mountains and playing golf with friends, several
of whom believed that retired Coca Cola and Pepsi executives living side by side represented diversity. I was most
amazed that a few seemingly intelligent guys considered
pill-popping, failed disc jockey, Rush Limbaugh, a sage. As
regular viewers of "fair and balanced" Fox News," they were
also fans of professional asshole Bill O'Reilly, loony Sean
Hannity, and right-wing fruitcake, Ann Coulter. What was
the world of public affairs coming to?

Anyway, a funny thing happened on the way to exile. Ten days into my life of leisure, I received a dinner hour call from Tom Johnson. After a bit of chitchat, he asked if I were interested in doing a freelance project, an odd question since the ink was barely dry on a termination agreement he signed. Curious, I asked what he had in mind.

"I'm tired of people calling CNN the "Clinton News Network. I want to end the myth once and for all." I agreed that the network was unduly accused. But short of sneaking into Rush Limbaugh's office and stealing his supply of Oxycontin, I couldn't imagine what Tom expected me to do. However, he had a plan. "I want you to go to Little Rock and determine if Bill Clinton fathered a black child." He couldn't be serious.

Scores of reporters—some even claiming to be legitimate journalists—wasted years chasing the rumor. It was old news, the kind of gossip that had been spread from the first day Clinton ran for public office in Arkansas two decades before. Being the pappy of a mixed-race love child is the oldest form of mudslinging in Southern politics. Except for the late South Carolina Senator Strom Thurmond, the rumors were rarely true.

Tom's inspiration for contacting me was a story in a tabloid falsely claiming it had located a young man of African-American heritage, who called the leader of the free world, "Daddy'o." I really didn't care if Clinton had undisclosed progeny, no matter what race, color or creed. So I said, "Thanks, but no thanks."

It was a fitting end to my fulltime career. Although I've produced PBS documentaries and continue to do consulting work since leaving CNN, I realize the heyday of television muckraking as I define it has ended. Perhaps never to return.

For twenty-five-years, beginning in the post Watergate epoch, I witnessed the best of TV investigative reporting. And the worst. But after taking the money for all those years, complaining that "It ain't what it used to be" exposes me as a grouchy old man.

And maybe it never was as I remember. If not, let me enjoy the delusion.

EPILOGUE

I hope my odyssey as a "derelict gunslinger" had meaning. Especially in search of my own true character. Professional success was an adjunct to sobriety. Every principle I learned in Alcoholics Anonymous applied to investigative reporting—faith, trust, honesty, courage and the biggest obstacle of all for me and many muckrakers— humility. I don't claim to have mastered any of these virtues.

But as a student of decent living, I am now more adept at distinguishing the differences between truths, half-truths and hoped for truths. The distinctions are the most difficult challenges that confront ambitious investigative reporters. None of us like facts to get in the way of a good story.

Many people I've encountered will take issue with my self-assessment of honesty. Targets of exposés see themselves differently than depicted by investigative reporters. As a consequence, the "derelict gunslinger" label attached to my name by former Louisiana Governor Edwin Edwards is tame compared to other characterizations.

..."yellow journalist." (Janet Reno in Miami, 1975, and many other critics)
..."a tool of organized crime" (U.S. Attorney Edward Harrington in Boston, 1979)

..."a fool," "a snake and reprobate" (Jimmy Swaggart, various occasions)
..."a hatchet man" (Ross Perot, 1992)
..."an investigative reporter wannabe" (James Squires, 1993)
..."a Clinton apologist" (a widespread portrayal from 1994 forward)
..."asshole" (everybody unable to come up with a better description)

The pejoratives are accurate in the minds of critics. And may even be true in some instances. The shame is that I took pride in being described in such terms. Like a child acting up to get attention, I needed to be recognized, whether the attention was good or bad. I wanted to fulfill my parents dream for me to become "somebody."

The definition of what constitutes "somebody" is a matter of perspective. For years, my perception was blurred by booze and self-absorption in which I put my needs ahead of my family and everyone around me. Then, the miracle in 1971 at a rundown halfway house altered my quest to be "somebody." I learned to be me. Most of the time.

Miracles are often explained as beneficent coincidences. But the eyes of the beholder are all that really counts. I see miracles in the people who arrive at the doors of AA without hope, then recover their lives. I see miracles on *60 Minutes* when elderly correspondents like Mike Wallace shuffle along without the aid of walkers. It reminds me that

I still have a few years remaining in my role as a mini-Mike Wallace.

I've had more than my share of unexplained events that I call miracles. One of the strangest occurred in April, 1977 when I received a call from the chief competitor of WBRZ, my future destination in Baton Rouge. The News Director wanted to interview me for a job that coalesced the roles of investigative reporter and Assistant News Director. I had been in Boston at the nation's "best local TV station" only seven months. But I was unhappy over broken promises and agreed fly to Baton Rouge for a meeting.

This was an opportunity for one last visit with my father, who was near death from cancer and severe emphysema. After twice racing to his death bed in recent months, we realized that the end was unpredictable. Each time he astonished doctors by pulling through. Still, they said there was nothing more they could do and sent him home to die.

After arriving in Baton Rouge on Thursday evening, I went straight to my parents' mobile home. Momma nearly keeled over when she opened the door. Daddy had been lapsing in and out of a coma. However, only minutes before I got there, he had turned to her and said, "Johnny is coming." She assumed he was hallucinating.

Seeing daddy was heartbreaking. I did not realize the ghastly state of his condition, or momma's burden in trying to comfort him. He weighed less than ninety pounds. Gasping for breath and requiring twenty-four-hour oxygen therapy, his body was ravaged by cancer. As I sat next to the bed, he opened his eyes and feebly reached for my hand. Momma grasped the other hand and asked me to pray.

Except for the opening *Serenity Prayer* and closing *Lord's Prayer* at AA meetings, I rarely prayed aloud. Choking back sobs, I made an effort this time. I was flooded by memories of the tough times we had gone through, and the pain I caused my parents before I stopped drinking and began making amends. Though heavily sedated, daddy's eyes focused on me.

"It's going to be fine, Johnny," he whispered. Those were his last words I heard.

After taking care of business at the TV station, I stayed with my parents until Sunday morning. On Saturday, while a home health nurse tended to dad, momma and I arranged for the funeral. I wanted to stay, but he had surprised us so many times before. This time, there was no surprise. Two hours after arriving home in Boston, the phone rang. Daddy's pain was over. By midnight, I was back in Baton Rouge.

What makes the unforeseen visit to dad's bedside so peculiar is the fact that the job offer was withdrawn. My salary requirements were discussed prior to the Louisiana trip. The station owner, however, tried to bargain downward and the deal fell through. Miracle? Coincidence? Whatever way it's spun, the circumstances were odd.

For years, my immediate reaction after receiving journalism prizes had been to call daddy. Even long after his death, I caught myself reaching for the phone. I believed the accolades were proof that I had become "somebody." But while helping mother dispose of his belongings, I discovered that I misinterpreted his definition of being somebody. I came across an audio tape he planned to send to a family member.

"Johnny has stopped drinking and seems to have gotten his life together. He is happy and we are really proud of him." The journalism prizes in which I took so much pride were never mentioned. He talked only of my personal happiness.

No doubt, he and momma delighted in my professional recognition—momma in particular. Before leaving Baton Rouge for CNN a dozen years after dad's death, I received a three a.m. call that she was experiencing severe chest pains and had been taken to a hospital by ambulance. At the Emergency Room, I heard her moans. She breathed a deep sigh of relief as I entered the treatment room.

"Do you watch my son on television?" momma asked the examining doctor.

With momma, my children and others, I struggled before and after my sobriety to break through an internal obstacle that prevented me from unselfishly giving of myself. I had difficulty performing even the simplest personal tasks for those I loved.

During a hospital visit to dad, mother asked me to shave him. As I hemmed and hawed about a minor personal service, daddy saw my discomfort and took me off the hook.

He said he preferred to shave himself. I was haunted by my inability to show him love by doing something that was so simple.

As a measure of progress, I began edging across the barrier before momma died. In 1995, she was diagnosed with terminal lung cancer. I made regular visits from Atlanta and sat by her bedside patiently feeding her.

"Just one more bite to build your strength." It was a huge breakthrough for me. I hope that was the "real John."

Thirty-three years after my perceived epiphany in a halfway house, I saw the manifestation of another miracle. I stood only a few feet from what had been the location of a coffee-room couch where I slept after many drunken nights of carousing. WJBO was gone. The radio station had been demolished and a church assembly hall built on the site.

I stood behind a podium in the auditorium speaking to scores of past and present clients of O'Brien House—a harbor for indigent alcoholics that I helped found in 1971. As I told of my odyssey from a New Orleans curbside to sobriety, I was suddenly struck by the significance of this place and time. Almost overcome with emotion, I needed to pause for a few moments to gather my thoughts.

The next day, I spoke at an O'Brien House fundraising breakfast. Hurricane Ivan was in the Gulf of Mexico. Although landfall was uncertain, the Interstate was clogged with thousands of evacuating New Orleans residents. It was a false alarm, which may have slowed the evacuation when Katrina struck a year later.

I had expected a low turnout, maybe even a cancellation. Instead, the hotel ballroom was filled with public officials, businessmen and friends of O'Brien House. A place that started as a glorified "flop house," had become one of nation's premier treatment centers for homeless alcoholics. Many people cultivated its growth. But by some miracle, a Power I choose to call God selected me to plant the seed. It is my legacy.

Returning to Georgia, Annette and I sensed that it was time to go home. Two months later, we sold our house in the mountains and returned to the place where we found the miracle of sobriety—and each other.

We look forward to new miracles.

AUTHORS COMMENTS

Because of the subjective nature of this book, I have not included footnotes. Most sources of my material are self-evident. Besides, who reads footnotes? Nonetheless, back-up documents are available on request at www.derelictgunslinger.com.

As a believer in redemption and the notion that time heals all or most wounds, I have been selective in identifying by name some people who I disparaged over the years. Several are dead. Others only flashed across the TV screen, and are so obscure that most folks would not recognize the names — or even care if they did. But inquiries about identities will be answered at my website if there is a purpose beyond curiosity.

The majority of the direct quotes in this book were lifted from scripts of my investigations, transcripts of interviews left on the cutting room floor, and video/audio tapes gathered in researching stories. I've also reprised a few of my own quotes from publications that quoted me. I hope this is not stealing. For narrative purposes, I have reconstructed some conversations based on notes and memory. In those instances, I confirmed my recollections with former producers, photographers and others who were either present at the time, or to whom I contemporaneously repeated the conversations.

Omissions are an inherent danger in making acknowledgements. I've tried to give due credit to people I worked with over the years. But like most TV correspondents, I tend to take too much credit for work that succeeded through a team effort. In moments of truth, I realize my walls would be bare of awards without the support of colleagues, and a few courageous employers willing to take a chance on me.

They have my lasting gratitude for helping an under-educated, ex-drunk escape his trailer-trash destiny.

INDEX

Abrams, Floyd: 467
Acceturo, Anthony (Tumac): 113, 269, 272-273, 275, 341
Accuracy in Media: 63, 124
Adams,(Camp)Glenda:188, 301
Aiken, Pete: 271-273
Alcoholics Anonymous: 21, 52, 146, 166, 194, 253, 289, 308, 353, 370-371, 375, 475
Ali, Muhammad: 462
Alter, Jonathan: 11
American Spectator: 32, 34, 125
Anderson, Jack: 7, 127
Ansin, Edmund: 296
Armistead, Rex: 52-53
Arnett, Peter: 443-444, 446, 449, 468
Ash, Marty: 258
Aynesworth, Hugh: 216

Bailey, Chauncy: 280
Bakker, Jim: 175, 355-356
Bakker, Tammy Faye: 356
Balboni, Phil: 295, 332
Bardwell, Stanford: 70, 74, 95, 108, 110
Barger, Brian: 387
Barrett, David: 41
Bates, Felix: 86
Bergen, Peter: 388
Bergman, Lowell: 384
Bernard, Sherman: 233-235, 238, 367
Bernstein, Carl: 256
Bilonick, Ricardo: 411

Bishop, Art: 451
Blair, Jim: 43
Blandon, Jose: 397, 405
Bode, Ken: 387
Bolles, Don: 280
Boni, Frank: 279
Bonilla, Rodigo Lara: 75, 84
Bossie, David: 26, 50
Boston Broadcasters: 331-332
Bottoms, William (Bare): 120
Bowen, Ralph: 311
Brezon, Chris: 73, 75
Brock, David: 32
Brown, Dale: 392
Brown, Floyd: 62
Brown, L.D.: 34, 125, 126
Brown, Ossie: 236, 238
Bucha, Paul: 422
Bulger, James (Whitey): 111-112, 432
Burton, Dan: 36, 50, 56
Busbee, Walter L.: 449
Bush, George Herbert: 78, 123, 397, 425
Bush, George W.: 12, 17, 384, 408, 441
Bustamonte, "Lito": 90
Byrd (Camp), Patricia: 52, 193

Cafiero, Carmel: 298
Callahan, John B.: 111-112
Camp, Emil: 82-83, 114, 117, 120
Camp, Harry Uncle: 310
Campbell, Donald: 108, 122
Carter, Lew: 198, 207

Carville, James: 373-374

Champion Insurance Company: 366, 368

Chiapprone: Paul: 422

Chico, California: 328

Choate, Dave: 73, 251

Christic Istitute: 118

CIA: 55, 63-64, 67, 76, 78, 79, 82, 86, 89, 107-108, 114, 117-119, 121-122, 124-127, 396, 447, 454-455, 461-462, 464-466

Cisneros, Henry: 41

Citizens United: 23, 26, 62

Clinton Rules: 11-12, 126

Clinton, Bill and Hillary: 50

Clinton, Roger: 57

Close Up: 8, 270, 348-350, 383, 389, 393

CNN: 1, 9, 13-14, 31-35, 37, 39, 47, 54, 56, 59, 62, 69, 82, 123-124, 129, 239, 298, 374, 376-379, 381-383, 385, 387-390, 392, 394-397, 399-407, 409-410, 413, 415, 418, 420, 426-428, 430-432, 436, 439-451, 453, 458, 460, 467-473, 479

Cohen, William Defense Secretary: 448

Colbert, Stephen: 467

Collins, Robert: 209

Columbia Journalism Review: 34, 389, 394

Columbia School of Broadcasting: 309

Compromised: Clinton, Bush and the CIA: 124

Conason, Joe: 33, 39

Conger, Lester Colonel: 460

Connolly, John, FBI Agent: 111

Connor, Jim: 388, 471

Connor, Myles: 110, 113, 345, 347-349

Cooley, Earl: 347, 349

Coulter, Ann: 471

Courtney, Bob: 148, 209

d'Hemecourt, Jules: 221, 223

Davis, Jimmy: 220

Davison, Roger: 188

DEA: 64-65, 69, 72, 74-76, 79, 83, 86-94, 97, 99-100, 102, 105, 110, 117, 119, 122, 128, 292, 397

Delahunt, William: 344

Delio, Emilio (The Count): 271, 282

Denton, Sally: 126

DiNorciscio, Jackie (Fat Jack): 273

Doan, Harry: 88

Dornan, Robert, U.S. Rep.: 56

Double-Crossed: The Barry Seal Story: 119

Drudge Report: 12

Drysdale, Don: 307, 312

Dukakis, Michael: 23

Duke, David: 145, 227-228

Duncan, Bill, IRS Agent: 115, 121, 127

DuPont Columbia: 366

Eperson, Peter: 82, 89, 120

Edwards, Edwin: 136, 138, 144, 238, 370, 375, 475

Ellis, Tom: 339

Epps, Wooten: 61

Escobar, Pablo: 75, 84, 86, 88-90, 92-93, 103, 107
Espy, Michael: 41
Evans, Joe: 116, 120-121, 124
Evans-Pritchard, Ambrose: 127
Ewing, Hickman: 17, 47-48, 50, 54, 60
Exodus: 428-429

Falwell, Jerry: 51, 56, 124, 162, 356, 361
Faulk, Walter: 27, 30, 33
Feldstein, Mark: 387
Fernandez, Marlene: 397
Fiske, Robert: 15, 36, 49
Fitzhugh, Michael: 121
Foster, Vincent: 17, 19, 23, 56
Fox News: 12, 298, 439, 470, 471
French Quarter: 4, 193, 197

Gardner Museum theft: 350
Garfinkle, Howard: 266
Gaylord, Bill: 422
Gerstein, Richard: 256-257, 262, 283
Gerth, Jeff: 25-26, 29, 39, 43
Gillers, Stephen: 398
Gilley, Mickey: 158
Gingrich, Newt: 12
Give Me That Big Time Religion: 163, 169, 172-173, 355, 360
Goodhart. David, Judge: 257, 261-262
Gore, Albert, Jr. (Al Gore): 425
Gore, Albert, Sr.: 425
Graham, Billy: 142, 153, 166, 195
Grassley, Charles, Senator: 173

Green, Douglas, Insurance Commissioner: 366
Greenfield, Jeff: 443
Gregorie, Dick: 121-122, 398
Greist, Ralph: 311, 313, 315-317, 319, 321-323, 454, 456, 458-459, 460-461, 463
Grutman, Norman Roy: 357, 360
Gugliotta, Guy: 119
Guste, William, Louisiana Attorney General: 192, 213

Hahn, Jessica: 356
Haley, Mike: 389
Hampton, Fred: 116-117, 120-121, 125
Handlin, Oscar: 294, 332
Hannity, Sean: 471
Harrington, Ed: 475
Harris, Art: 386-387
Hasenfus, Eugene: 119
Helms, Jesse, Senator: 49
Hill, Pamela: 31, 59, 383, 385, 388-390, 401, 411, 417, 467
Hinn, Bennie: 173, 433-434
Hoeveler, William, Judge: 400-404, 407, 409-410, 412
Hoffa, James: 223
Hoover, J. Edgar: 137
Hopper, Dennis: 119
Hubbell, Webb: 16
Hunting of the President: 11

International Assemblies of God: 174, 177, 184, 356
International Association of Chiefs of Police: 414

Investigative Reporters and Editors: 280, 351, 377, 385, 394

I-Team: 334-335, 350, 351

Jackson, Brooks: 387
Jackson, Sailor: 73, 80, 83, 169, 172
Jacobson, (Jake) Ernst: 75, 92
Jacobson, Natalie: 339-340
James. Anderson: 233, 235
Jernigan, George: 151-152, 153, 166
Johnson, Sam, U.S. Rep.:
Johnson, Tom: 400-401, 404, 407, 409-410, 411, 412, 443, 467-469, 472
Jones, Paula: 14, 21, 49
Jumper, Bill: 194

Kaplan, Rick: 443, 445, 469-470
Kasarda, Amy: 458
Keeter, Jack: 452
Kelly, Virginia: 58
Kendall, David: 39
Kerry, John: 13, 51
Keys to the Vault: 135-136, 138, 140, 142-147
King, Larry: 224, 418-419, 424
Kings of Cocaine: 119
Kohler, David: 445, 467
Kohn, Aaron: 226
Korn, Steve: 406
Koughan, Marty: 402, 404, 407
KPAY: 328
KUBA: 323, 325, 327-328
Kurtz, Howard: 11
KVML: 2, 310-318, 323

Lane, John: 388, 469
Lansky, Meyer: 250, 257-258, 264, 276, 281-282
Lasater, Dan: 55-56, 58, 60, 62-63, 67, 108
Layton, Charles: 202
Lazar, Hyman: 258
Leach, Jim: 28, 54, 78
Ledher, Carlos: 84-85, 87
Leen, Jeff: 119
Lewinsky, Monica: 11, 14, 21
Lewis, Anthony: 387
Lewis, David: 387
Lewis, Jerry Lee: 148, 158, 172
Lewis, John, U.S. Representative: 475
Limbaugh, Rush: 1, 52, 472
Long, Earl: 219-220
Long, Huey: 217-219, 221
Long, Russell: 134, 217, 219
Los Angeles Times: 57, 59, 63, 401
Luce, Tom: 422, 423
Luciano, Charles (Lucky): 259
Lyons, Gene: 33, 39

Madison Guaranty: 23, 25, 27, 28, 50
Mafia: 4, 67, 111, 113, 226, 249, 259, 260, 265, 266, 267, 268, 270, 272, 275, 278, 279, 281
Mahvi, Abolfath: 421
Manship, Douglas: 133, 134, 139, 140, 143, 147, 237, 238, 297, 359
Manship, Richard: 359
Marcello, Carlos: 67, 224
Marriott, Mike: 457
Martin, William: 153

May, John: 412

McCarley, Eugene: 447

McDougal, James: 16, 20, 39, 43, 82, 111, 214, 223, 233, 235, 373, 374, 389, 476

McDougal, Susan: 21, 35, 38

McKeithen, John: 221, 222, 224

McKenzie, Ellis: 74, 85, 90, 93, 103

Meese, Edwin Attorney General: 108

Mena, Arkansas: 55, 63, 77, 78, 79, 80, 82, 108, 114-121, 123-128

Messick, Graham: 433

Middleton, Frank: 139

Minton, Denver: 453

Moorer, Thomas Admiral: 446, 447, 448, 450, 451, 457, 468

Morris, Roger: 124

Morrison, Micah: 127

My Lai Massacre: 236

National Association of Chiefs of Police: 414

National Association of Insurance Commissioners: 396

Nealy, Dan: 214

Nerve gas: 385, 440, 443, 444, 446, 447, 449-452, 454, 456, 457, 459, 460, 461, 463, 464, 467

New York Times: 8, 13, 14, 19-22, 31, 35, 36, 38, 43, 235, 294, 331, 387, 394, 404

NewsStand: 440, 442, 443, 444, 445, 447, 450, 451, 452, 453, 456, 457, 459, 467

Newsweek: 57, 59, 216, 338, 412, 451, 452

Nightline: 176, 177, 178, 361, 417, 443

Noriega, Manuel: 396, 397, 398, 403, 407-413

North, Oliver, Colonel: 91, 128

O'Brien House: 205, 480

O'Brien, Pat: 205

O'Reilly, Bill: 471

Oakley, Phil: 208

Obama, Barack: 12, 62

Ochoa, Jorge: 86, 92, 102

Oliver, April: 443, 445, 450, 467

Palin Sarah: 424

Partin, Ed Grady: 223, 226

Partners in Crime: 126

Paterno, Joseph: 267, 270, 271

Peabody Awards: 3, 8, 18, 250, 265, 282, 294, 299, 387

Perot, Ross: 418, 426, 476

Phoenix: 455, 461, 465, 466

Pickard, Larry: 295, 332

Pierson, Stuart: 402

Plante, Bill: 128

Polk, James: 389

Polozola, Frank Judge: 98, 100, 102, 104, 108, 110

Poorvu, Bill: 295, 299, 332

Provenzano, Anthony (Tony Pro): 291

Provincial Reconnaisance Unit (PRU): 454, 456, 459

Rarick, John, Congressman: 227

Rather, Dan: 384, 442

Reagan, Ronald: 70, 78, 107, 123, 326

Reed, Terry: 124, 125, 127, 128

Regunberg, Michal: 335

Reinhardt, Burt: 400

Reno, Janet: 40, 256, 283, 475

Rico, Paul, FBI Agent: 112

Riddick, Winston: 368

Rivera, Geraldo: 364

Roberts, Oral: 358

Robertson, James Judge: 43

Robertson, Pat: 151, 162

Robinson, Jackie: 199

Roettger, Norman Judge: 99

Romano, Frank and Thomas: 290

Rose Law Firm: 16, 18, 21

Rosen, E. David: 217

Ross, Brian: 256

Rubino, Frank: 398, 399, 400, 404, 412

Saal, Matt: 19, 24, 26, 29, 61, 389, 431

Salon: 54

Samuels, Bill: 226

Sandinista: 65, 69, 86, 91, 92, 119

Scaife: Richard Mellon: 54

Schaffer, Archie: 42

Schaffer, Beverly Bassett: 25-30, 33, 40

Schmidt, Susan: 35

Sclafani, Tom: 101

Screen, Pat: 373

Scroggins, Noble: 166

Seal, Barry: 63, 65, 66, 68, 74, 76, 78, 79, 81, 82, 91, 92, 93, 94, 98, 105, 108, 109, 110, 113, 117, 118, 119, 121, 124, 125, 126, 127, 128, 365, 370, 396, 412

Seal, Deborah: 99, 106

Sentelle, David Judge: 49

Shaw, Bernard: 403, 404, 443

Sheehan, Daniel: 118

Shiffman, Ken: 389

Siegel, Benjamin (Bugsy): 259

Simpson, O.J.: 59

SixtyMinutes:

Slobogin, Kathy: 389, 398

Smaltz, Donald: 41, 43, 44, 51

Smee, Bill: 389, 414, 419

Smith, Jack: 445, 450, 452, 456, 467, 469

Smith, Perry: 448

Snelling, Eugene: 204

Snipes, John: 448

Sonnett, Neal: 398

Sonora, California: 339, 365, 377

Spain, John: 72, 140, 143, 351, 359, 379

Sperrazza, Tommy: 344

Squires, Jim: 423, 426

St. Jean, Harvey: 285

Starr, Kenneth: 15, 16, 18, 36, 39, 40, 47, 49, 50, 51

Stempel, John: 421, 422

Stewart, James: 39

Strul, Gene: 239, 249, 268, 275, 296, 297

Studies and Observations Group (SOG): 443

Swaggart, Donnie: 150, 168, 169, 180, 359, 362, 364, 436

Swaggart, Frances: 150, 168, 169, 171, 179, 357, 363, 412
Swaggart, Jimmy: 4, 13, 148-152, 155-178, 181-185, 191-236, 291, 292, 304, 355, 356, 357, 359, 360, 361-365, 387, 433, 435, 436, 476
Swift Boat: 13, 30

Tailwind: 440-442, 445, 448, 450, 451, 452, 453, 454, 458, 460, 467-470
Tapp, Charles: 204
Taylor, Dorothy: 362
Teresa, Vincent (Fat Vinnie): 259
that Thing: 184, 185, 363
The Best Insurance Commissioner Money Can Buy: 366, 395
The Clinton Chronicles: 47, 50, 52, 55, 57, 59, 60, 63, 124
The Departed: 112
The Mena Myth: 79, 80, 108, 114, 117, 118, 123, 128
The Secret Life of Bill Clinton: 127
Thistle, Jim: 295, 332
Thomas, Evan: 451
Thomason, Harry: 11
Thomason, Patsy: 56
Thornberg, Richard: 428
Time magazine: 44, 417
Treeby, William: 182
Tucker, Jim Guy: 16, 38
Turner, Ed: 31, 376-378, 427
Turner, Ted: 388, 391, 401, 427
Tuscaloosa High School: 39, 215, 294, 300, 386
Tyson Foods: 41-43
Tyson, John: 51

Uncle Sam Wants You: 93, 94, 96, 98-100, 110, 115, 120, 122
Unglesby, Lewis: 98, 101, 105
University of Alabama: 6, 20

Van Buskirk, Robert: 446, 447, 451, 452, 453
Vance, Zoe: 164
Vaughan, Federico: 86, 88, 90, 92, 107
Vinet, Raymond: 234
Voice of the Mother Lode: 2, 9, 310, 311, 315, 318, 324, 365, 390, 413, 439

Waas, Murray: 54
Wall Street Journal: 18, 24, 34, 41, 55, 127, 387
Wallace, Mike (mini): 8, 372, 379, 476, 477
Wallace, Mike: 372
Warner, Ken: 389
Washington Post: 19, 24, 31, 35, 256, 386, 394, 412
Washington Times: 19, 24, 31
Watergate: 5, 7, 13, 134, 252, 256, 389
WBRZ: 65, 72, 75, 103, 104, 110, 113, 134, 135, 143, 147, 163, 172, 208, 296, 359, 362, 364, 365, 370, 376, 377, 378, 382, 391, 395, 435, 477
WBZ: 334
WCVB: 295, 299, 331-334, 338-340, 347, 348, 382
Webb, Kenneth: 94
Weinberg, Steve: 394

Weisman, Alan: 388
Welch, Russell: 115, 128
Wheaton, Eugene: 118
White, Frank: 62
Whitewater: 12-25, 28-40, 47-52, 54, 60, 62, 66, 128, 139, 389, 431
Wicker, Tom: 383
Wilson, Luther (Bill): 142
WJBO: 133, 134, 189, 198, 199, 203, 207, 208, 209, 213, 221, 222, 226, 229, 231, 235, 238, 329, 480
Woerner, Frederick General: 408
Wolfie's: 258
Womack, Kenneth Sr.: 136, 137, 138, 145
Woodward, Bob: 256
WXOK: 198, 200, 201, 203, 207

Yuba City, California: 323-325, 328, 329

3904502

Made in the USA